Public Health Policy

To my father, Drummond Hunter, 1918–2002

* * *

Health is very much a political issue (with a big 'P' and a small 'p'), and will not change unless those who have political power at all levels wish it to do so and the population want it to happen and see value in it. Almost all change is wrought through people, as individuals and as groups.

(Calman 1998: 263)

To date, health care policy has in most societies dominated health policy, because of its greater immediacy and apparently more secure scientific base.... One lesson from international experience in the post-Lalonde era is that appropriate conceptualisation of the determinants of health is a necessary, but not a sufficient, condition for serious reform of health policy. Intellectual frameworks ... are only a beginning. Simply put, to be useful, they must be used.

(Evans and Stoddart 1990: 119)

Public Health Policy

David J. Hunter

polity

First published in 2003 by Polity Press in association with Blackwell Publishing
Ltd

Reprinted 2004

Editorial office:
Polity Press
65 Bridge Street
Cambridge CB2 1UR, UK

Marketing and production:
Blackwell Publishing Ltd
108 Cowley Road
Oxford OX4 1JF, UK

Distributed in the USA by
Blackwell Publishing Inc.
350 Main Street
Malden, MA 02148, USA

A catalogue record for this book is available from the British Library.

   Library of Congress Cataloging-in-Publication Data

Hunter, David J.
Public health policy / David J. Hunter.
     p. cm.
Includes bibliographical references and index.
ISBN 0-7456-2646-7—ISBN 0-7456 2647-5 (pb)
1. Medical policy—Great Britain. I. Title.
RA395.G6 H863 2003
362.1′0941—dc21

                                                              2002155695

Typeset in 10.5 on 12 pt Palatino
by Kolam Information Services Pvt. Ltd, Pondicherry, India.
Printed and bound in Great Britain by TJ International, Padstow, Cornwall

For further information on Polity, visit our website: www.polity.co.uk

Contents

Figures and Boxes

Preface

I came late in my academic career to public health, having spent most of my early years undertaking research and policy analysis on the National Health Service and on health-care systems in other countries. Work as an adviser to the World Health Organization in the 1980s and 1990s began to broaden my interests in respect of the determinants of health and how little the vast expenditure on health-care services both in the UK and elsewhere actually appears to impact on improved population health. At least, if it does, we seem to lack good evidence that the significant spending is justified by the return on that investment. This is not to argue that health-care services do not contribute to better health – clearly they do – but policy-makers, the media and the public often seem to have unreasonable expectations of them in this regard.

I have become increasingly intrigued at the difficulty of making a paradigm shift from a preoccupation with 'downstream' health care to 'upstream' health. For many years in the UK it proved impossible even to have such a discussion, but the change in government in 1997 altered all that – at least in terms of the rhetoric being used and the willingness to engage in open discussion about the poor state of health and widening 'health gap' between rich and poor. The incoming government talked convincingly and passionately about health and health inequalities, and acknowledged that their determinants had more to do with other sectors of public policy besides health-care services.

But despite that initial commitment, the reality has proved less encouraging as the usual preoccupation with health-care delivery issues and systems restructuring has been reasserted and has dominated the attention of policy-makers, managers and practitioners. Public health issues seem to have been eclipsed. In addition, their implementation has proved more difficult than was perhaps appreciated. All around, there remains concern that the government's early enthusiasm has waned.

Why progress has been so unimpressive, even with a government seemingly well disposed to pursuing a public health agenda, is the subject of this book. Of course there are many good and useful initiatives under way (some would argue too many!) to demonstrate the government's good faith, but these seem unlikely to make real inroads into the problem and will not, by themselves, bring about the sought-after paradigm shift in health policy. It is also fair to argue that by their very nature there cannot be a quick return on interventions to improve health, since most will take many years to bear fruit.

The impediments to progress are often seen to lie in the poor state of the evidence base, and while there may be some justification for this stance it is insufficient to explain the lack of progress. Indeed, the state of the evidence can all too easily become a smokescreen for inaction. It is my thesis that the real barriers to change are more likely to be political in origin and have more to do with existing power plays among particular interests. The book is an attempt to redress the balance and get away from a rather naïve belief that if only we could sort out the evidence then we will make rapid progress.

I owe many debts in the production of this book, too numerous to list here. But I ought to single out a few for special mention. My years as co-chair of the Association for Public Health (APH) and, more recently, my role as a council member of the UK Public Health Association (which replaced the APH and Public Health Alliance) have offered me many opportunities to listen to, and participate in, discussions about public health, its status and its future. They form both a background to this book and a source of material. My role as one of four specialist advisers to the House of Commons Health Committee in its inquiry on public health, completed in 2001, also provided a unique opportunity to review the latest evidence and thinking on public health. Finally, I have been fortunate over the years in being a member of various groups and committees within the Department of Health and the Health Development Agency which have been concerned with various aspects of public health. All of these roles and commitments have provided valuable material and insights which have significantly influenced the content and conclusions of what follows. No one, of course, is in any way responsible for the views expressed here. They are solely my own.

I have dedicated this book to my father, who died suddenly in April 2002 before I had completed the manuscript. He has been an inspiration throughout my professional life and was certainly a factor in my interest in health policy. He was an NHS manager for most of his career. At the time of the 1974 NHS reorganization, he became a senior civil servant in what was then the Scottish Home and Health Department in the Scottish Office. Putting kinship bias aside, he was one of the few health-care managers I know who never lost sight of the bigger picture and of the overriding importance of improving the public's health, towards which health care was but one means among many. He introduced me to much of the literature on organization theory, on management and on complexity, some of which I cite in the book. As first secretary of the Scottish Health Service Planning Council in 1974, he was committed to the notion of 'planning for health' – one that is now back on the post-devolution policy agenda in Scotland. Indeed, he once wrote: *'health service* planning is dead – long live planning for health!'.

Finally, I should like to give my deepest thanks to my wife, Jacqui, and children, Eve and Miles, for their unstinting support and encouragement throughout this project. Inevitably writing a book intrudes into domestic life and involves sacrifices. They will have been worthwhile if the book helps to keep alive and strengthen the resolve of those who believe that we must end our obsession with the NHS and health-care services and think more widely and creatively about health.

David J. Hunter
University of Durham

Acknowledgements

The author and publishers wish to thank the following for permission to use copyright material:

World Health Organization Regional Office for Europe for figure 2.1, based on G. Dahlgren, *European Health Policy Conference: Opportunities for the Future*, Volume II: *Intersectoral Action for Health*. WHO Regional Office for Europe, 1995.

HMSO for material from National Audit Office, *Health of the Nation: A Progress Report*, 1996, and Department of Health, Executive Summary: *The Health of the Nation – A Policy Assessed*, 1998. Crown copyright material is reproduced with the permission of the Controller of HMSO and the Queen's Printer for Scotland.

1 Introduction and Approach

This book has been written at a time when concern over the public's health in the United Kingdom, having remained in the shadows for many years, has arguably never been greater. Mounting public disquiet over a range of public health crises, including foot and mouth, BSE and other food safety issues, obesity, pollution and the environment, the poor state of public transport and so on, has fuelled this renewed interest. There is also the growing 'health gap' between the richest and poorest sections of society. The government came to power in 1997 pledged to tackle health inequalities – a topic which had been effectively barred from public discussion under the previous Conservative administration.

Some respected commentators, such as the Institute for Fiscal Studies and the London School of Economics, claim that inequality, including the 'health gap', has continued to widen under New Labour despite its commitment to arrest and, in time, narrow the gap. Some evidence for this is presented in a review of trends in life expectancy by social class based on the Office for National Statistics Longitudinal Study for England and Wales over the period 1972 to 1999 (Donkin et al. 2002). A key finding is that inequalities in male and female life expectancy by social class have persisted since the 1970s, with those in non-manual classes living longer than those in manual classes.

Other commentators are less pessimistic or dismissive and believe the government's actions are yielding 'some tangible results'. However, they concede 'the picture is mixed' and that it will be at least another five years before the measures introduced to combat health inequalities will make a significant impact (Appleby and Coote 2002: 121). Moreover, while it may be that the government's own specific targets and objectives will not be met, the interventions could well yield benefits of a less tangible or measurable nature (Walker 2002).

In the midst of these claims and counter-claims, there is an overall sense that early enthusiasm for improving health and tackling health inequalities has waned and that health, as distinct from health care, has become a second-order issue. The sense of disappointment is palpable and is not lost on the government. Addressing the annual conference of the Faculty of Public Health Medicine in June 2002, the Minister for Public Health, Hazel Blears, highlighted the challenge we all face in improving health and combating inequalities. 'It is a big step, and hard, for governments to publicly acknowledge this challenge. No other country has taken the course of facing up to health inequalities as we have' (Blears 2002). But is the government seriously facing up to the challenge? Or is it indulging in symbolic or gesture politics where there are admittedly some signs of progress at the margins but where the underlying structural determinants of health and power imbalances persist more or less intact?

The Secretary of State for Health took up the mantle of public health in an upbeat speech to the Faculty of Public Health Medicine in late 2002. Before a somewhat astonished audience, he asserted that the time has come 'to put renewed emphasis on prevention as well as treatment so that we develop in our country health services and not just sickness services. It is time for a sea change in attitudes' (Milburn 2002: 1). He made the link between good health and economic prosperity and expressed impatience with 'a sometimes paralysing debate about whether we could do anything to tackle health inequalities at all' (ibid.: 5). He ended on a triumphant note, proclaiming that 'we are engaged in a major national effort to tackle health inequality and improve public health' (ibid.: 13). Echoing the speech of his public health minister referred to above, he stressed that the government was doing what no government had ever done, namely, to improve the health of the country. Almost as an afterthought, he showed awareness that many people might be inclined to dismiss the renewed commitment to public health 'as a road merely paved with good intentions'. We shall see.

A former Chief Medical Officer for England (and before that for Scotland), Sir Kenneth Calman, wrote a book in 1998 with the title

The Potential for Health. Its purpose was to demonstrate that 'more might be achieved *now* to improve health, health care and quality of life, if we were able to use our existing knowledge more effectively' (Calman 1998: 1). He was firmly of the view that

> existing knowledge about improving health already provides the means to change, and while it will always be useful to have more evidence, getting started is important. New knowledge will always be 'just around the corner', but there should be no delay in beginning. (Ibid.: 26)

A purpose of this book is to review New Labour's record in respect of its determination to shift the health policy agenda towards health and away from health care, and to target its policies on the poorest social groups in an attempt to raise their health status at a faster rate than that of other social groups. Without such positive discrimination in favour of the poor the health gap will always remain and will almost certainly widen.

But the book has another and deeper purpose, namely, to explore the fault-line that runs through health policy between an 'upstream' focus on the one hand and a 'downstream' focus on the other. Governments may openly speak the language of an upstream agenda, seeking to improve the health of populations, but they invariably act according to a downstream agenda that is rooted in the delivery of health-care services and centred largely on acute hospital care. Tinkering with health-care systems may not be entirely irrelevant to improving population health (at least in terms of quality of life, if not longevity) but its impact may be rather more limited than the investment of time, money and human resources would suggest. There are powerful forces at work which governments ignore at their peril. These are largely responsible for the consistent, and persistent, bias in health policy towards health care.

Such a state of affairs is by no means unique to the UK. A similar policy dynamic is at work in virtually every other country (World Health Organization 2002). Apart from possibly Finland, Canada has made the most earnest efforts to shift the focus of health policy to embrace the wider public health agenda but, sadly, with very limited success (Glouberman 2000; Legowski and McKay 2000). Indeed, if policy failure is evident in countries such as Finland and Canada, which have served as vanguards to other countries, then what grounds can there be for optimism that such a shift in health policy is either possible or sustainable elsewhere?

Source material for the book comes from my involvement in, and commentaries on, various aspects of public health policy over many years from both research and policy analytic perspectives. In addition, I was one of four specialist advisers appointed to assist the House of Commons Health Committee with its major inquiry into the public health function conducted between October 2000 and March 2001. The committee received around 100 written memoranda of evidence and took oral evidence from a wide range of government officials, NHS and local authority managers and practitioners, voluntary organizations, academics and others. It also made a number of visits throughout the UK and one overseas, to Cuba. Its report appeared in March 2001, before the general election (House of Commons 2001a). The extensive, and in many ways unique, evidence base assembled in the course of the inquiry, comprising both written and oral submissions from the majority of the key organizations and individuals concerned with public health policy and practice in the UK, has not been systematically analysed (House of Commons 2001b). It provides a rich source of material for this book.

It is customary for texts on health policy to devote most of their attention to describing and analysing health-care services or delivery systems. They may turn their attention briefly to wider notions of health and to its determinants, acknowledging that while health-care systems have a critical role to play in health improvement they do not have an exclusive one. However, the balance of discussion for the most part remains heavily in the direction of health-care services. The imbalance probably reflects the actual state of health policy and its preoccupation with health services, so may not be entirely unreasonable or illogical. Moreover, it is not just governments that show a bias towards health care. The public and media are similarly biased.

At the same time, the policy issues to which health services give rise are particularly acute. Are they under- or, perhaps, even over-funded? Is their quality sufficient? Why are doctors so difficult to manage? Why is getting effective working across the primary/secondary divide so difficult to achieve? Do managed clinical networks offer a solution? Why is the demand for services rising so sharply? Are patients less stoical and resilient than they used to be? Are they more irresponsible in their lifestyle choices despite better information about the risks of over-eating, lack of exercise, smoking, etc.? Do people simply assume that health services will be there for them to access when needed, thereby absolving them of having to bear any responsibility for their own health?

These, and similar, questions are of course important and should not be lightly dismissed, although they are not the subject of this study. There is another set of questions to be asked around why health receives less attention than ill health and disease. These tend to receive less of an airing. It is the purpose of this book to restore some sense of balance to the discussion of health policy by focusing on *health* rather than *health care*. A simple justi-fication for adopting this stance is that there is already a surfeit of texts that set out to describe the complexities and successive restructurings of health-care systems. What is lacking, though Baggott's book on public health comes close (Baggott 2000), is a text that attempts to explore at some length why health policy gets captured or colonized by health-care policy. These two strands of health policy, though overlapping to a degree, and without wishing artificially or unhelpfully to polarize them, are also quite distinct. For instance, a policy centred on health would have as its primary focus an 'upstream' agenda aimed at provid-ing the conditions that need to exist in order to keep populations healthy. In contrast, health-care policy tends to take as its starting point a 'downstream' preoccupation with service delivery matters. Once people fall ill, how can resources – human, organ-izational and financial – best be mobilized in order to rescue them from their predicament, irrespective of its causes?

Some 'simple truths' about health systems

In any attempt to refocus health policy on health there is a prior need to understand the key drivers and dynamics of modern health-care systems. They are where the real power in the forma-tion of health policy resides, and the simple truths listed below demonstrate how extraordinarily difficult it is to shift the policy agenda away from them. These can act as a brake on radical change and on shifting the paradigm from an ill health to a health system. No matter how enlightened and visionary the policy frameworks, they will count for little if the mode of implementa-tion is not addressed, and the need to disturb, if not undermine, the prevailing power base is not accepted as an essential pre-requisite.

As an aside, in the UK it has always seemed curious that the NHS should be accorded the lead role for improving health when its whole *raison d'être* is treating sickness rather than promoting health. Moreover, it has become a cliché that the factors determining health are more the responsibility of agencies such as local government and the private sector than the NHS. Such a 'whole systems' approach may be central to the government's notion of 'joined-up' policy, but it remains an aspiration. Little will change until there is greater honesty about the dynamics of, and power plays at work within, health-care systems. There are six 'simple truths' to appreciate (Lewis et al. 2000). Each of them is briefly introduced in turn.

- *Health-care systems want to grow*: they are naturally expansionist and create vested interests intent on survival and growth.
- *Higher health spending does not necessarily lead to higher health status*: cross-national comparisons of expenditure and outcome reveal some puzzling patterns, with lower-spending countries such as Japan having better health status than higher-spending countries such as the USA. However, as the World Health Organization (WHO) points out, it is the distribution of funds that may be a more important determinant of the success of a health system. There is no correct level of funding to allocate to the health system, although there may well be a minimum per capita level – a baseline investment – below which health care is not going to be adequate (World Health Organization 2000). The World Bank, in its global review of the relationship between spending on health services and population health, concluded that although higher health spending should yield better health there is no evidence of such a link (World Bank 1993).
- *Universal access to health care does not lead to universally good health*: it has done little to change the way health status is distributed across population groups, with the wealthy continuing to remain healthier than those who are poor. This is certainly an issue the government is keen to address through its commitment to narrowing the health gap between social groups.
- *Public awareness of risks to health has greatly improved*: a mid-century preoccupation with medical science gave rise by the 1970s in many countries such as Canada and, to a lesser

extent, the UK to a renewed focus on individual risk factors and lifestyle choices. 'Upstream' approaches to health were promoted, with the result that public awareness was raised about individual risk factors. Few people nowadays are ignorant of the dangers of smoking, drug and alcohol misuse, drink-driving, fatty diets, risky sexual behaviour and so on, even if they choose to ignore the advice on offer and the consequences of their own actions.

- *Health care almost always wins out in the competition for resources*: this remains the case even when governments proclaim their commitment to improving health – it is not backed by a significant shift of resources. It is not too difficult to understand why this should remain the case. Health improvement promises *future* not *immediate* gains, and it also challenges the status quo and the vested interests that profit from it. Whereas a switch from health care to improving health may strengthen social capital, the reverse may be true in the case of political capital. The public, unless they were reprogrammed or their expectations were transformed, would not look kindly upon politicians who failed to meet their perceived need for health-care services.

- *Changing the distribution of health status through 'upstream' strategies is extraordinarily difficult*: interventions intended to benefit the disadvantaged disproportionately benefit the already advantaged, thereby widening disparities and the health gap. More than 'upstream' single-sector interventions are required – rather, the policy focus needs to be on multi-sectoral strategies that address the broader determinants of health.

Underpinning these six simple truths are two further truths (Lewis et al. 2000). They concern *timing* and *epistemology*, and might be termed 'meta' truths. As was stated earlier, governments, trapped in five-year electoral cycles, are increasingly driven by short-term pressures and considerations. A health agenda demands a longer term horizon, and there are risks in expecting too much short-term progress. How this temporal tension is to be resolved, and a new balance of interests arrived at, must surely constitute one of the more intractable policy dilemmas facing not just governments but also those seeking to influence the agenda in favour of a longer term, public health approach.

Second, there is the epistemological dilemma. It centres on what constitutes evidence in public health and its degree of scientific robustness and solidity. Evidence-based medicine (EBM) has taken off as a major movement in the UK, principally in the context of clinical governance and the cost-effectiveness of health care. It is also attractive to policy-makers because it is seen as a means of resolving the rationing dilemma (Hunter 1997). Interventions denied patients should be those of proven ineffectiveness, thereby releasing resources for allocating to interventions of demonstrable efficacy.

EBM is heavily reliant on randomized control trials (RCTs) as being the 'gold standard' of evidence. RCTs have their place in the repertoire of methodological approaches, but in the context of broader health policy and interventions aimed at modifying behaviour patterns and lifestyles they are inappropriate or quite irrelevant (Perkins et al. 1999; Fulop et al. 2001). Here, causality is inferred or inductively derived, not experimentally demonstrated. Since health care and medicine aspire to the status of a natural science, health policy is expected to adhere to similar standards of scientific rigour and proof as well as causation. But this is unfair, since like is not being compared with like. However, not all social scientists are persuaded by the arguments against RCTs and experiments in social interventions. Macintyre and Petticrew, for example, reject much of the antipathy to EBM and RCTs in social science and public health. 'Rather than thinking of EBM as a biomedical orthodoxy whose applications to social policy, education, the criminal justice system, etc., should be resisted, we believe that the *thoughtful* extension of evidence-based principles to all those realms of public policy is important for all those who wish to improve human well-being' (Macintyre and Petticrew 2000: 803; my italics). The key word here is 'thoughtful'. It is the unthinking bias in favour of EBM and RCTs and their application to all evaluation questions that is the source of, sometimes heated, dispute within the social science research community. As Bakker and Mackenbach put it, 'opportunities for learning should not be foregone only on the basis of the impossibility of a traditional research design' (Bakker and Mackenbach 2002: 337). Klein is more directly critical of the unfounded faith in 'the new scientism' and argues that is a delusion rather than a solution (Klein 1996). The rhetoric of a science-based health policy is likely only 'to arouse excessive and unrealizable expectations' (ibid.: 85). There is too much uncertainty and too many context-specific factors at play for research to produce unequivocal conclusions that can be generalized across the NHS or health policy more generally.

Another problem with evidence-based public health interventions has been identified by Cummins and Macintyre (2002). Using the example of 'food deserts' to make the point, they argue that many ideas become accepted as fact and form the basis of policy even though they may not be true. 'They become "factoids": assumptions or speculations reported and repeated so often that they are popularly considered true; they are simulated or imagined facts' (ibid.: 436). The aim of the paper is to raise 'important questions about how evidence in public health is produced, interpreted, and reproduced when making health policy' (ibid.: 438). The researchers call for a move away from 'an unquestioning acceptance of conventional wisdom and "expert" advice and cast a more critical and objective eye over the facts' (ibid.). Whatever the merits of this argument, it would be unreasonable to claim that they are confined to public health interventions or that the tenets of evidence-based medicine, which the researchers suggest should apply with equal rigour to public health interventions, are uncontested in regard to their implications for health policy. Much of Cummins and Macintyre's argument is actually a more general comment on the state and practice of public policy and the use of evidence (Black 2001).

In any event, as was suggested earlier, the state of the evidence base in public health is not the only, or even always the principal, reason why progress in shifting from a health-care to a health agenda is proving so difficult to achieve. This is not to deny the very real methodological challenges that exist and face those seeking to improve the quality of evidence. Nor does it deny the existence of 'factoids'. But none of these dilemmas is a major concern of this book. Even where there is robust evidence about what might contribute to better health there remain deep-seated forces at work that serve as intractable barriers to change. A good example is the government's prevarication and back-tracking over the banning of tobacco advertising. Belatedly, such a ban became law in Britain in February 2003. That it happened at all was in large part because the government was forced into backing a private member's bill introduced in the House of Lords. Yet, Labour entered government in 1997 unequivocally committed to ending tobacco advertising. Until now, the UK had lagged behind many other European countries in introducing such a ban despite the extensive evidence that a ban would be highly effective in reducing tobacco consumption.

There is other evidence, too, of the dissonance between research rhetoric and health service reality. Research shows that, locally,

GPs and hospital doctors do not follow guidelines or adopt whatever it is that EBM is promoting as best practice (Davis and Howden-Chapman 1996; Haynes and Haines 1998). As Kernick, himself a GP, puts it, GPs 'make do with pragmatic, adaptive characteristics implementing small changes that they consider as evolving and improving on current systems' (Kernick 2001: 275). Davis and Howden-Chapman point to the contrasting relationships between research and policy and, by implication, governments' ambivalent relationship to evidence.

> In the case of health restructuring there is ample evidence of sustained and vigorous policy development across a broad range of health systems, but this seems to have occurred largely in the absence of any clear and compelling body of research. By contrast, in the case of the evidence-based medicine movement we have a highly motivated, organised and productive research enterprise, yet one that seems to be making little headway in influencing the bulk of clinical work. (Davis and Howden-Chapman 1996: 866)

So, even if the temporal and epistemological challenges identified above could be met, as well as those arising from the six truths listed earlier, it does not follow that there would be overwhelming government support for action if powerful vested interests, to which there is some sensitivity, considered themselves to be adversely affected by it.

Moreover, it is by no means clear that there exists widespread public support for such a radical reconfiguration of health policy, although a ban on tobacco advertising might prove an exception. Indeed, this could turn out to be the biggest impediment of all. Adopting a population health perspective may be desirable for the reasons given concerning the limits to health care in improving health. But neither are health-care systems wholly irrelevant in the pursuit of improved health, contributing, some claim, significantly to it (Bunker 2001). It does not therefore follow that the public would axiomatically prefer or support a population-based health perspective if they perceived it to endanger or compromise the quality, or accessibility, of health-care services to which they have become accustomed.

So if it is all so difficult and negative, and all is rotten in the realm of party politics where immediate electoral gratification takes precedence over what might make better sense in policy terms, why this book? What hope is there for shifting the paradigm in health policy firmly and unswervingly towards health and in a way that proves sustainable over time and not a mere passing fad perhaps triggered by a spasm of conscience on the part of centre-left-leaning politicians?

Well, there are glimmers of hope and a growing realization that 'more of the same' may not be the answer, despite its having served politicians, if not the country, pretty well in the post-World War II period. This is certainly a conclusion to be drawn from an important review of the NHS and its financing set up by the Treasury (Wanless 2002). Under the chairmanship of Derek Wanless, a former banker, the inquiry acknowledged the importance of public health in preventing ill health and promoting healthier populations, thereby easing pressures on health-care services. The inquiry team also acknowledged the gaps in knowledge and the absence of sound evidence which might help direct health policy to those areas where real long-term benefits could be achieved. But, as noted earlier, this is only partially true. Wanless concedes that, for all the methodological difficulties and so on, 'there is evidence suggesting that some health promotion interventions are not only effective but also cost-effective over both short and longer time periods' (ibid.: §3.41, 47). For example, according to McPherson (2001), and cited by Wanless, 25 per cent of all cancers and 30 per cent of cases of coronary heart disease are preventable through public health measures. If that is the evidence, then why is it not being acted upon in a vigorous and sustained fashion? By the end of the book, the hope is that the reader will be somewhat clearer on this point, will better comprehend the issues involved, and will be able to provide a convincing answer to the question.

If it is conceded that the future cannot, or should not, simply be an extension of the present, then the difficult part begins. What policy instruments exist for refocusing the policy agenda on health? *Do* they exist? Do we have the evidence base, or at least sufficient elements of one, to convince policy-makers of the soundness of their judgements and actions, and direct investment into interventions that will be likely to succeed? Or is the evidence so heavily contested that it is virtually meaningless as a reliable aid to politicians ostensibly committed and eager to act? Or, as was pointed out above, are we using rules of evidence that are paradoxically part of the problem because they are applicable only to some aspects of health-care interventions and quite inappropriate in judging the impact or outcome of interventions aimed at modifying behaviour and improving the health of communities? The evidence base may be imperfect but it will *never* be perfect. Notwithstanding this, we might need to widen the repertoire of what constitutes acceptable evidence if we are to embrace health as distinct from health care. In particular, the precautionary principle might be a better guide to action than a misplaced faith in absolute scientific proof. Adopting this stance means being clear about what is understood by the precautionary principle and where it ought to be invoked and where it perhaps should not.

All these issues have been circulating around academic departments, and occasionally some government departments, for many years. What is different about the current policy climate is that these issues are taking on a greater urgency as the government seeks answers to help guide its policy-making and lead to action. Perhaps one of the great failures of public health, which is addressed later in the book as one of its central themes, has been its inability, and also that of those who practise it, to seize the initiative on the numerous occasions when it has had the opportunity to do so. Had it proved able to deliver, it might have been better placed to provide the ammunition needed to give confidence to policy-makers and help ensure that they do not lose their nerve. Because it is a loss of nerve and a failure to 'speak truth to power' that seem to be the central problems confronted by those who seek a shift in health policy from health care to health.

Policy dilemmas and 'wicked issues'

In the UK, the last decade or so has witnessed an attempt by successive governments to grapple with the central policy tension in health noted earlier, that is, the 'upstream' versus 'downstream' thrust of policy. Even when at a rhetorical level governments seek to shift attention from health care to health, they struggle to maintain the emphasis and invariably become preoccupied with the language and accoutrements associated with modern health-care services, including the numbers of doctors and nurses needed, the number of hospital beds required, the length of waiting lists and times, and so on.

The reasons for the extraordinary difficulties encountered in trying to shift the emphasis from health care to health are multiple and complex. At a political level, the electoral cycle, a media much more alert to health-care issues and quick to pontificate on the NHS's shortcomings, and a public impatient for results and demanding immediate relief when afflicted by health problems all point towards governments being consumed by a search for short-term solutions or palliatives to problems that may in fact demand a longer time-frame and a wholly different approach. Focusing on health-care delivery issues such as numbers of doctors, nurses and beds, and seeking to make services more responsive to user preferences, is somehow more visible and has the potential for immediate pay-off. In contrast, going 'upstream' to tackle the root causes of ill health is complex, invisible and less likely to result in immediate or easily identifiable change or improvement.

In short, the longer term needs of health policy are at odds with the short-term pressures on governments to deliver and show results according to the success criteria judged to be appropriate by an ever-sceptical electorate, and by a media ever hungry for news and ever ready to criticize the actions of government. It is a major policy conundrum facing modern governments globally. No matter how genuine or sincere politicians may be in their resolve to lead change, they invariably capitulate to the overwhelming pressures on them to follow opinion. In fact, so anxious are they to appear successful and as high achievers that they ratchet up the very expectations to which the public and media then holds them to account for failing to meet. So the vicious circle is formed.

The implementation gap between policy aspiration on the one hand and the reality all too often experienced by the public on the other hand has to be one of the more intractable dilemmas of modern government (Chapman 2002). Indeed, one renowned observer of organizational behaviour has posed the question: 'why does it appear that the ability to get decisions implemented is becoming increasingly rare?' (Pfeffer 1992: 23). In seeking to answer the question, Pfeffer believes that implementation is becoming more difficult for two principal reasons:

- changing social norms and greater interdependence within organizations have made traditional, formal authority less effective than it once was
- developing a common vision is increasingly difficult in organizations comprised of heterogeneous members. (Ibid.: 28)

Pfeffer adds a third reason – an ambivalence about power and the fact that training in its use is far from widespread. For him, learning to manage with power is an essential prerequisite to ensure effective implementation.

It is the thesis of this book that a policy shift from health-care services to health is rendered difficult, if not almost impossible, because

- there is a lack of power to effect change in the status quo
- traditional policy and management models, with their emphasis on mechanistic, reductionist, command and control approaches, are quite inappropriate for addressing the complexities intrinsic to health policy.

Unless these two issues are acknowledged and confronted, then progress will continue to be piecemeal and generally absent. This book is therefore not about the state of the evidence base in respect of public health, nor about the gaps in knowledge which, many assert, constitute the principal reasons for lack of progress in moving 'upstream'. 'If only we had the evidence' is a frequent refrain, implying that its absence is the only or chief impediment to action. The Minister for Public Health takes up the refrain when she says 'evidence is vital, not least because I am well aware that there are sceptics who suggest that none of this effort makes any difference to the health of the public' (Blears 2002). But the reality is decidedly less simple, since there are also many (other) sceptics who for some time have questioned the vast sums spent on health-care interventions that are of dubious efficacy. They appear to be subject to different rules of evidence. Clearly, some sceptics have more influence on policy than others. Hence the book's focus on the barriers to getting things done and to making progress on the basis of the knowledge that already exists. The barriers have their origins in a power imbalance in respect of those interests engaged in health policy. The dominant interests are intent upon preserving the primacy of attention on health-care services. As the marketization of public services, such as health, continues apace, these dominant interests will become ever more powerful.

However, the position is even more complicated than this. After all, the government is exercised about delivery and implementation and has expressed its growing frustration over the slow pace of change. Indeed, the mantra of its second term in office has been 'delivery! delivery! delivery!'. But, and this is the second major theme of the book, the management model adopted to steer and enact the government's chosen policies is not proving 'fit for purpose'. Government talk of 'joined-up' policy is not matched by 'joined-up' management. Indeed, the government's favoured approach to implementation, based on a battery of centrally devised and imposed targets, indicators and performance management arrangements, is leading in precisely the opposite direction, that is, towards greater fragmentation and disjointedness. The approach is also seriously alienating those upon whom the government is reliant to do its bidding.

The models and theories of change successive governments have adopted, although perhaps without the conviction and single-mindedness displayed by New Labour, are based on a misconception of how change in complex systems occurs or can be manipulated. Governments remain wedded to an outmoded, hierarchical, linear rational model of command and control. The model is surrounded by an armoury of targets, performance indicators and performance management systems all designed to ensure that it is adhered to and achieves the desired outcomes (or outputs, since often outcomes cannot be specified with any degree of precision or are too far off in the future to be of interest to ministers, who have an average lifespan in office of two to three years).

Despite growing evidence, reviewed later in the book, that such an approach is deeply flawed and destined ultimately to fail, the government has so far appeared to be impervious to such criticism, believing that defects in implementation have more to do with the application of the model and its associated tools rather than the model itself. Either that or the competence of managers to deliver has been questioned. However, even if there is some truth in the claim that management is mediocre, government must accept some responsibility for permitting such a state of affairs to exist. Moreover, the charge of poor management is not confined to the NHS or even to the public sector. As has been claimed, following the government's 2002 spending review, 'in the UK, management isn't the solution to the underperforming economy: it's the £61 billion problem' (Caulkin 2002).[1]

---

[1] The sum of £61 billion is the amount the government has allocated following the 2002 comprehensive spending review to improve public services, including the NHS, by the time of the next election in 2006.

There is another way of looking at change and policy implementation. The tenets of complexity science and complex adaptive
systems are introduced and explored in an attempt to demonstrate how a shift in health policy to health could be made to
work if governments were prepared to jettison much of the man-
agerialist baggage with which they have become encumbered
over the years. Much of this baggage is in any case of dubious
value, owing much to the changing fads and fashion in management (Collins 2000; Marmor 2001). If these fads were subjected
to the same tests of evidence that sceptical policy-makers seek to
apply to public health interventions, then few would be likely
to survive the scrutiny. As it is, policy-makers seem to lose their
critical faculties and embrace the latest management fad as if it
really is going to be the panacea or technical fix for which they
have been searching (Loughlin 2002). The fact that many of these
fads have their origins in the private sector seems only to increase
their appeal and to imbue them with an even greater allure for a
government that has unashamedly and uncritically embraced
business and business management principles.

Policy dilemmas are often aggravated by the tendency of governments, despite the rhetoric of being 'joined up', to become a
series of separate units or silos, each focused on a limited or specific task without sufficient capacity to work across the units in a
co-ordinated way. The problem has been recognized from time to
time over the years by successive governments, but, despite various attempts and innovative devices to address the problem, what
a former minister, Gerald Kaufman, has termed 'departmentalitis'
remains a virulent disease within Whitehall (Kaufman 1997). The
disease 'stems from a preoccupation with the department to which
the minister is assigned, to the exclusion of all other considerations
including the fortunes of the government as a whole' (ibid.: 14).
'Joined-up' government is well nigh impossible in a context where
a symptom of departmentalitis is the ruthless pursuit of 'your own
department's interests even if another department has a better
case: quite simply, your department must win. You will often not
even be interested in, let alone care, whether your department's
activities impinge adversely on those of a colleague' (ibid.: 14–15).
For Kaufman, none of this is surprising or unexpected, since 'the
department is where you spend most of your time. Your office is
there, your staff is there, your officials are there' (ibid.: 15).

The dilemma arises because many, if not the majority, of the
policy problems affecting society cannot be neatly compartmental-

ized along departmental lines. They invariably cross departmental boundaries both vertically and horizontally, because action is often required by more than one department. Such complex problems have been termed 'wicked issues' (Rittel and Webber 1973). As Stewart (1998: 19) describes them, 'wicked issues are the deeply intractable issues which are imperfectly understood and to which solutions are not clear.' Such issues include aspects of the public's health, such as community safety, the environment and sustainable development, social exclusion and the regeneration of neighbourhoods. These are not 'tamed issues' to which there is an obvious and clear response. Almost by definition public health issues are wicked issues. Because the fragmentation of government reduces the capacity to identify and respond to these problems, they become less attractive to handle and get chucked into the 'too difficult to solve' category.

It is partly because the 'wicked issue' of the public's health is so complex that governments retreat from a sustained assault on it and seek safety in the relative familiarity of health-care delivery problems. These may be troublesome enough and have certainly succeeded in seeing off a succession of secretaries of state for health while remaining largely unchanged. But at least the problems appear to have reasonably clear boundaries, and ministers believe that they can influence the pace and direction of events. The fact that they seldom can, or perhaps can do so only in unintended ways, is a salutary lesson that they generally do not survive in office long enough to learn, let alone act upon. In any event, they are all too aware that the public will judge them above all else on the degree to which they have contributed to an effective health service which reduces pain and suffering rather than on whether the latest smoking cessation programme has prevented many thousands of deaths.

The politics of health policy

There are many theories of policy – how it is formed and implemented, or not (Hogwood and Gunn 1984). Policy involves inaction as well as action. In Heclo's words: 'a policy can consist of what is not being done' (Heclo 1972). An example might be the thwarted attempts to shift policy from a focus on health care to one on health. There is a policy of sorts, if judged by the outpouring of policy statements and commitments that governments have issued over the years. But if a policy is not acted upon or does not meet its stated objectives then it may as well not exist. As Hogwood and Gunn observe, pinning down and analysing policy as inaction is much more difficult than policy as action. Yet there is mounting evidence, accumulated over several decades, that policy failure has been the hallmark of attempts by successive governments to enact a policy for health as distinct from health care.

The theory of policy, including its implementation, adopted in this book is one that treats it as a *political* process. Policy is not a rational, objective, neutral activity devoid of values or the play of power. It is central to this conception of policy that individuals and groups within organizations charged with formulating and implementing policy often have multiple and conflicting objectives and interests, and that their desire to defend these is an important determinant of behaviour and policy outcomes. Indeed, Bakker and Mackenbach make exactly this point when they state:

> the link between the political context and the policies devised is important. If we wish to understand the health policy process in a realistic manner, political ideology and economic interests of key players in the health decision-making process cannot be avoided. (Bakker and Mackenbach 2002: 338)

But policy-making is also affected by puzzlement and uncertainty. These should not be overlooked as determining factors in policy formulation and implementation where the play of power in conflict terms may not be present. These issues are returned to below.

Power

The concept of power has been developed over more than thirty years of academic inquiry. In a short introduction such as this it is not possible to do justice to the history of the concept. The intention, therefore, is to do no more than offer a plausible account for its application to a study of health policy. At its simplest, the exercise of power is evident most clearly where there is observable overt conflict, that is, where B is seen to offer resistance which is subsequently overcome by A. But, as Bachrach and Baratz (1962) first pointed out, while such a view of power may be adequate for the analysis of specific incidents, it is misleading when applied across a whole polity, including a policy sector such as health and health care. This is because conclusions about the distribution of power across the whole would rest solely upon the (presumably) small minority of issues over which overt conflict occurred. In other words, such an analysis would have built into it the unwarranted assumption that a virtual consensus existed on all matters that were not the subject of overt conflict.

In order to correct this perceived bias, Bachrach and Baratz proposed to supplement this rather limited, or 'first face', view of the display of power with what they termed a 'second face' of power:

> Power is also exercised when A devotes his [*sic*] energies to creating or reinforcing social and political values and institutional practices that limit the scope of the political process to public consideration of only those issues which are comparatively innocuous to A. (Bachrach and Baratz 1970: 7)

If this seems a little abstract, the flavour of what Bachrach and Baratz have in mind can be tasted by the stratagems employed by the NHS to ensure that the focus on health-care services does not get seriously challenged in the battle for resources. Aided by possibly unwitting collusion with the public, health policy is seen to consist of hospitals, beds and clinical treatments/interventions. This process of agenda-structuring is in principle observable, though it is not always related to specific decisions or issues or events; a dominant group or organization may control agendas in such a way as to promote and protect its general dominance, even if not consciously responding to a direct or potential challenge.

So, as the next chapter shows, a stream of policy documents testifying to the importance of an 'upstream' health policy agenda has had little impact on the decisions or resources of those within the health-care system. The fact that local government could have attempted to seize the initiative and confront the NHS on the grounds that it had failed to put health before health care suggests either that, as a sector, it has been too disorganized to put forward a convincing or coherent case, or that it has regarded itself as being in a subordinate or minority position, or that it has not recognized the language of public health as relevant to its activities. Whatever the explanation, and it is possibly a mix of all three factors, it has decided not to make an issue of something that it calculates it is unlikely to win. Thus the powerful remain powerful without ever having to act. Indeed, 'simply supporting the established political process tends to have this effect' (Bachrach and Baratz 1970: 50).

At a more macro level, a third dimension of power may be at work. Lukes suggests that

> [A] exercises power over [B] by influencing, shaping or determining his [*sic*] very wants. Indeed, is it not the supreme exercise of power to get another or others to have the desires you want them to have – that is, to secure their compliance by controlling their thoughts and desires? (Lukes 1974: 23)

The standard objection to Lukes's position is that, since by definition the third dimension of power involves B's values and preferences being shaped by A, there remain no observable conflicts of values and therefore there is no observable exercise of power. Lukes defends his position by arguing that it is valid for an observer to make a judgement about the 'real' ('objective') interests of actors: to reach, for instance, a conclusion that B has been manipulated into adopting preferences which are actually against B's interests. The problem of observation would be much reduced if A were actually to admit what was going on: if attempts to shape B's values and preferences were acknowledged to be such. There are examples where such an admission is evident. For instance, much of the government's NHS modernization project is predicated on changing organizational and professional cultures within health-care services so that the work is done differently and, hopefully, more effectively.

Another example closer to public health is the way in which the specialty of public health medicine has, since 1974, been tied, or more precisely allowed itself to be tied, to the fortunes of the NHS and a managerial agenda that is concerned primarily with improving acute health-care services rather than health. Many would argue that such a focus has stripped the specialty of its core purpose, namely, the pursuit of the public's health in all its complexity, pluralism and interconnectedness. Many would also argue that this narrowing of public health within what has amounted to an NHS ghetto has suited those whose interests and preferences dominate the health policy agenda and who happen to be powerful advocates of not merely maintaining but also expanding acute care services. Of course, it may have suited public health to collude with these dominant interests and to appear to secure its position at a time when the specialty was experiencing a lack of confidence and considerable uncertainty about its future. These matters are explored further in chapter 4. Suffice it to state here that the effect of these power plays has been to reinforce and compound the 'downstream' agenda in health policy rather than the 'upstream' one that has been advocated by governments from time to time.

A final comment on power draws attention to the fact that some groups are strong and others weak and that this may be more a matter of luck than power. As just noted, historically public health has been weak in the NHS, lurking in the shadows of the more powerful and prestigious specialties within health care. But the events of 11 September 2001, when terrorists struck at the heart of global capitalism in New York with an unprecedented attack on the World Trade Center, changed at least part of the power imbalance between the interest groups. Suddenly, the risks associated with bio-terrorism rose rapidly up the policy agenda and health protection from terrorism became a hot topic for ministers. Public health specialists came in from the cold and suddenly found themselves at the centre of policy concern. To a lesser degree, recent food safety scares as a result of BSE have also put public health concerns – notably absent while the crisis was raging – higher on the policy agenda. They were certainly instrumental in the formulation of a new public health strategy for the European Union (see chapter 5).

Puzzlement and uncertainty

Politics is not all about conflict and power, whether covert or overt. Puzzlement and uncertainty are common features in respect of policy-making and implementation. It is a blinkered view of politics to believe that it is only present where there is disagreement about who gets what, when and how. As Heclo (1975: 305) succinctly put it: 'politics finds its sources not only in power but also in uncertainty – men [*sic*] collectively wondering what to do.' Governments and their agents not only indulge in power play or power – they also puzzle. Heclo again: 'policy-making is a form of collective puzzlement on society's behalf; it entails both deciding and knowing.' References to competing claims should not be taken to imply that all, or even the predominant feature of, social politics is conflict and the play of power. Because the issues faced in social politics are so complex, the major difficulty may be not the exercise of political will, but the determination of what that will is, or ought to be. In other words, the situation confronting decision-makers may be less one of competing for power and more one of coping with uncertainty or the 'possibly unwinnable dilemmas of social policy' (ibid.: 152). A pure power approach is insufficient to explain all the outputs from the 'black box' that is called policy. Rivlin reaches a similar conclusion in her claim that social problems remain unsolved

> because we do not know how to do it...The difficulties do not primarily involve conflicts among different groups of people, although these exist. Rather, current social problems are difficult because they involve conflicts among objectives that almost everyone holds. (Rivlin 1971)

The contribution of the 'health problem' to puzzlement and uncertainty cannot be overstated. The problem stems from a series of fundamental uncertainties (Thompson 1981). For a start, the health status of a population, as well as the means for improving it, remains cloudy (Mooney and Loft 1989). It is not necessary to travel far down the road of trying to discover answers to these puzzles before quickly becoming embroiled in the complexities involved in assessing whether greater public investment in health care actually produces a healthier population. As Mooney and Loft argue:

> medical decision-making attempts, inter alia, to analyse the often difficult relationship between certain types of health care inputs (for example, those comparing certain treatment regimes) and certain types of health outputs – and in a world of uncertainty. How this is actually done is itself shrouded in uncertainty or more accurately ignorance. (Mooney and Loft 1989: 21)

But the health problem in the UK goes further and concerns the very purpose of the NHS. Does it exist to deal with ill health or to promote health? Very different strategies are implied by each. Moreover, and some of the policy pronouncements in respect of improved health rather than health care fall into this camp, many goals are articulated at an idealized level of abstraction which makes their achievement problematic. Sometimes, the goals may be ambiguous and/or abstract in order to bury conflicts or, at any rate, to ensure they remain latent, like the tendency for health care to predominate over and above a health agenda. Hence, the concept of power may be responsible for, or at least be a contributory factor to, the ambiguity that is evident. But it is also plausible to argue that a major source of ambiguity lies in puzzlement, or in what Lipsky calls 'social service technologies'. Accordingly,

> when there are uncertainties over what will or will not work, there is greater room for admitting and tolerating a variety of approaches and objectives. In such an intention there is often a hunger for discovering successful techniques. (Lipsky 1980: 41)

In health policy, one of the reasons why it has proved difficult to shift the focus of attention (and resources) from health care to health is the difficulty of knowing which interventions are effective. As mentioned earlier, the Minister for Public Health has admitted as much (Blears 2002). The available evidence on the effectiveness of policies and interventions to improve health and reduce socio-economic inequalities in health, while not wholly lacking, remains very limited (Mackenbach and Bakker 2002). Most research in these fields has described and explained the problem of poor health and of a widening health gap between rich and poor. There has been a relative paucity of studies evaluating the effect of interventions and policies. Nonetheless, as Calman (quoted near the start of this chapter) has pointed out, given what we already know, do we not possess sufficient knowledge and therefore grounds for action?

The depoliticization of health policy

As noted already, the difficulties confronting those who seek to accord health policy a higher priority, and who are intent on moving beyond the mere articulation of policy to its implementation, do not merely reside in the evidence. There has been a tendency in this fiercely managerial and technocratic age to reduce problems to technical ones and, in effect, to depoliticize them. So defects in the evidence base can all too easily become an excuse or a pretext for inaction while further research is conducted to find the answers, assuming there are answers to be discovered. Much of the difficulty lies in power plays between stakeholders – covert rather than overt – but it is also a product of a continuing, and misplaced, adherence to a rational, linear model of policy-making and implementation. Such a model, which itself is a good example of Lukes's third dimension of power, creates expectations, and tensions arise when these remain unfulfilled.

A rational model of policy, as Allison (1971), among others, has suggested, presupposes the existence of a consensus within an organization among those involved in making policy. Basically, the greater the degree of rationality in a policy process, the greater the emphasis on consensus, on harmony, on a corporate approach to decision-making, and on 'technical' criteria for the evaluation of proposals. Conversely, the less the degree of rationality, the greater the emphasis on political 'wheeling and dealing' and incrementalism. This unitary perspective and conception of policy and implementation denies the existence of sectional and/or conflicting interests. In contrast, a pluralistic approach acknowledges differences between stakeholders and accepts that not all are equal. Moreover, there is no unitary mode of action but rather a pluralistic mode where there are many strategies for solving a particular problem. The pluralist view sees organizations as containing a number of related but separate interests and objectives which must be maintained in some kind of equilibrium. 'Instead of the concept of a corporate unity reflected in one source of authority and loyalty, there exist rival sources of leadership and attachment' (Dimmock and Barnard 1977: 85).

Even incrementalism risks imputing to policy-making a greater degree of stability and orderliness than is warranted. It can oversimplify social complexity – a view shared by Chapman, who argues that in many domains of public policy

> the world in which the policy-maker aims to intervene is beyond complete comprehension. The complexity involved precludes the possibility of being able to predict the consequences of an intervention. Under these conditions the linear rational model of policy making fails to guide the policy-maker. (Chapman 2002: 19–20)

Complexity, according to Chapman, is not simply about there being 'many moving parts' but about what happens when these parts interact in ways which cannot be predicted but which will nonetheless heavily influence or shape the probabilities of later events. Without the ability to predict the outcomes of policies, the policy-maker has no rational basis for choice. If this is a dilemma besetting many public policy sectors, or 'wicked issues', then the pursuit of improved health must rank high on the list. It is clearly a policy domain that is beyond complete comprehension. Shifting the paradigm in respect of health policy therefore also entails a new paradigm for making policy. Achieving one without the other is not possible. It is this realization, and the tension caused by not easily admitting or accepting it, that lies at the heart of the policy paradox that is in evidence. On the one hand, there is plenty of policy advocating a rebalancing of priorities and a 'joined-up' approach in favour of a health agenda and a commitment to improving the public's health in ways that go well beyond the NHS and its competence. But, on the other hand, there appear to be insurmountable obstacles that prevent such a holistic approach from taking root. The preoccupation among policy-makers reverts all too easily to the status quo. So, in the case of health policy, the focus remains unswervingly on the NHS despite an acknowledgement that good health is not the sole responsibility of the NHS. Nevertheless, the NHS still has an important role beyond providing acute care and needs to be reminded of this now and then. These issues are revisited in chapters 4 and 6.

Finally, as chapter 2 will demonstrate, the development in many countries, including the UK and its constituent parts – Wales, Scotland and Northern Ireland – of their health strategies has not taken adequate account of the non-linear, non-rational and complex process of policy development (Glouberman 2000). As Glouberman asserts, 'there is little doubt that the many factors that are relevant to health and the interaction between many areas of specialisation lead inexorably to the conclusion that the health field constitutes a complex environment' (ibid.: 50). He may be correct in claiming that there can be few government officials or policy analysts who any longer believe in the idea that policy formation follows a traditional linear, rational policy-making framework. However, it is also the case that the notion of complexity is still regarded in some quarters as unorthodox and has yet to enter the mainstream in respect of discourses about policy formation and implementation. But he surely has a valid point when he notes that, despite widespread recognition of the complex nature of policy, those engaged in the process still feel compelled to reduce the complexity to a simpler, if not simplistic, framework. Pursuing a similar theme, Cornford asserts that a rational model of policy-making may not yield a satisfactory account of the policy process, but it is nevertheless part of it, since it underlies the public language in which politicians must argue and provides the legitimation of their bargains from whatever motives and interests these result. (Cornford 1974: 246)

Cornford goes on to suggest that, even if all policy represents a compromise among competing interests, those engaged in the activity 'would still be obliged to argue in the language of [a rational model] of the national interest [since some approximation of the model underlies much of [their] own understanding and judgement of politics].'

So, the rational model of policy-making cannot simply be discarded; nor does government show any signs of doing so, despite growing concern about policy failure and a recognition that a new approach to policy is needed. Indeed, a report on policy-making prepared by a Cabinet Office team in 1999 stated that

the world for which policy makers have to develop policies is becoming increasingly complex, uncertain and unpredictable... Key policy issues, such as social exclusion and reducing crime, overlap and have proved resistant to previous attempts to tackle them, yet the world is increasingly inter-connected and interdependent. ... Government is asking policy makers to focus on solutions that work across existing organisational boundaries and on bringing about change in the real world. (Quoted in Chapman 2002: 22)

However, while diagnosing the problem facing modern policy, the report did not offer any guidance on how these attributes might be realized. Chapman argues that 'a new intellectual underpinning for policy is required' (ibid.: 23). This must also include the means of delivery, since current approaches derived from 'new public management' thinking, itself based on mechanistic, market-style liberalism in which people are treated in instrumental ways, are proving dysfunctional (see further chapter 3 below). Such hard-line command and control managerialism has swept through public policy in the UK over the past decade or so with damaging effect, especially in respect of a massive failure either to comprehend or to manage social complexity. A result of the approach has been an inability to make sustained progress in improving the public's health. Much of the book is a critique of this approach to policy and its implementation and is a call to those seeking to replace it with an approach that is 'fit for purpose' and one that recognizes the essentially political nature of the policy process. As Pfeffer concludes,

> it is not clear that by ignoring the social realities of power and influence we can make them go away, or that by trying to build simpler, less interdependent social structures we succeed in building organisations that are more effective or that have greater survival value. (Pfeffer 1992: 10)

For Pfeffer, problems of implementation are often problems in developing political will and expertise in order to get things done. In their absence, there is an implementation gap that appears to be getting wider. The slow and uneven progress made in improving the population's health is a powerful illustration of these deficits at work. It is the purpose of this book to draw attention to this missing dimension of the policy problem. The problem is not principally a technical one and has little to do with the state of the evidence base. Rather the state of the evidence base reflects the absence of the politicization of policy. If there is a single key message from this book to leave with readers it is this: the time has come to repoliticize public policy in general and health policy in particular. Only then might the shift from a health-care to a health agenda be possible.

The plan of the book

This introductory chapter has set the context, and provided the conceptual underpinning, for the remainder of the book. It has also identified the key themes that form the substantive core of the argument. To restate the themes, they are as follows:

- the continuing tension between health and health-care policies respectively, which, though linked, are also distinct, and the extent to which New Labour has succeeded in placing a greater emphasis on health as distinct from health care
- the evidence for an implementation gap in moving 'upstream' from a 'downstream' preoccupation with health-care services, and possible explanations for such a gap derived from notions of politics and power as important drivers of policy action and/or inaction

- the evidence base for public health and whether its incompleteness and contested nature are convincing causes of implementation failure or perhaps merely convenient excuses for inaction – the view adopted in this book is that it is probably the latter
- a failure on the part of the specialty of public health medicine to remain focused on a public health agenda while at the same time allowing itself to be captured by a 'downstream' NHS acute-health-care dominated management agenda
- a flawed model of change management which remains rooted in an outmoded mechanistic, reductionist, apolitical command and control approach and which has so far failed to embrace the implications of complexity science and of viewing the health policy domain as a complex adaptive system where the play of politics and power should be heeded as a perfectly natural activity that demands to be managed appropriately.

Subsequent chapters develop each of these key themes in more detail.

Chapter 2 examines the relationship between health and health care, and the policy tensions evident. A key tension in UK health policy, as noted above, has been the dominance of the NHS since its creation in 1948. Whatever the strengths of the NHS as a system of financing and delivering health care, its very existence has served to mask proper consideration of the wider determinants of health and of the actions required in public policy to address them. Confusion has surrounded the purpose of the NHS from the outset. In reality it has never sought to promote health, as its title might suggest it should, but rather has endeavoured to repair ill health. As long as there is a sense, or pretence, that the NHS exists to promote the well-being of the collective and has a population-wide focus, it can only serve to conceal the reality, which is a national sickness service that reacts to individuals' problems as these arise. Perhaps this perfectly legitimate function should not be combined, or confused, with a wider remit aimed at improving the public's health. The fact that they have been collapsed into the one organization may not be helpful but merely sows the seeds of goal displacement.

This tension lies at the centre of policy debates about the place of population health in health policy and whether the NHS or some other agency, notably local government, is the optimal vehicle to lead on it.

Chapter 3 reflects on the rise of managerialism in medicine from the 1960s to the present. The NHS has been subjected to successive waves of reorganization since the 1970s, all of which have had as a common theme running through them the shift of the frontier of management further into territory traditionally occupied by the medical profession. The particular brand of managerialism favoured, known as 'new public management', is drawn from the business sector and has been directed towards health-care delivery concerns around cost containment, service configuration and improving efficiency. Managers are judged on their ability to manage institutions, not to manage the health of communities or populations.

As suggested earlier, the managerial model introduced into the NHS from the 1970s on and endorsed by successive governments from across the political spectrum may not be appropriate in shifting the policy paradigm from a focus on health care to health. Even where governments will the ends, they invariably employ inappropriate means to realize their goal. The consequence, not surprisingly, is a maintenance of the status quo in policy and a massive failure to appreciate the complexities around delivering on a population health agenda.

Chapter 4 examines the new paradigm which may be termed 'managing for health'. As has been pointed out already, advancing the public's health has always been the stated goal of health policy, even if in practice it has taken second place to responding to ill health. The reasons for this paradox are explored, including a review of the public health function which has largely failed to put health on the agenda but instead has allowed itself to become captured by an NHS management agenda with its focus firmly on health-care delivery, including clinical effectiveness and evidence-based medicine.

The chapter will also review the government's 'whole systems' approach and its commitment to 'joined-up' policy whereby complex problems demand 'joined-up' solutions. Partnership working and integrated care are viewed as the principal means by which these policy objectives can be achieved. They have a long history in health policy which will be examined. The government's key initiatives aimed at achieving effective cross-sectoral partnership working, notably Health Action Zones and Health Improvement Programmes (HImPs) and their successors, Health Improvement and Modernization Programmes and, more recently, Local Strategic Partnerships, will be critically assessed.

For a shift in focus from managing health care to managing for health to be possible, a number of prerequisites are necessary. They are detailed and their chances of success assessed.

Chapter 5 is concerned with developments in health policy in a comparative context within the UK. The arrival of political devolution in 2000 has given rise to a potentially and increasingly disunited kingdom. Health is one of the major areas of policy that have been devolved. Therefore it might be expected that greater divergence across the UK would be likely, although it remains early days as far as detecting major policy differences are concerned. The material here draws on a three-year study (in progress) of devolution and health being conducted by the Constitution Unit at University College London. It is likely, too, that before long elected regional government in England may begin to take root, albeit at a measured pace and on the basis of local referenda to assess the strength of public opinion in favour of an elected assembly at regional level. Whether such an entity would in time be granted responsibility for health remains uncertain. There are lobbies both for and against such an expansion of its remit and powers.

From the subnational level, the chapter moves to the supranational level, since the growing influence of the EU on health policy within member states and on its own emerging policy in this area should not be overlooked, even if it invariably is. With devolution now a feature of the UK political scene it brings us into line with other European countries with devolved systems of government. The extent to which a Europe of regions, in which the nation state ceases to be so central to issues of governance, may have implications for health policy is considered. Within a global political system it is argued that the nation state is both too large for some policy imperatives (e.g., public involvement) and too small for others (e.g., health and environment) which transcend national boundaries. As the slogan puts it, the political pressures are to think globally and act locally.

Chapter 6 pulls together the main strands of the various issues and arguments considered and explored in the preceding chapters. It speculates on likely future prospects in respect of pursuing a wider health agenda that is not forever overshadowed, or blown off course, by a constant preoccupation with a narrow 'downstream' health-care agenda in which delivery issues centring on waiting lists, hospital beds, and so on take precedence.

2 The Relationship between Health and Health Care

Introduction

Although disease prevention and the promotion of health has assumed greater importance in both health policy and the wider social culture, this attention is not reflected in the public health infrastructure required to realize the ambitious policy aspirations that have arisen. The situation is in sharp contrast to the attention lavished upon the health service and the means of delivering care. Why should this be so? Why is a disabling feature of the National Health Service its predisposition to mask proper consideration of the wider determinants of health and to ignore the powerful evidence testifying to the almost entirely preventable nature of the major killer diseases such as cancer and coronary heart disease?

The answers to these and similar questions are by no means simple. Rather like the solutions to which they point, they are multiple and multi-faceted. This chapter does not pretend to be exhaustive in its analysis of possible explanations. It limits its search to the bitter-sweet relationship between health and health care. Unless we understand, and ultimately confront, this relationship and its internal dynamic and power plays it is unlikely that significant progress will ever be made in shifting the policy paradigm from a 'downstream' to an 'upstream' focus. We also need to understand, and learn the lessons from, the so far largely failed attempts that have been made both in the UK and internationally to give a higher priority to an 'upstream' agenda.

Defining health

It is commonly agreed that defining health is 'perhaps the most perplexing and ambiguous issue in the study of health since its inception centuries or millennia ago' (Kelman 1975: 625). Most definitions of health take as their starting point the WHO definition: 'health is a state of complete physical and mental well-being and not merely the absence of disease or infirmity.' The definition has been heavily criticized for being naïve, unrealistic and utopian; Calman, however, reckons it provides a good starting point, though not the only one (Calman 1998). What it usefully does is imply that health is multi-dimensional and holistic, embracing all aspects of individual and collective existence. A healthy person is one who enjoys a harmonious existence within themselves and within their societal context. Physical, emotional, psychological, social and intellectual factors are all important. This suggests that health is 'a relative term and cannot be regarded as an absolute in that it can always be improved' (ibid.: 4).

If defining health is a difficult business, the determinants of health are just as, if not more, complex (Lewis et al. 2000). Figure 2.1 illustrates the range of determinants of health and their interactions. It can be seen that virtually all public policy has an impact on health. Moreover, as the model also clearly shows, producing health is not the same as providing health care to address illness, despite the fact that responsibility for tackling both objectives can sometimes fall to the same structural arrangements, as in the case of the NHS.

It is difficult to discuss improving health without reference to health inequalities, although the two issues should not be confused. They have a separate existence. Nevertheless, in this discussion they are considered together because their persistence is seen by some as the biggest public health issue facing government (Mackenbach 1995; 2002). Social inequalities in health have persisted over decades and have widened significantly over the past twenty years or so (Appleby and Coote 2002). The UK's record is among the worst in the developed world, especially in respect of child poverty. As measured by the proportion of children living in households with incomes less than half the average, child poverty ranges from less than 4 per cent in Sweden and Norway to about 20 per cent in the UK and Italy (UNICEF 2000).

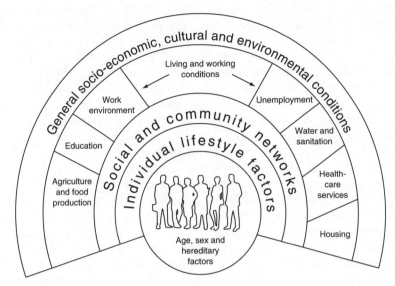

Figure 2.1 The main determinants of health
Source: Dahlgren (1995)

There is a major ongoing debate over the degree to which investment in health care contributes to health. Recent research by Bunker claims that around 50 per cent of health expenditure is directed towards health improvement of an 'upstream' nature (Bunker 2001). Others, such as the Health Development Agency in England and the former US Surgeon-General, take the view that health-care provision contributes only around 20 per cent to improved health. In their opinion, traditional health-care practice has had a minimal impact on health status. Hence the need for radical changes in policy and practice.

Mackenbach casts a more circumspect eye over the 'upstream' versus 'downstream' dichotomy (Mackenbach 2002). In assessing the relative merits of investing in 'upstream' or 'downstream' solutions, he argues that 'at first sight offering extra health care is not the most attractive option for reducing inequalities in health' (ibid. 2002: 1783). It is costly, and really effective health-care interventions are few. 'In contrast, changing the basic socio-economic distributions is intuitively much more attractive. Where one knows the fundamental causes of health problems, it is appropriate to address these directly' (ibid.). But despite the 'intuitive comparison' offered by Mackenbach, which on balance favours 'upstream' solutions, there is one very real practical problem, and that is the absence of 'empirical evidence to support the claim that "upstream" interventions are more effective for reducing health inequalities than "downstream" interventions' (ibid.: 1784).

Reporting the results of a unique initiative in the Netherlands which focused on interventions and their evaluations, Mackenbach and Stronks concluded that, although the programme of research on a range of 'upstream' and 'downstream' interventions provided evidence on their effectiveness and showed some positive results, 'there remained important gaps in the knowledge base, both in coverage of various policy options and strength of evidence' (Mackenbach and Stronks 2002: 1029). The majority of intervention studies were quasi-experimental in design and compared health outcomes or process measures in an experimental and a control group. It was felt that since further evidence was unlikely to become available it would be possible to recommend a combination of 'promising' interventions with continued evaluation efforts. At the end of the process, and because the intervention studies were limited to twelve rather small-scale studies funded from a modest budget, Mackenbach and Stronks acknowledged that the contribution of the intervention studies to strategy development was modest.

Where the evidence is lacking, incomplete or indicative rather than conclusive, choices will have to be made on other grounds, including political will and feasibility or promise. As was pointed out in the last chapter, the notion that perfect evidence of what works and is effective will be forthcoming is an unrealistic one and cannot be a sensible guide for policy intent upon action. It all too easily becomes an excuse for inaction. Of course, investment in research must be stepped up, but our expectations of what it will demonstrate by way of solutions must be modest.

This is the starting point for the discussion in this chapter. The arguments in favour of a preventive approach to health policy have been well documented elsewhere and are not rehearsed at length here (see, for example, Ritsatakis et al. 2000). Certainly there remains heated debate about aspects of the argument and, as Mackenbach quoted above and others have argued, about the degree to which a preventive approach does work. But some of these issues are further complicated because they relate to the nature of the evidence itself and the methodologies underpinning it. Often this is equally contentious given the in-built biases or assumptions contained in particular methodologies and the so-called hierarchy of evidence (Fulop et al. 2001).

The emergence of the new public health

Concepts concerning the 'new public health' and new approaches to health policy began to emerge in the 1970s both in the UK and elsewhere (for the UK, see Department of Health and Social Security 1976; for Canada, see Lalonde 1974; and for Europe, see the country case studies in Ritsatakis et al. 2000). These analyses acknowledged the limits to medicine as the dominant driver of health policy and the reductionist focus on hospital and medical services to the exclusion of a broader conception of health. Improving population health could not be achieved through medicine and health-care interventions alone. Governments were becoming increasingly anxious about the cost implications of continuing to pour already huge and growing sums of money into increasingly expensive health-care technologies. Apart from anything else, many of these innovations had yet to prove themselves, and there was a serious absence of systematic cost-effective evaluation of their efficacy.[1]

In the UK there is a blurring of the notions of health and public health with the existence of the public health function (by which is meant principally the specialty of public health medicine). Sometimes the use of the term 'public health' is disabling or dysfunctional, and there are issues about what, if anything, it means to the general public. In the course of its inquiry into public health, the House of Commons Health Committee was told that public health can be variously defined so as to cover trends of disease in a population, the provision of preventive and health-improving care, or a range of health-impacting factors, including or excluding the NHS (House of Commons 2001a).

While giving a lecture at the LSE in March 2000, in one of very few speeches he has given devoted to the subject, the Secretary of

---

[1] It was for this reason that the National Institute for Clinical Excellence (NICE) was established in April 1999 'to give new coherence and prominence to information about clinical and cost-effectiveness' (Department of Health 1997). It produces and disseminates clinical guidelines based on relevant evidence of clinical and cost-effectiveness. It has produced numerous reports on the effectiveness of new drugs and treatments.

State for Health, Alan Milburn, took up the challenge of what public health actually is. He drew attention to the problem of definition and its implications.

> The time has come to take public health out of the ghetto. For too long the overarching label 'public health' has served to bundle together functions and occupations in a way that actually marginalises them from the NHS and other health partners... Public health understood as the epidemiological analysis of the patterns and causes of population health and ill health gets confused with 'public health' understood as population-level health promotion, which in turn gets confused with 'public health' understood as health professionals trained in medicine. (Milburn 2000)

The minister believed that such a train of argument played into the hands of those seeking to equate public health with the medical model.

> By a series of definitional sleights of hand the argument runs that the health of the population should be mainly improved by population-level health promotion and prevention which in turn is best delivered – or at least overseen and managed – by medical consultants in public health. (Ibid.)

He denounced such a view as 'occupational protectionism'.

It is a view reinforced by the weight of evidence submitted to the Health Committee. Time and time again the point was made that health is determined by a wide range of factors and not predominantly by curative services within the NHS – although they have an important part to play in respect of improving access to services aimed at saving, and improving the quality of, lives. For instance, in its evidence to the committee, the Nuffield Trust argued that the term 'public health' was 'restrictive' and inhibited the broader agenda of 'the health of the public' and the quality of life lived rather than the absence of illness. In its view, a culture shift was needed away from 'public health' and towards 'the health of the people'. This was justified on the grounds that 'the public health function has been insufficiently effective' and that 'public health is a broader church than public health medicine' (House of Commons 2001b: 469).

In similar vein, the Chartered Institute of Environmental Health Officers affirmed that 'mass vaccination programmes, the engineering works of the mid 19th century and the creation of social and welfare structures that addressed the needs of the poor' underlay the greatest strides in public health (House of Commons 2001b: 389). The institute was scathing about the NHS's pretence that it was a *health* service at all.

> The emergence of the inappropriately named National HEALTH Service in 1948 while welcomed unreservedly, actually did a disservice to the work undertaken by others over the previous century and deflected attention away from the work still to be done to protect and promote public health. In reality the NHS was not concerned with health but with ill health. (Ibid.: 393)

The Health Development Agency, set up in 2000 to replace the Health Education Authority and strengthen the evidence base in public health, pointed to estimates that 'over 70 per cent of what determines a people's health lies outside the domain of health services and in their demographic, social, economic and environmental conditions' (House of Commons 2001b: 124).

Despite much of the evidence, both written and oral, reaffirming the view that the model of public health in the NHS was not sustainable because it was starved of resources demanded by the insatiable 'treat and cure' model of care, the Secretary of State for Health in his evidence to the committee dismissed such criticisms. He held the view that the NHS had to change so that people realized that it was not merely a 'service to treat sick people'. He mentioned the commitment to both primary and secondary prevention. More recently, the Minister for Public Health, Hazel Blears, has developed this theme. She sees public health

> at the centre of exciting and challenging times, not least in making sense of the new NHS in a way that enhances the public health voice and influences its future shape. This includes 'mainstreaming' the public health message within the NHS and beyond into other parts of central and local government. (Blears 2002)

Despite such assurances, the Health Committee remained unconvinced that the mindset of the NHS permitted it to go as far beyond the medical model as the health secretary implied. Even when talking of public health interventions, the examples given were all of a medical, disease-focused nature. The Royal College of Nursing (RCN) was not alone in believing that the very culture of the NHS was not conducive to its dealing with public health (House of Commons 2001b: 213). Its core business was perceived by both those working within the service and the public to be the care or cure of individuals who are ill. Public health remained on the margins of NHS activity. The RCN noted that Department of Health circulars prioritized issues such as waiting lists but failed to prioritize public health issues such as the involvement of local communities in health promotion.

The Local Government Association (LGA) was critical of the government in failing to follow through with its determination to 'break with the past' and 'move beyond the old arguments and tired debates' that surround public health (House of Commons 2001b: 143). The LGA did not believe the government's health strategy represented a break with the past but rather more of the same, with a 'constricted view of health' dominant. To concentrate on the 'downstream manifestations of ill health and early death' was not helpful in realizing the broader public health strategy.

The Health Committee did not consider that greater impetus would be given to public health in the UK while it continued to be largely locked into the medical community. As it also pointed out, within the medical fraternity public health is regarded as a marginal discipline. Indeed, as will be argued in chapter 4, it is this very marginality which may have contributed to public health allowing itself to become drawn into the NHS management agenda at the expense of pursuing its core business. Perhaps the price to pay for acceptance by the NHS has entailed a dilution of the public health function, with a loss of direction and focus as a result.

But as more has become known about the structural determinants of health and the impact on health of public policies in other sectors besides health care, the reductionist interpretation of the public health function within the NHS has increasingly been found wanting. This began to become apparent in many Western industrialized countries during the 1970s, when the pouring of vast sums into health-care systems began to be questioned as the best or only means of addressing health problems.

The health field concept

With the economies of Western countries slowing down or going into retrenchment in the early 1970s, there was even greater pressure on governments critically to examine their health-care

systems. Many took the easy route and simply capped expenditure without asking too many questions about how resources
were being used and to what effect. It fell to the Canadians to
take a more radical and, at the time, enlightened scrutiny of
modern health-care systems. In 1974, the then Minister for Health
and Welfare, Marc Lalonde, published what was to become a
seminal report entitled *A New Perspective on the Health of
Canadians*. As has been noted, 'it was the first government document in the Western world to acknowledge that the current
emphasis upon a biomedical health care system is not entirely
desirable for the enhancement of health, nor particularly relevant
to prevention' (Research Unit in Health and Behavioural Change
1989: 140). At the core of what became known as the Lalonde
report lay an emphasis, radical at the time, on an 'upstream'
policy agenda. It was suggested that future improvements in the
health of Canadians would come mainly from improvements in
the environment, moderating risky lifestyles, and increasing our
understanding of human biology. Its intellectual inspiration came
from the work of Thomas McKeown, who was based at the
University of Birmingham. His seminal critique of modern medicine and health care was first published in 1976, and a second
edition appeared in 1979 (McKeown 1979). His thesis was that
modern medicine was too disease focused and was overly concerned with the individual at the expense of taking a holistic
view. It ignored the wider socio-economic and environmental determinants of health.

The Lalonde report introduced the 'health field concept' as the
theoretical justification for reorienting health policy. The concept
comprised four broad elements as important in health:

- *human biology* – the genetic inheritance of the individual, the
  process of aging, and so on
- *environment* – defined as the influences on health which are
  external to the human body and over which the individual
  has little or no control
- *lifestyle* – defined as the individual's capacity to make decisions which affect their health and over which they more or
  less have control
- *health-care organization* – consisting of the quality, quantity,
  arrangements, nature and resources, both human and financial, in the provision of health care.

Calman (1998), in his consideration of what constitutes health, adds a fifth category – social and economic factors – which under Lalonde are subsumed within the environment. By these, Calman means different cultural backgrounds, employment status, income, housing, and social class, all of which have an important bearing on health status.

The Lalonde report claimed that the majority of health spending has gone to health-care services, while the major potential for prevention and health promotion is rooted in the other three (or four in Calman's typology) elements of the health field concept.

Criticism of this concept, and of other reports which have placed an emphasis on lifestyle factors, has centred on the imprecision of the lifestyle element and the failure to acknowledge the complex interactions between socio-economic factors and individual decision-making. Lifestyle choices may be less within the control of individuals than Lalonde suggested. Moreover, as has been witnessed throughout the West, unhealthy lifestyles have become widespread as a consequence of many factors, not all of which are amenable to individual decision. For example, obesity is on the increase in the UK, as it is in the USA, where over 60 per cent of Americans are alleged to be overweight. The problem is particularly acute among children. A major contributory factor is the sedentary lifestyles people lead both at work and at home. Ironically, the rise has coincided with a massive explosion of the health and fitness and leisure industry. But often these facilities attract the middle classes, who tend to be more health conscious in any case. Those who might be most at risk, and possibly experiencing serious health problems, may be unable to join a gym or fitness club on account of cost or family commitments or for other reasons.

Criticisms of the Lalonde report were far outweighed by the welcome and support it received from around the world. It marked a turning point in thinking about health policy and did much to boost the 'new public health' movement emerging at the time. The health field framework emphasized the centrality of health and the fact that health care was only one among several components of public policy that might realize this objective. The report is still often referred to and has become a touchstone for all those committed to a 'whole systems' approach to health policy, in which there is a new-found equilibrium between health-care considerations and those affecting the wider health of the population.

Yet for all the enthusiasm which greeted it, nearly thirty years on the record of achievement remains unimpressive. As Legowski and McKay (2000: vii) rather delicately put it, since the Lalonde report appeared there as been 'a logjam in health policy'. The Lalonde report, while doing much to modify the way in which people and governments think about health policy and to raise the consciousness of the public health movement, failed to break the mould or shift the paradigm. Public policy changed little in respect of the environment and inequalities between social classes. The prevailing bias towards health-care services and the vested interests associated with them has continued more or less unabated. At most, the Canadian government, like other governments subsequently, including that of the UK, backed healthy lifestyles, and resources were found to launch public campaigns aimed at modifying individual behaviour. Most of these have centred on smoking, drug addiction and drinking. As Legowski and McKay concluded: 'it was not enough to conceive of an idea for it to be implemented, nor perhaps was implementation always the intention of policy documents' (ibid.: 44).

In seeking an explanation for this disappointing outcome, Evans and Stoddart (1990) suggest that the appropriate policy response was less clear than the diagnosis of the problem because the report could be read in a number of different ways. 'At one end of the ideological spectrum, it was seen as a call for a much more interventionist set of social policies, going well beyond the public provision of health care per se in the effort to improve the health of the Canadian population and relieve the burden of morbidity and mortality' (ibid.: 111).

At the other end of the spectrum is an assumption, or so many perceived it to be the case, that people are largely responsible for their own health and have chosen to indulge in unhealthy or risky lifestyles of their own volition. On this interpretation of the Lalonde report the justification for collective action becomes less self-evident. As Evans and Stoddart (1990: 111) conclude, regardless of the intention of the authors of the report, 'the [health field] framework lends itself to "victim-blaming" as well as to arguments for more comprehensive social reform.'

Indeed, most of the policy activity post-Lalonde centred on interventions and programmes to modify individual behaviour, particularly addictions. In the late 1980s in Canada health promotion broadened beyond an emphasis on lifestyle to include environmental determinants. Similar approaches have been adopted in the UK.

In the early 1990s the notion of population health entered the policy mainstream. It focused on the impact of the social and economic environment on health. The challenge for the UK, Canada and other countries is whether population health can succeed in refocusing the health policy agenda so that it is not dominated by health-care policy. So far, the indications are mixed. At the level of policy-making and political posturing there is indeed commitment to a 'whole systems' health policy, but this has yet to be translated into effective implementation. The problem may be that merely having a policy, no matter how enlightened or radical, need not mean the same thing as being serious about changing anything in line with the policy. For ministers, simply having a policy can often be an end in itself, as the observation on the fate of the Lalonde report from Legowski and McKay (2000) quoted above suggests may have been the case. But it is also possible that the problem lies elsewhere, for example, in the absence of sufficient capacity and/or capability to achieve effective change in practice. In short, the commitment to implementing the policy may be genuine but the necessary means may be deficient. Chapter 4 returns to this issue, while the first problem just mentioned – policy as a symbolic gesture rather than as a precursor of real change – is considered further below.

If there is a single overriding lesson from the post-Lalonde era it is this: that appropriate theorizing and conceptualization, though important preconditions for reform of health policy, are insufficient on their own. They are but a beginning. Evans and Stoddart (1990: 119) again: 'Simply put, to be useful, they must be used.'

Barriers to progress

If the case for shifting the policy focus from health care to health has been made repeatedly over the years, then why do governments find it so difficult to make the shift? Why do their commitments remain at a largely rhetorical level while the reality is one of continued expansion of health-care services, even when it is conceded that these are directed principally towards salvage and repair? If governments are ambiguous about their intentions then why bother at all? Why pretend to do something that they know will not happen?

Writing in a Canadian context, Legowski and McKay (2000: vi) identify the following barriers to health policy initiatives:

- fiscal restraint often thwarts new policy development
- jurisdictional issues arising from federal–provincial–territorial relations have a considerable influence on the extent and way in which health policy is realized in Canada
- health care continues to dominate the agenda, pushing preventive efforts such as health promotion and population health to a secondary rank
- there is a greater willingness to fund narrow, issue-specific, time-limited strategies rather than long-term, broad approaches aimed at all citizens.

With the possible exception of the second barrier, though the impact of devolution could over time change things, the other barriers could apply equally to the (largely unfulfilled) efforts in the UK to shift health policy in the direction of health.

But simply listing the barriers does not help us understand or confront the underlying causes. Why should these barriers appear so embedded and insurmountable? It is necessary to dig deeper to uncover the forces giving energy to the barriers. Their origins may be found in three linked concerns. First, there is what has been termed the 'surface appeal' of the public's health, which conceals the very real difficulties and uncertainties surrounding policies for shifting the balance in favour of a policy for health. Second, there is the nature of the territory itself, which cannot neatly be placed within a single department's remit. This fragmentation and diffusion of responsibility poses problems of who, if anyone, is providing the lead for action. And, third, there is the messiness of producing health as distinct from health care and knowing not only when it has been achieved but also what interventions have contributed to this achievement, how and for whom. The complexities and uncertainties of medical science appear insignificant when set alongside those encountered in improving the public's health beyond health-care services. It defies precision or tidy categorization. The temptation is always to narrow down the options to render the issues researchable in measurable and quantifiable terms. Such an approach is potentially misleading and certainly incomplete. It risks doing a grave disservice to the multi-faceted nature of health and its inherent complexity.

With respect to the surface appeal of a policy propounding the importance of health, it sometimes seems as if there are too many fine ringing phrases for the policy to be taken seriously. They can serve as a substitute for rigorous and detailed attention derived from practice on how the various good intentions might be delivered. For example, calls to partnership or intersectoral working across discrete professions and organizations have been made repeatedly over many decades, but to little avail. Partnership working remains patchy and uneven despite repeated calls for it. Yet whenever there is a breakdown in the seamless provision of care, inquiry after inquiry and report after report come up *ad nauseam* with the standard set of recommendations. Top of the list is usually another exhortation to work in partnership and a plea for professions to get out of their silos and work across professional and organizational boundaries. The problem is that a call to work across sectors is rarely accompanied by detailed guidance on how such co-ordination might best be achieved in order to improve health. It is as if by stating that partnership working is important it will then follow, as night follows day. Astonishingly, this remains the case despite all the evidence from numerous failed national policies and accompanying exhortations. Policy-learning, at least in the area of partnerships, appears not to have taken place despite a reasonably robust evidence base identifying the causes of failure and offering possible solutions and criteria for success (Hardy et al. 2000).

Second, unlike health-care policy, health policy cannot conveniently be made the responsibility of a single agency or department. It is, as a UK government report put it in the mid-1970s, 'everybody's business' (Department of Health and Social Security 1976). While on the one hand this acceptance might act as a powerful spur to action, on the other it has a rather debilitating effect, since the risk is that if health policy is everybody's business it becomes no one's responsibility. This is the weakness of the WHO's definition of health. It is too all-embracing in its implication that *all* public policy is health policy and accounts for why the definition 'has accordingly been honoured in repetition, but rarely in application' (Evans and Stoddart 1990: 1347). Hence the vexed issue of leadership for health has left governments with a dilemma. Most have simply ducked the issue and given the lead role to their health-care systems without much further thought as to the consequences of such an action or the likely perversities to flow from it.

In the UK, much of the failure to take health policy seriously is a consequence of having accorded the NHS the lead role for both health and health care. This is one of the key findings to emerge from an evaluation of the impact of the first ever English health strategy, *The Health of the Nation*, which was operational between 1992 and 1997 (Department of Health 1998a). While there is a certain logic and rationale behind the decision to give the NHS the lead role, since health-care services do have an important preventive role and can improve health status and quality of life (e.g., hip-joint replacements), the day-to-day reality is that health-care services are concerned primarily with ill health and disease. The simple truths described in chapter 1 all point unequivocally in this direction, as does virtually all the evidence submitted to the Health Committee in the course of its inquiry into public health. The pressures for change are not felt as acutely or given the same expression as those emanating from the health-care system, with their accompanying calls for more resources and expansion.

Some lessons from Lalonde

The Lalonde report affords lessons from the time of its publication that are highly relevant to current debates not only in Canada but elsewhere, too. Legowski and McKay (2000: vi–vii) identify the following:

- champions for new ideas are critical to move them onto and up the policy agenda and into policy statements and implementation
- dedicated time is essential to enable staff to reflect, think and generate new ideas
- publishing an official report does not always signal a commitment to implementation – governments are littered with policies which never (or which may never have been intended to) get implemented
- divisions between proponents of health promotion, population health, public health and health care remain alive and do not help the cause of refocusing health policy on health
- the population health approach has yielded evidence without identifying a policy instrument, which helps explain why it has proved difficult to move from theory to practice
- many of the influences on health lie outside the policy domain of health departments, and there is therefore a need

for 'joined-up' policy *and* management despite the considerable difficulties in achieving this
- there is much government can do to improve the determinants of health, and efficient resource allocation would prioritize health not health care.

The last of these is the most significant. Yet governments have yet to learn most of these lessons or to apply the fruits of their learning. So where are we heading some thirty years after Lalonde? The analysis of its strengths and weaknesses and its aftermath resonate strongly with developments in other countries such as the UK.

The post-Lalonde era

As was pointed out above, the Lalonde report, with its health field framework, had shortcomings, in particular the lack of attention given to the structural or socio-economic determinants of health. It placed too much emphasis on individuals as rational actors in control of their lives and capable of assuming far greater responsibility for their health. The impact of forces such as culture and poverty on lifestyle was largely ignored. Although it did succeed in broadening the perspective on health to go beyond health care, it remained too rooted in an individualistic interpretation of health-inducing behaviour and actions.

Perhaps the most significant contribution of the Lalonde report was its acknowledgement that if the health of the population was to be improved then the scope of health policy had to be expanded beyond traditional public health measures and health-care, disease-focused services. It was a major achievement that countries such as the UK tentatively followed some years later. Their efforts were encouraged by WHO's (1985) *Health for All* strategy and related work such as that by Dahlgren and Whitehead (1992) on policies and strategies to promote social equity in health.

Since then there has been a much greater appreciation of the complexities of health as a concept. The health field framework was an attempt to capture some of these complexities, but it fell short of appreciating just how complex the interplay was in reality between nature and nurture, personal lifestyles and structural determinants. As Glouberman (2000: 19), who has studied the history of the Lalonde report, puts it, today health is recognized as a complex concept but it has new meaning: 'As we have begun to delve into the nature of complexity we recognise that complex concepts are not reducible to their contemporary characteristics, but often display emergent qualities unforeseen by analysis.' The notion of complexity is fundamental to making progress in shifting the focus of attention from health care to health, and chapter 3 provides an elaboration of it. Before then it is necessary to review policy developments in the UK as far as health is concerned.

The UK experience

In the UK, the policy document that came closest to resembling at least part of the content of the Lalonde report was published two years after Lalonde, in 1976, and was entitled *Prevention and Health: Everybody's Business* (Department of Health and Social Security 1976). Its subtitle was also interesting: *A Reassessment of Public and Personal Health*. Like Lalonde, its appearance was a product of economic restraint and pressures on resources. Although it marked something of a new departure in British health policy, it did not have the freshness or broad appeal of Lalonde. Its impact remained muted, perhaps because the document did not seek to recommend specific programmes or actions but was intended to 'to start people thinking and talking about the place of prevention in the overall, longer term development of the health and related services' (ibid.: 7). Nevertheless, it did attempt to shift attention from an exclusive focus on curative medicine – 'we need to interest individuals, communities and society as a whole in the idea that prevention is better than cure' (ibid.: 9) – and paved the way some sixteen years later, alongside other reports (including the 1988 Acheson report on public health in England), for the first ever health strategy for England, *The Health of the Nation*. Both reports are commented upon further below.

In the foreword to *Prevention and Health: Everybody's Business*, the four UK health ministers stated that 'the time has come for a re-appraisal of the possibilities inherent in prevention' (Department of Health and Social Security 1976: 6). They surmised that 'curative medicine may be increasingly subject to the law of diminishing returns' (ibid.). They were at pains to point out that they were not proposing a new initiative but 'a re-exploration of a well-tested, traditional approach' (ibid.). The health ministers also noted that responsibility for prevention had transferred from local authorities to the NHS in 1974 at the time of the service's first major reorganization since its inception. However, this move was not intended to imply that a preventive approach was to be confined to health services. 'The re-organised NHS, however, provides an improved administrative framework within which it is now possible to look at priorities more comprehensively and to plan the allocation of resources more effectively both at local and national levels' (ibid.).

While *Prevention and Health* was in many ways a thoughtful document raising many issues for discussion, including the interesting notion at a time when evidence-based policy and practice is in vogue that even incomplete knowledge may be adequate for the purpose of preventive action, it is hard to conclude that it resulted in any marked change of direction on the part of the NHS or health policy more generally. In which case, this must mean the document failed, since it closed with the words: '[this paper] will have failed in its purpose if this discussion does not lead in turn to positive action to promote health' (Department of Health and Social Security 1976: 96). Such action was to include reorienting the NHS to give a greater emphasis to prevention. The fact that precisely the same debate is being waged over twenty-five years later suggests that health policy has advanced little and that prevention and promoting the public's health remain in the shadows.

The Acheson report on public health

The Acheson report on the future development of the public health function in England which appeared in the late 1980s was the first such review since the report of the Royal Sanitary Commission in 1871 (Acheson 1988). Under the chairmanship of the Chief Medical Officer for England at the time, Donald Acheson, the review was set up principally in response to two major outbreaks of communicable disease, but the committee interpreted its brief more broadly to embrace the entire public health function, since there were widespread concerns about the growing crisis in the specialty of community medicine. The crisis was the result of the fate of public health following the 1974 NHS reorganization, when it was transferred from local government control (see chapter 4). The committee adopted a broad definition of public health as 'the science and art of preventing disease, prolonging life and promoting health through organised efforts of society'.

The committee drew attention to five main problem areas:

- lack of co-ordinated information on which to base policy decisions about the health of the population at national and local levels
- lack of emphasis on the promotion of health and healthy living and the prevention of disease
- widespread confusion about the role and responsibilities of public health doctors – both within the health service and more broadly
- confusion about responsibility for the control of communicable disease and poor communication between the various agencies involved
- weakness in the capacity of health authorities to evaluate the outcome of their activities.

In the light of these deficiencies, the committee wanted health authorities to be reminded of their public health responsibilities and review regularly the health of their populations, to relate their decisions about resource use to their impact on the health status of the population, and to work with other agencies to promote health. It envisaged that improvements in the health of the local population would be used as an indicator of health authority performance. Medically qualified public health specialists were regarded as key figures in the pursuit of improved population health. Indeed, the whole purpose of the Acheson inquiry was to restore the status of public health medicine (Baggott 2000: 85).

'The Health of the Nation'

If there was a sense that public health was not being taken sufficiently seriously by the NHS and suffered from an absence of strategic focus, then the appearance of the first ever health strategy in England ought to have marked a turning point for advocates of a public health approach.

The Health of the Nation (HOTN) was all the more remarkable for being produced by a Conservative government not renowned for its commitment either to strategic planning or to the broader health agenda (Secretary of State for Health 1992). After all, this was an administration that did not subscribe to the notion of health inequalities or believe that poverty might have something to do with the widening health gap between social groups. Moreover, it had directed most of its efforts to the health-care agenda and to introducing an internal market (or, to be more precise, the semblance of one) in order to improve the efficiency of hospitals through injecting some competition into their transactions. A consequence was the introduction of a purchaser–provider separation. It quickly became apparent that there was a strategic vacuum and that the purchasing authorities required a framework within which to agree their priorities and make decisions. Notions of improving the health of the population and health gain therefore took hold in a context where there seemed to be a vacuum in respect of what the purpose of the NHS was and how it could best be achieved.

In his deconstruction of the notion of 'health gain', Loughlin (2002) argues that the language of the term never took off in the way that the language of 'quality' has. He speculates on why this is the case, suggesting that the term itself is too specific in making direct reference to 'health'.

> In contrast, if the desired 'output' of health service activity is 'quality' and there already exists a developed language of 'quality' in the commercial sector, then it is possible to think of the goal of healthcare in the very same terms as one conceives of the goals of commercial enterprises. (Loughlin 2002: 104)

While quality is the goal of any production process, health gain applies only to the area of health. According to Loughlin, therefore, 'quality' is much more effective if the overall purpose is to make every aspect of public policy and professional life 'comprehensible in terms of the same, free market, ideology' (ibid.). Loughlin's critique is explored further in chapter 3 when we consider the nature of the managerial revolution in public services, including the NHS. This also owes its origins to a belief that business practices can be applied with equal success to public services.

However, in the early 1990s, there was an attempt to talk openly about the importance of health rather than health care in isolation, and the *Health of the Nation* strategy was seen as the principal means by which such a refocusing of policy would occur. At the time of *HOTN*, health ministers proclaimed that it was 'shifting the focus from NHS institutions and service inputs to people and health' (Mawhinney and Nichol 1993: 45). *HOTN* acknowledged its debt to WHO's *Health for All* approach in its overarching goal

> to secure continuing improvement in the general health of the population of England by: adding years to life: an increase in life expectancy and reduction in premature death; and adding life to years: increasing years lived free from ill health, reducing or minimising the adverse effects of illness and disability, promoting healthy lifestyles, physical and social environments and, overall, improving quality of life.

The emphasis of the strategy was on improving and maintaining health, not simply health care. Five key areas of health and associated objectives were identified (see box 2.1). They were chosen because

- they were major causes of premature death or avoidable ill health
- they were ones where effective interventions offering significant scope for improvement in health should be possible
- it was possible to set objectives and targets in the areas and monitor progress towards them.

The five key areas and associated twenty-eight objectives and national targets were tools for achieving the wider strategic aims of *HOTN*, which were to improve the nation's health. Settings such as schools, homes and workplaces were also identified where health promotion could show useful progress.

HOTN sought to widen the responsibility for health, and this emphasis was reflected in the ministerial committee set up to oversee the development, implementation and monitoring of the strategy. The committee, chaired by a senior cabinet minister (Lord President of the Council), was comprised of ministers or junior ministers from twelve government departments, including health, social security, employment and the environment (those

---

Box 2.1   *The Health of the Nation:* five key areas and main objectives

Coronary heart disease and stroke	To reduce the level of ill health and death caused by CHD and stroke and the risk factors associated with them
Cancer	To reduce death and ill health from breast cancer, cervical cancer and skin cancer
Mental Illness	To reduce ill health and death caused by mental illness
HIV/AIDS and sexual health	To reduce the incidence of HIV infection and sexually transmitted diseases; to provide effective diagnosis and treatment for HIV and STDs; to provide effective family planning services and to reduce the number of unwanted pregnancies
Accidents	To reduce ill health, disability and death caused by accidents

---

Source: National Audit Office (1996)

---

from home affairs, transport and education were to receive papers and invited to attend as appropriate). There is no evidence that this committee ever met (Robinson et al. 1996).

The committee was supported by three working groups which focused on the public health dimensions of *HOTN*; the monitoring and review of progress towards the achievement of targets; and the contribution of the NHS to the implementation of *HOTN*. At the local level, health authorities were given the responsibility for co-ordination and implementation of the strategy through alliances with other organizations such as local authorities, voluntary agencies, and the private sector.

HOTN was generally welcomed, principally on the grounds that the emergence of an explicit national health strategy marked a significant turning point in seeking to shift the emphasis in health policy from health care to health. However, it was criticized for not taking into account the socio-economic determinants of health, and the strategy and targets were criticized for following mainly a disease-based model. The different views have been summarized as follows:

> for some it was a bold initiative, setting out specific health targets for cutting mortality from the major causes of death and reducing risk factors across a range of illnesses and diseases. For others, [it] side-stepped issues such as the need to tackle poverty and deal effectively with equity. (Appleby 1997: 24)

The UK Faculty of Public Health Medicine was reported as wanting 'the targets and activities to focus on the factors that led to ill health – smoking, poverty, inadequate housing, for example, rather than on the diseases and conditions that resulted' (Holland and Stewart 1998: 154).

HOTN heralded a commitment to target-setting that was to be continued under the Labour government which assumed office in May 1997. There are critics of an approach based on targets, especially those imposed from the centre (Hunter 2002a). For instance, a survey of health authorities carried out in early 1992, just prior to *HOTN* taking root, found that an overly prescriptive approach and the imposition of inflexible targets from the centre were seen as inhibiting implementation (Barnes and Rathwell 1993). Many respondents stressed the need to tailor targets to local needs while recognizing that this could be done within the overall framework of a national strategy. Some commentators, notably the Faculty of Public Health Medicine, had more general concerns about a target-based approach on the grounds that it resulted in a concentration on those things that could be measured and quantified to the neglect of those things that could not. The preoccupation with targets in central government policy-making has become one of the central tenets of the new public management as applied to public service reform in the UK. It is considered further in chapter 3.

The impact of 'The Health of the Nation'   In its review of the health strategy, the National Audit Office (NAO) hailed the initiative as 'ambitious and far-reaching' (National Audit Office 1996: 9). It claimed that the effect of *HOTN* on the NHS as a whole 'has been substantial' (ibid.). However, it did not elaborate on what precisely it meant by this. It is certainly true that the strategy was generally welcomed despite its somewhat narrow conception of health, and despite a focus that remained largely biomedical and concerned with disease prevention and avoidance of premature death rather than with the attributes which kept people healthy in the first place.

However, a key finding from an independent evaluation of the impact of *HOTN* commissioned by the Department of Health was that interest in the strategy waned when it became apparent that *HOTN* did not seem to matter when the performance of the NHS was being judged (Department of Health 1998a). What mattered far more were the by now familiar preoccupations of bringing down waiting lists, ensuring speedy access to hospital beds, and keeping within budget. Managers were not brought to heel for failing to meet *HOTN* targets. By 1997 hopes were fast fading that *HOTN* would bring about the promised paradigm shift in health policy.

There was controversy about how the targets had been set within each of the five key areas. Some argued that the targets, notably those for coronary heart disease and stroke, were set too low, as rates were already decreasing in line with the target set. Progress towards targets was mixed – three targets had gone in the opposite direction: obesity, teenage pregnancies, and smoking among young people. The NAO felt that it was too soon to say how far the strategy 'will ultimately succeed' and urged the Department of Health to keep the targets under close review, both those that had already been met and those where progress 'is slow or trends are running counter to targets to see what further action should be taken' (National Audit Office 1996: 10).

Health policy as shaped by *HOTN* largely emphasized the individual. As noted earlier, it was not widely acknowledged in government that socio-economic factors affect the health of individuals or communities. No targets were based on equity, community development or environmental protection. The focus of the strategy was on containing disease rather than on risk/behaviour modification (Holland and Stewart 1998).

Prior to introducing its own health strategy to replace *HOTN*, the incoming Labour government in 1997 commissioned a review of the impact of *HOTN* at local level in order to learn lessons which could then be reflected in its own approach. The evaluation was commissioned in September 1997 and, to fit in with the ministers' timetable, had to be completed within nine months or so. To ease the research task and allow a larger sample of sites to participate, two research teams were invited to undertake the study. One was based at the London School of Hygiene and Tropical Medicine, and the other at the Nuffield Institute for Health at the University of Leeds in collaboration with a team from the University of Glamorgan. Their respective reports were published separately in one volume, with a joint summary, by the Department of Health in late 1998, by which time the government's own health strategy was well advanced (Department of Health 1998a).

As has already been pointed out, and as the Health Committee heard many times in the evidence it received during its inquiry into public health, whatever the strengths may be, having the Department of Health and the NHS lead on health policy when their focus is primarily on health-care services can lead to tensions and to a marginalization of health policy. There were reservations over the extent to which the NHS would in practice be capable of detaching itself from the pressures of providing health services in order to give priority to a notion of health which went far beyond its boundaries. Given the NHS's generally poor track record in the area of promoting and protecting the public's health, few were convinced that it could or would make the necessary shift in thinking or resources. Regardless of whether or not it is right and proper for the NHS to operate in this way, it has had a disabling effect on health policy (Harrison et al. 1991). The tendency to look upon the NHS as a catch-all for all aspects of health – cure, care, prevention/promotion – may result in unreasonable, if not impossible, demands being placed upon it.

A related problem with *HOTN*, which was picked up in the evaluation and by others (McInnes and Barnes 2000), was the need to take care to ensure that it was not seen only as a national Department of Health initiative or, locally, as falling only within the remit of public health departments located in health authorities.

Despite this caution, the evaluation concluded that *HOTN* was indeed regarded as largely a Department of Health initiative that lacked cross-departmental commitment and ownership. At local level, it was seen principally as a health service document and lacked local government ownership. Interviewees would have liked central government to take a stronger role in improving health and to avoid conflicts between policies of different government departments. 'Shared ownership, therefore, at all levels, both horizontally and vertically, was stressed as essential for success' (Department of Health 1998a: 1). An earlier survey of local authorities' views on *HOTN* conducted for the Health Education Authority and the Local Government Management Board confirmed these findings (Moran 1996). It demonstrated that much of the criticism of the health strategy centred on four main issues (ibid.: 47):

- the health strategy was too narrowly focused on disease models and measurable disease-reduction targets, and failed to promote a positive view of health
- *HOTN* neglected key socio-economic and environmental determinants of health
- because of its reductionist approach, the health strategy failed to appreciate the potential local authority contribution to a national health strategy; local authorities had difficulty reconciling rhetoric about 'healthy alliances' with the allocation of lead responsibility to the Department of Health and the NHS
- no new resources were forthcoming to progress the health strategy.

Although credited with some progress in respect of prevention policy, overall *HOTN* was deemed to have failed over its five-year lifespan to realize its full potential and was handicapped from the outset by numerous flaws of both a conceptual and a process-type nature. Its impact on policy generally peaked as early as 1993, and by 1997 its impact on local policy-making was negligible. It was not seen to count, while other priorities, for example, waiting lists and balancing the books, took precedence.

The architects of *HOTN* understandably took a more optimistic view, although they were mindful of some of its shortcomings in areas such as obesity and teenage smoking rates where the trends were disappointing (McInnes and Barnes 2000). But progress was evident, too. Calman, for instance, who was Chief Medical Officer at the time of *HOTN* and one of its staunchest advocates, notes the advances made towards achieving the targets in several areas, notably coronary heart disease, breast cancer and lung cancer in men (Calman 1998). However, as noted above, critics of the strategy argued that several of the targets would have been met anyway even if there had been no *HOTN*.

Perhaps the most significant contribution made by *HOTN* was simply its *being* there. The fact that it existed at all, particularly given the hostile nature of the political environment at the time, provided an instrument through which to continue lobbying government to do more to improve health. Up until its arrival there had been nothing by way of explicit policy to form the basis of a dialogue with policy-makers to assess progress. Also, the fact of its very existence made it difficult for future governments simply to jettison the strategy without putting something in its place. To this extent, therefore, *HOTN* served as something of a benchmark to those seeking to replace it. It certainly provided the basis for the Labour government's new health strategy issued initially as a consultation paper in early 1998, less than a year after its arrival in office, under the leadership of the newly appointed first ever Minister for Public Health.

New government, new health strategy

The incoming Labour government in May 1997 appointed the Minister for Public Health, Tessa Jowell, as a member of the health department ministerial team. Her remit only covered England as plans for devolution to Scotland, Wales and Northern Ireland were already well advanced. The new government, and minister, were keen to map out a new approach to health policy to demonstrate their commitment to a more socially equitable and cohesive society. For the first time, the responsibility for improved health in this wider sense was not seen as being the sole responsibility of the health department. Rather, it was a cross-cutting theme running through virtually all of public policy, with the public health minister working with and through other government departments to make progress in areas such as child poverty, neighbourhood renewal, community safety and so on. A Social Exclusion Unit was set up in the Prime Minister's office and chaired by the Prime Minister to demonstrate the government's resolve to halt, and in time narrow, the growing health gap between rich and poor. The policy response, therefore, was multiple and complex and embraced many central departments besides health. The Treasury under the Chancellor of the Exchequer, Gordon Brown, assumed a prominent role in the assault on poverty and inequality. A notable initiative to tackle child poverty with a view to eliminating it over the next twenty years was the Sure Start programme. A summary of other policy initiatives that are intended to contribute to a reduction of socio-economic inequalities in health is provided in box 2.2.

Box 2.2   Policy initiatives in the UK designed to reduce socio-economic inequalities in health

Employment-related initiatives

- Welfare-to-work programme ('New Deal'): increasing the skills and employability of unemployed people
- Working Family Tax Credit: more entitlements, more generous benefits
- National minimum wage

Area-focused initiatives

- Health Action Zones: twenty-six disadvantaged areas receive funding for innovative health policy

Initiatives to tackle social exclusion

- National Strategy for Neighbourhood Renewal: 'New Deal for Communities'

Source: Graham et al. (1999)

For all the rhetoric of 'joined-up' government and 'whole systems' thinking, the focus of attention in respect of this new approach to health remained firmly within the Department of Health, and the NHS retained its lead role in taking the government's strategy forward. Furthermore, the Minister for Public Health had no budget, and her influence was therefore largely dependent on her interpersonal skills and ability to be persuasive with colleagues, who, for the most part, did not wish to see any of their budgets going into areas for which they had no direct responsibility or particular interest. As was pointed out in chapter 1, it was a case of 'departmentalitis' confounding the government's desire for 'joined-up' government. One of the findings from an earlier attempt at 'joined-up' thinking and working – known as the joint approach to social policy – in the mid-1970s was that prising ministers away from their departmental base and mindset proved more difficult than had been envisaged (Blackstone and Plowden 1988). Yet, without that political leadership to work across boundaries, any attempt to do so was destined to be short-lived.

In addition to commissioning an evaluation of *HOTN*, the new Minister for Public Health commissioned a former Chief Medical

Officer, Sir Donald Acheson, to chair an independent inquiry into inequalities with a view to demonstrating where the scientific evidence showed interventions to be effective in tackling inequalities (*Independent Inquiry into Inequalities in Health 1998*). The Acheson inquiry made thirty-nine recommendations, only three of which directly concerned the NHS or were within its power to influence directly (Macintyre 2000).

The three priority areas identified by the Acheson inquiry provide guidance on where sustained effort by government and its agents should be focused. These are:

- all policies likely to have an impact on health should be evaluated in terms of their impact on health inequalities
- a high priority should be given to the health of families with children
- further steps should be taken to reduce income inequalities and improve the living standards of poor households (*Independent Inquiry into Inequalities in Health 1998*: xi).

Among the other recommendations were: incorporating inequality within health impact assessment; additional resources for schools in deprived areas; policies to increase work opportunities, better housing and public transport; and policies to tackle ethnic and gender inequalities.

'Our Healthier Nation'

The new health strategy to succeed *HOTN* was entitled *Our Healthier Nation* and unashamedly used the language of health inequalities and social equity. For political and ideological reasons these had had to be subtly sneaked into *HOTN*. The final strategy document had its title slightly modified, so that before *Our Healthier Nation* (*OHN*) came the words *Saving Lives*. Some commentators suggested that the inclusion of these two words brought the strategy firmly within the health-care model, which was less about supporting communities to remain healthy than about keeping individuals alive (Fulop and Hunter 1999). Moreover, the new strategy focuses mainly on disease-based areas (see box 2.3), despite criticism from many quarters and the findings of the review of the *HOTN* strategy (see below). Unlike *HOTN*, the new strategy concentrates on four (not five) key areas and just four targets instead of twenty-seven.

Box 2.3   *Our Healthier Nation:* four key areas and main objectives

Cancer	To reduce the death rate in people under seventy-five
Coronary heart disease/stroke	To reduce the death rate in people under seventy-five
Accidents	To reduce the death rate and serious injury
Mental illness	To reduce the death rate from suicide and undetermined injury

---

Source: Secretary of State for Health (1999)

Fulop and Hunter (1999: 140), who respectively had led the two evaluation studies of *HOTN* reported earlier, suggested that the priority areas and targets remained primarily disease based. 'Our review of the *HOTN* found that the predominance of the medical model underlying the strategy was a major barrier to its ownership by agencies outside the health sector, notably local government and voluntary agencies.' They argued that a sound and logical case could be made for local government rather than the NHS taking the lead role in the local implementation of *OHN*. This was a theme taken up by the Local Government Association (LGA) and the UK Public Health Association (UKPHA) in 2000 in their joint response to *Saving Lives: Our Healthier Nation*. They concluded that 'the traditional concerns of public health medicine focused primarily on alleviating sickness and preventing premature death' remained a 'dominant and overly narrow perspective' in the strategy (ibid.: 2). It accounted for the contribution of agencies outside the NHS not being sufficiently understood or acknowledged. 'Too little attention is paid to the need to integrate local planning mechanisms in order to achieve true joint strategies for health improvement' (ibid.).

The then Chief Medical Officer for England, Sir Kenneth Calman, noted the emphasis in the new health strategy on social exclusion, inequalities in health, and the importance of housing, employment and the environment (Calman 1998). He particularly commented on the fact that *OHN* was to be an 'across-government' strategy focused on improving the outcomes of interventions to change the health of the population.

Not surprisingly, considerable enthusiasm from the health lobby greeted the consultative document, but it proved difficult to maintain this level of support when the final policy statement eventually appeared. It was long overdue, and when it did finally appear the event was something of an anti-climax after months of waiting. Moreover, while it contained much that was significant in respect of a health agenda, parts of it still seemed rooted in a medical model of health prevention and promotion that distracted attention from the wider socio-economic determinants of health. At about this time, too, the government was becoming increasingly preoccupied with its plans to reform the NHS. Initially it was opposed to another 'big bang' approach to structural change, preferring instead to introduce changes incrementally. However, as ministers began to appreciate how extensive and deep-seated the problems of the NHS were, as a result of under-investment and neglect of its infrastructure stretching back over nearly twenty years, their attention was inevitably, and almost wholly, directed to addressing these in the full knowledge that the NHS was a key electoral issue. For it to remain an electoral asset rather than become a liability required ministers to devote most of their attention to it, probably to a greater degree than had been anticipated.

As mentioned earlier, the government wanted its health strategy to be informed by the lessons from the valuation of *HOTN*, especially as these applied at local level. The study certainly contained a number of pointers for the new public health strategy (see box 2.4). To a degree, these were taken into account by the government following several briefings with officials and one including the Minister for Public Health. But the proof of the pudding is not so much in getting the words right, although this helps. It is in translating those words into action. Since the publication of the final strategy in 1999, over a year after the consultation document, the principal issue has centred on implementation. Subsequent chapters will return to this issue and are critical of the degree to which the pointers listed in box 2.4 have been addressed. At the same time, there have been numerous other initiatives which have had a direct, or indirect, impact on achieving the targets and objectives set out in *OHN*. Indeed, the government has been accused of suffering from 'initiativitis', so frequent have been the announcements of new initiatives and policies from the centre.

Box 2.4   Pointers for the new public health strategy

Greater success is likely with integrated central leadership and committed local ownership.
Government needs to:

- send out clear, consistent 'corporate' signals and ensure cross-departmental ownership
- develop an integrated framework for new initiatives, e.g., HAZs, HImPs, HLCs, SRB, Agenda 21 etc., thereby addressing effectively the underlying determinants of ill health
- establish shared ownership, horizontally and vertically, with a statutory framework and accountability, and widen ownership outside the NHS
- spell out agency expectations, tasks and responsibilities
- give consideration to a joint lead role locally between health and local authorities
- encourage a wide range of programme approaches at the local level.

Building and sustaining local intersectoral partnerships and alliances will be important.
There is a need:

- to develop and use a matrix approach involving diseases, population groups and community settings
- for a development strategy to equip managers and practitioners with the requisite skills and competencies
- to acknowledge and take into account the different cultures in health and local authorities
- to use existing evidence on alliance building
- to involve all key stakeholders and to include the public through the voluntary sector and other means.

Developing the evidence base for both target-setting and other implementation activities should be a key priority.
There is a need to consider:

- the further development of evidence-based targets
- mechanisms for the dissemination of evidence in respect of public health interventions to the NHS, local government and the voluntary sector
- local target-setting using the evidence base
- re-examination of the inclusion of the suicide target, or the addition of items stressing measures of well-being

- new approaches to implementation which combine individual life-style change and community development
- strengthening the public health information and intelligence function to operate widely across health and local authorities
- setting up new data capture mechanisms, including relating resource use to outcome, for future evaluation purposes.

Without the requirement for substantial performance management, particularly at local level, a new public health programme's chances of success will be reduced significantly.
There is a need to:

- require the development of local strategies and targets, together with a timetable, involving health and local authorities and the voluntary sector
- hold each group responsible for its contributions – both process and outcomes
- make public health part of the core business, by embedding it in the organizational culture
- consider instituting regular and independent policy audit, to include a cost–benefit approach
- consider a new role for the Health Education Authority in strengthening the performance infrastructure[a]
- keep the public health function under regular review
- include *Our Healthier Nation* in the new performance management framework, with measures of process as well as outcomes.

[a] The Health Education Authority was formally replaced by the Health Development Agency in April 2000.

Source: Department of Health (1998a)

Developments in the NHS since 'Saving Lives: Our Healthier Nation'

The publication of the government's health strategy, coming on top of plans for improving the performance of the NHS, did not complete its policy-making. Indeed, as the NHS rose higher up the political agenda as a result of many well-publicized failures in health care, the flow of policy statements seemed to increase. In chronological order, beginning with *The NHS Plan*, the turn of the century has witnessed a considerable outpouring of policy direction, advice and guidance. Most of it has been directed at the NHS and health care, with the consequence that health policy issues have been overshadowed or marginalized.

The NHS Plan   Concern over the lack of progress in modernizing the NHS, and growing awareness of the scale of the challenge if it was to fulfil any of its promises to the public, led the government to produce a ten-year plan for the NHS. It appeared in July 2000 and was the work principally of the health secretary personally and a handful of trusted advisers. A number of modernization action teams also contributed to the plan. The plan announced a compendium of desirable, and many overdue, developments to improve the operation of the NHS. But, with its principal focus on health care, the public's health did not figure prominently.

A slim chapter buried deep in the plan was devoted to improving health and reducing inequalities. There was recognition of the fact that the NHS acting alone could do little to deliver on such a challenging agenda. 'Improving health is now a key priority for all government departments. Action will be taken to step up the cross-departmental focus on health and inequalities' (Department of Health 2000: §13.2). The plan was rather vague on the specifics of what this 'action' might be or the form it would take. At local level, new partnerships to tackle inequality were announced – Local Strategic Partnerships – in recognition of the fact that 'the NHS cannot tackle health inequalities alone. The wider determinants of ill health and inequality call for a new partnership between health and local services. *That is the key strategic role for health authorities'* (ibid.: §13.22; my italics). The implication in the plan that the NHS will lead on this crusade finds little support in recent history that it will either happen or prove possible.

Of particular importance for the public's health are three developments announced in the plan. First is the commitment to devising national targets for health inequalities that were subsequently announced in March 2001 (see below). These are intended to complement the local targets called for in the health strategy *Saving Lives: Our Healthier Nation*. The targets will be delivered by a combination of specific health policies and broader government policies, including abolishing child poverty through Sure Start, and action on cancer and coronary heart disease to be taken through the national service frameworks.

Second is the setting up of a Healthy Communities Collaborative (HCC), which is aimed at identifying ways of achieving innovation and spreading best practice. The model for this is the Primary Care Collaborative, which has been hailed a great success in imparting change management skills to those in primary care, although an unpublished evaluation of this initiative commissioned by the Department of Health is allegedly rather sceptical of the impact of collaboratives in bringing about long-term sustainable change. Moreover, little has been heard from the HCC since its introduction.

Finally, in recognition of the importance of the regional dimension, new single, integrated public health groups have been introduced across NHS regional offices and government offices of the regions. These forums are intended to encourage an approach to neighbourhood renewal and regeneration that combines social and economic development with health concerns. The importance of this link is reinforced by the pivotal role of the NHS as employer in local communities. Often the NHS is the major employer and almost always a significant one. Therefore, it has, or should have, a crucial role to play in the regeneration of particular neighbourhoods.

The purpose of all these changes is to 'help embed work on prevention and health inequalities within the core of what the NHS does' (Department of Health 2000: §13.28). Above all, successful implementation is what matters.

But when all is said and done, the limited role of the NHS in influencing or having much impact on the wider health agenda becomes a recurring theme. As mentioned above, only three of the Acheson inquiry's thirty-nine recommendations directly concerned the NHS.

'Shifting the Balance of Power' In response to critics who accused the government of control freakery over its NHS reforms and a top-down, command-and-control style of management which was deemed wholly inappropriate to the needs of a complex adaptive system, the government announced its intention to devolve responsibility and shift the balance of power from centre to periphery. Following a speech along these lines in April 2001 by the health secretary, which took his own officials by surprise, the government moved swiftly to publish its plans following the election in June 2001 under the heading *Shifting the Balance of Power* (*StBOP*) (Department of Health 2001a). The changes plunged the NHS into the most extensive structural upheaval since its birth and ushered in a period of instability and uncertainty with which it is still coming to terms. Whatever their ultimate purpose and impact, the *StBOP* changes have served to distract attention from the implementation of the NHS plan while employees worry

about their futures in a service that is changing dramatically and unpredictably at every level.

Several of the changes have implications for health policy, although their main impact will be on the delivery and performance management of health-care services. Primary Care Trusts (PCTs) are the new front line of the NHS and from April 2003 assumed responsibility for 75 per cent of the NHS budget, as well as responsibility for commissioning care for their local populations. High among PCTs' stated objectives are assessing, with a view to improving, the health of their communities. Each PCT board has appointed a director of public health. However, early studies of the operation of PCTs suggest that, while some progress in this direction has been made, most lack the sustained leadership essential for the successful pursuit of the policy (Gillam et al. 2001). Moreover, it seems reasonable to predict that PCTs will be under extreme pressure to deliver on the government's NHS modernization agenda, with its stress on improving access to health care, bringing down waiting lists, and keeping within budget. Of course, improving access to health care can help provide better health for those denied access for whatever reason. But improving health care, as has been argued throughout, is insufficient if the policy goal is to adopt a holistic view of health.

The other key development arising from *StBOP*, and mentioned above, is the strengthening of public health at regional level. Four new health and social care regions have replaced the existing eight NHS regional offices, although these are being disbanded and their functions absorbed by the Strategic Health Authorities. But the regional directors of public health (RDsPH) have been located within the regional government offices, where they will liaise with a range of regional functions concerned with economic and social development. The intention is that they will tackle the wider determinants of poor health and inequalities. As the guidance on next steps puts it, 'for the first time, the RDsPH and their teams will be uniquely positioned to work with other Government Departments in the regions to build a strong health component into regional programmes in areas such as transport, environment and urban regeneration' (Department of Health 2002a: §18b). Such a move could indeed herald a new era for public health and begin to put health on the agenda of regional bodies and, possibly in time, elected assemblies (see chapter 5). But question marks remain over whether the public health function as currently configured will be able to meet the challenge.

The implications of *StBOP* for the health agenda will be considered further in chapter 4.

'Tackling Health Inequalities' and 'Vision to Reality' Two Department of Health documents on public health appeared in the summer of 2001, perhaps in response to a perception externally that the government had taken its eye off the health ball as distinct from the health-care one. It wanted to reassure its critics that this was not so. The first document, *Tackling Health Inequalities,* was produced to consult on the action needed to achieve the two national health inequalities targets announced in March 2001 (Department of Health 2001b). The targets were aimed at narrowing the gap in childhood and throughout life between socio-economic groups and between the most deprived areas and the rest of the country. To deliver the targets, six priority themes were proposed:

- providing a sure foundation through a healthy pregnancy and early childhood
- improving opportunity for children and young people
- improving NHS primary care services
- tackling the major killer diseases: coronary heart disease and cancer
- strengthening disadvantaged communities
- tackling the wider determinants of health inequalities.

Apart from the two national targets a number of other targets impacted on health inequalities, including the national targets on child poverty, smoking and teenage pregnancy, all of which are central to supporting work on health inequalities.

The document reaffirmed the government's determination to act on health inequalities and noted that effective action requires joined-up working across government and across sectors at national, regional and local levels. The consultation exercise ended in November 2001, and almost 600 written responses were received. In addition to these, a series of regional consultation conferences and related events attracted a combined audience of 1000 people. The results of the consultation exercise were published in a follow-up report in June 2002 (Department of Health 2002b).

The responses were generally supportive of the six priorities listed above and of the government's recognition of the importance of health inequalities. The overriding challenge, however, would lie in translating this priority into a sustained commitment and programme of action across government. Respondents also urged that the strategy should look beyond the NHS to the influence of the wider determinants of health inequalities. The Treasury-led cross-cutting spending review on health inequalities, completed in July 2002, was seen as crucial in widening the perspective of an emerging strategy (HM Treasury 2002).

Concerns were expressed over the ability of PCTs to meet the challenge and act as vehicles for reducing health inequalities; over continuing gaps in the evidence base about the effectiveness of interventions to tackle health inequalities; over the need to learn from other initiatives, build on good practice, consolidate the many different initiatives (rather than introduce new ones) and strengthen partnerships; over the need for a sustained and long-term approach rather than one based on short-term, time-limited projects and initiatives; and over developing a sufficiently comprehensive approach.

Feedback on the consultation document was critical of its largely NHS and medical focus, despite the occasional mention of wider public health issues and the role of other agencies. In particular there was concern that the contribution to be made by local government had been given insufficient attention and weight and needed to be made more explicit. This should include its duty to develop community strategies and its health scrutiny role. Local strategic partnerships were seen as key vehicles for involving both the NHS and local government in the health inequalities agenda.

In terms of delivering on the agenda, the feedback from respondents was that the document was unbalanced and gave too much prominence to the NHS and too little attention to the territory beyond. Involving local government and the voluntary sector was also seen as a way of developing greater public health capacity to deliver on the policy agenda.

There was particular criticism of the heavy reliance on projects and initiatives, the majority of which were too short term and small in scale. They also served as a distraction for staff that was counter-productive. Lessons from existing initiatives should inform mainstream developments. Too often they did not, and mainstream activities continued unaffected or unchallenged.

The second document, *Vision to Reality*, took the form of a progress report from the public health minister and the CMO on developments since the Acheson inquiry on inequalities, the *Our Healthier Nation* strategy, *The NHS Plan*, and the CMOs's report on strengthening the public health function (Department of Health 2001c). As such, it did not contain any new policy thinking but a reaffirmation of the government's commitment to a modernized health service and public health service that 'will lay even greater emphasis on the protection and improvement of the population's health, and which will at last start to reduce the gap between the best and worst off in society.' The document adopts a slightly defensive tone when the minister and CMO in their joint fore-word note that 'for too long the NHS has been seen as a sickness service not a health service. We believe that the role of the NHS in partnership across the community, should be to prevent sickness and ill health, as well as treating problems once they arise.' The new PCTs are singled out for special mention as 'the focus for delivery of public health programmes', working as part of local strategic partnerships 'to ensure co-ordination of planning and community engagement, integration of service delivery and input to the wider Government agenda.'

The Wanless review In March 2001, the Chancellor of the Exchequer commissioned a major review to examine future health trends and the resources required over the next twenty years to close gaps in performance and to deliver the NHS plan. The review team was led by Derek Wanless, former chair of the National Westminster Bank. An interim report was published in November 2001 (Wanless 2001), and the final report was pub-lished in April 2002 (Wanless 2002). The review team was given the following terms of reference:

1. To examine the technological, demographic and medical trends over the next two decades that may affect the health service in the UK as a whole.
2. In the light of (1), to identify the key factors which will deter-mine the financial and other resources required to ensure that the NHS can provide a publicly funded, comprehensive, high quality service available on the basis of clinical need and not ability to pay.
3. To report to the Chancellor by April 2002, to allow him to con-sider the possible implications of this analysis for the Government's wider fiscal and economic strategies in the medium term; and to inform decisions in the next public spending Review in 2002.

In its interim report, the review team made reference to the import-ance of public health (Wanless 2001). Following further consult-ation, the final report gave greater prominence to this theme. It argued that 'better public health measures could significantly affect the demand for health care' (Wanless 2002: §1.27). It quoted one response which claimed that 'the one major area of government activity that can, but mainly over the long term, reduce demand for health care and other related services is public health promotion and sickness prevention' (ibid.). Others whom the review team consulted said that investment in changing people's behaviour now, such as cutting out smoking, improving diet and encouraging more exercise, could significantly improve the population's health status. This would potentially reduce demand and postpone the average age at which health care would become expensive. On top of any health benefits, a focus on public health was also seen to bring wider benefits by increasing productivity and reducing inactivity in the working-age population. Also in its interim report, the review team was concerned that the poor evidence base in public health demonstrating the effectiveness of interventions made it difficult to conclude that investment in public health should be significantly increased. In its final report, it revised this conclusion and was more optimistic in its assessment of the potential for public health interventions. It nevertheless concluded that 'the likely impact of health promotion on overall demands for health care is difficult to assess' (ibid.: §3.41). There is a time lag between interventions and effect, and it is, and probably always will be, difficult to attribute changes in health status to an individual intervention. But the review team went on to state that, 'despite methodological difficulties and the length of time needed for research, there is evidence suggesting that some health promotion interventions are not only effective, but also cost-effective over both short and longer time periods' (ibid.). It quoted research findings showing that 25 per cent of all cancers and 30 per cent of cases of coronary heart disease are preventable through public health measures (McPherson 2001).

In its assessment of the balance of care, the review team was critical of the current balance, with care too focused on the acute hospital setting. In its conclusions, the review team suggested that one of the five factors which would result in lower projected overall resource requirements would be 'more success in public health' (Wanless 2002). The bias in health policy towards health care is not confined to the UK. The World Health Organization, in its *World Health Report 2002*, points out that much scientific effort and most health resources are directed towards treating disease rather than preventing it. It calls on governments, in their stewardship role, to achieve a much better balance between preventing disease and merely treating its consequences. It is a lack of political will, not knowledge, that is hindering progress.

Underlying the Wanless review was a conviction that good health is good economics and that, far from being a cost, investment in health is a benefit to individuals, employers and the government. Healthy communities attract investment, while unhealthy ones do not (Hunter 2002b). In particular, as mentioned above, health promotion and prevention play an important role in moderating the need for care.

The review developed three scenarios in order to identify the cost drivers and to help estimate the resources required to deliver a high quality health service (see box 2.5). Of the three scenarios, the Treasury has accepted the 'fully engaged' scenario. This is apparent from its cross-cutting review published in July 2002 (HM Treasury 2002), which includes a section on health inequalities. The 'fully engaged' scenario contains the most significant implications for public health, since it assumes it will improve

> dramatically with a sharp decline in key risk factors such as smoking and obesity, as people actively take ownership of their own health...People have better diets and exercise much more ...These reductions in risk factors are assumed to be largest where they are currently highest, among people in the most deprived areas. This contributes to further reductions in socio-economic inequalities in health. (Wanless 2002: 39)

Box 2.5   Three scenarios

- *Solid progress* – people become more engaged in relation to their health: life expectancy rises considerably, health status improves and people have confidence in the primary care system and use it more appropriately. The health service is responsive, with high rates of technology uptake and a more efficient use of resources.
- *Slow uptake* – there is no change in the level of public engagement: life expectancy rises by the lowest amount in all three scenarios and the health status of the population is constant or deteriorates. The health service is relatively unresponsive, with low rates of technology uptake and low productivity.
- *Fully engaged* – levels of public engagement in relation to their health are high: life expectancy increases go beyond current forecasts, health status improves dramatically and people are confident in the health system and demand high quality care. The health service is responsive, with high rates of technology uptake, particularly in relation to disease prevention. Use of resources is more efficient.

Source: Wanless (2002: 35)

As the review points out, this scenario is the most optimistic of the three and therefore the most challenging. If all goes according to the model and effective public health measures are applied, then NHS spending in 2022–3 will be £154 billion. Under the least optimistic 'slow progress' scenario, spending will be £184 billion – a gap of £30 billion. By accepting the 'fully engaged' scenario, the government has committed itself to significant improvements in public health that will benefit the high risk groups at a faster rate than the rest, thereby reducing the health gap.

Wanless was concerned only with the NHS, and his remit did not extend to other sectors or policy fields which have a significant impact on health. It is hardly surprising, therefore, to find that the approach adopted towards public health is somewhat narrow and confined largely to a medical model. Nevertheless, his report has given an important boost to those advocating a more assertive approach to public health interventions within government. The fact that it was produced by a businessman has served only to strengthen its message and has accorded it a credibility and edge that it might otherwise not have achieved.

Inevitably, the focus of media and public attention when the Wanless report was published was on its assessment of the funding issues in regard to the NHS, both the level of funding and the mechanism for raising it. Its comments on the importance of public health and improving the health status of the population as means to ease resource pressures on the NHS were largely ignored, thereby illustrating the problem of getting a balanced and informed public debate about the importance of looking at health policy as a 'whole system' rather than as a health-care system with the emphasis on acute care and hospital beds.

The Health Committee's inquiry into public health

Moving away a little from the heart of government, but still close to it, in May 2000 the House of Commons Health Committee announced its inquiry into public health with the following terms of reference:

> to examine the co-ordination between central government, local government, health authorities and PCGs/PCTs in promoting and delivering public health. In particular, the Committee will examine the organisational arrangements and will address:

- the inter-operation of Health Action Zones, Employment Action Zones, Healthy Living Centres, Education Action Zones, Health Improvement Programmes and Community Plans
- the role of the Health Development Agency
- the role of PCGs and PCTs
- the role and status of the Minister for Public Health
- the role of the Director of Public Health
- the extent to which current public health policy is reducing health inequalities.

The Committee will also study alternative models of public health provision.

The committee's terms of reference were extremely broad and wide-ranging – far more so than the majority of its inquiries. Yet, in many respects the subject demanded such an approach in order to ensure that all the issues were captured. By all accounts they were, and the report was generally well received despite its hard-hitting criticism of some aspects of the public health function.

Between July 2000 and January 2001 the committee took oral evidence from a wide range of organizations and individuals. It also received around 100 written memoranda, many of which proved influential in shaping the committee's conclusions and recommendations. A number of key themes emerged throughout the inquiry which are worth listing here. They were concerned with:

- achieving a balance in health policy between health and health care, 'upstream' and 'downstream' interventions
- strengthening public health leadership at all levels
- establishing strong partnerships at all levels for a broad-based approach to public health
- placing the emphasis on public health practice and implementation rather than on knowledge acquisition for its own sake
- avoiding distracting and probably counter-productive re-organization of structures imposed from the centre while allowing local initiatives to flourish
- creating incentives for health improvement activity
- building the evidence base in public health
- learning the lessons from past failures or partial successes in putting health before health care.

The committee was critical of government health policy in terms of its imbalance in favour of health care. Even in respect of those initiatives intended to promote health the committee was critical of the way in which they had been implemented. For example, while the objective to tackle health inequalities was welcomed, the means to realize this goal were found wanting. For example, Health Action Zones (HAZs) developed too slowly to spend all the money allocated to them in their first year. Each HAZ reviewed by the committee had its own intrinsic merits. The difficulties arose more from the sheer number of initiatives and their lack of integration. The committee did not consider these to be short-term glitches but rather that they reflected more profound systemic and structural problems which relate to the lack of co-ordination between different government departments, statutory agencies, elected authorities and the voluntary sector.

The committee also expressed concern over the existence of the plan charting a ten-year programme of reform for the NHS (see above). Though it welcomed the plan's commitment to health inequality targets, which were subsequently announced in February 2001, it nevertheless felt that 'a great opportunity to give public health a real impetus has been lost by the lack of emphasis on this area in the Plan' (House of Commons 2001a). The plan contained a slim and rather thin chapter on the wider public health issues, and this came quite late in the report. In contrast, the Scottish and Welsh equivalents led with a strong commitment to the public's health and to the need to support such a development (see chapter 5).

Members, somewhat reluctantly, accepted the Secretary of State for Health's assurance that *The NHS Plan* was of equal status to the health strategy *Saving Lives: Our Healthier Nation*, but they remained suspicious of the government's motives and felt that if *Saving Lives* had equal status with *The NHS Plan* then this should have been evident from the plan itself. In addition the government appeared to be dragging its heels over the report from the public health function review which was awaiting publication throughout the committee's inquiry The committee was not impressed by such comings and goings and recommended that publication of the previous CMO's report on the public health function be published without further delay. In fact, the report was published on the very same day as the Health Committee's report (Department of Health 2001d).

All in all, the committee considered policy to be out of kilter in respect of the balance between health care and health. 'For all the laudable Government rhetoric about dragging public health from the ghetto, in the race for resources it runs the risk of trailing well behind fix and mend medical services' (House of Commons 2001a: §47). The committee accepted the health secretary's view that the role of Minister for Public Health had not been downgraded following a change in title, while remaining concerned at the number of external organizations and individuals who thought otherwise. The committee was more concerned that the present arrangements do not adequately promote cross-government working. Though attracted to the notion of relocating the Minister for Public Health within government, perhaps into the Cabinet Office, the committee recommended that the public health function remain with the Department of Health 'for the present'. However, the committee wanted greater evidence that it had assumed priority within the department. 'If that is not forthcoming, we think the case for relocation would be much stronger' (ibid.: §237).

As it is required to do, the government replied to the Health Committee's report but refused to accept any criticism of its strategy or the balance (or imbalance) between health and health care (Department of Health 2001e). It trotted out all the policy initiatives it had launched as evidence of its commitment to a public health agenda (see box 2.2 for a summary of the key initiatives), and refused to acknowledge that there might be difficulties in implementation arising in part from the sheer volume of initiatives and because of the major structural changes occurring in the NHS and, to a lesser extent, in local government.

Chief Medical Officer's project to strengthen the public health function

One of the Health Committee's recommendations was for publication of the Chief Medical Officer's final report on the public health function. The report, commissioned from the former CMO, had been completed for months but had not been published for reasons which were never very clear. The delay may have had something to do with a new CMO coming into office who had different priorities: the public health function review was a project he inherited rather than launched. Whatever the reasons, the government obligingly published the final report on the same day as the Health Committee's report in March 2001 (Department of Health 2001d).

The function review was set up in response to the government's desire to improve the health of the population as a whole but especially that of the worst-off sections of society. It was argued that implementation would not succeed without a strong public health function. Doubts were expressed over whether the function was 'fit for purpose', given that the government's health strategy could be achieved only with a strong multi-disciplinary public health workforce in place.

Much had happened since the project began, including the publication of *The NHS Plan* in July 2000. An interim report had been published some three years earlier, in February 1998 (Department of Health 1998b). The final report reflected feedback from the interim report and summarized major recommendations from the project, achievements to date, and further action and development work needed. Five major themes emerged during the project as being essential for a successful public health function:

- a wider understanding of health and well-being
- better co-ordination and communication within the public health function
- effective joined-up working
- sustained community development and public involvement
- an increase in capacity and capabilities in the public health function.

More will be said about some of these themes in chapter 4, which considers the shift to a new paradigm, 'managing *for* health', and what this might entail in practice for the public health function to succeed.

The general response to the CMO's project report was to welcome it and its recommendations but to express concern that it had taken so long to get to the point of acknowledging the need to strengthen the capacity and capabilities of the public health function. The lengthy delay, it was feared, was indicative of the low priority which the government attached to the subject. Moreover, although the report made encouraging, though hardly new, noises about developing the public health workforce, it lacked detail on precisely how this would be done, by whom, and at what cost. Again, seasoned observers wondered how far the final report was an exercise in 'going through the motions' rather than heralding the start of a significant initiative to strengthen public health in order to deliver on the government's commitment to improve health and narrow the health gap. Was it merely another example of symbolic policy-making and gesture politics from which public health seemed to suffer more than its fair share?

What is worth noting about the review, despite justified criticism that it remain wedded to the public health function within the NHS and had under-representation on its working groups from sectors other than health care, is that it demonstrated the government's grasp of the importance of implementation and the need for a workforce appropriately skilled and in sufficient number to effect change on the ground. However, subsequent work on strengthening the function was overtaken by more urgent business affecting the NHS and its future, notably the preparation of the NHS plan. Events were moving swiftly, and once again in the history of health policy in the UK the NHS dominated the scene and moved centre stage. There was no let up as a major restructuring overwhelmed the NHS during 2001 and 2002 with the unfolding of the *StBOP* changes described above.

Conclusion

This chapter has reviewed the emergence and early twitches of a health policy as distinct from a health-care policy. There is an impressive weight of documentation setting out the case for rebalancing policy so that it gives proper attention to health. In the UK alone, since the early 1990s there has been a steadily growing acknowledgement of the importance of health and the specific issue of health inequalities. The New Labour government, elected in 1997, must take much of the credit for this shift in the climate of opinion. It also, as Appleby and Coote (2002: 121) point out, 'rehabilitated two concepts that are now widely recognised as essential to tackling health inequalities: locally-based partnerships that cross old boundaries, and community development.'

So far so good. But, if there has been a common complaint running through the various policy pronouncements it has been that there remains a bias in favour of the NHS and of avoiding ill health and disease rather than maintaining good health. The contribution other sectors and agencies can clearly make to the public health effort are too often overlooked or treated as an add-on. This has been a recurring complaint over the years. Such an approach, with its emphasis on the NHS, has not surprisingly failed to engage these other stakeholders in ways that are essential if the wider public health agenda is to be addressed.

Such a conclusion is reinforced by Webster's assessment of the government's approach to public health. Its

> paper plans for improving health and addressing inequalities in health cover a wide range and they are designed to look impressive. On the ground the government's initiatives look less impressive. They tend to be subject to the common criticism that on account of their token scale and especially because they fail to address the problems of economic disadvantage that lie at the roots of ill health, they are unlikely to achieve anything like the impact promised in the government's expensive publicity presentations. (Webster 2002: 221)

Despite attempts by many governments in countries such as Canada and the UK, progress in making a sustainable shift in policy from health care to health has proved disappointing. The next two chapters consider why this should be so.

3 Managing Medicine

Introduction

If, as the management thinker Peter Drucker claims, 'management world-wide has become the new social function' (Drucker 1990: 218), then this carries profound implications for all organizations, whether in the business or service sector. Regardless of whether organizations exist for profit or are non-profit, the responsibilities of the managers running them are essentially the same. They include: defining strategy and goals, developing people, measuring performance, and marketing the organization's services. But this is not to suggest that there are generic managers or universal ways of managing, or that what works in the private sector must also apply to the public sector. Context is all important, and simplistic assumptions about management are not helpful when dealing with complex adaptive systems, of which health and health care are good examples (Hunter 1999; Exworthy and Halford 1999; Plsek and Greenhalgh 2001; Chapman 2002). Indeed, there are those who insist that there can be no general 'science of managing' since managing is not a standardized activity (Whitley 1988). This is because

> managerial tasks and practices are dependent upon organizational arrangements and cannot easily be isolated from their context to form the object of research. They are not widely standardized and generalized across enterprises. (Ibid.: 56)

Within the health sector, there has been a global revolution in the organization of health services. Health-care reform 'is a transnational process that is intimately linked to the particular forms of socio-economic "globalisation" now in the ascendancy' (Twaddle 2002: 387). Management has been held up as the principal instrument through which the supply side objectives of health system reforms can be achieved as well as those which seek to shift the emphasis in health policy away from an exclusive concentration on health services and towards the notion of health in its wider sense. This and the next chapter review both of these facets of the rise of the management function in health policy and consider their implications for a shift in emphasis towards health.

In this chapter I examine management's preoccupation with health-care services and the way in which it has progressively intruded into clinical work. The next chapter switches the focus to examine managing *for* health, where the command-and-control and mechanistic model of management employed in health-care services is rejected as ill-fitted to the task. Arguably, such a model is also ill-suited to the needs of health-care services, which themselves are complex entities requiring a different style of management in respect of professional work. However, that is not my concern in this book. The point to stress is that it is essential to be clear about the type of management arrangements required if the policy objective is the pursuit of *health* as distinct from *health care*. Arguably, such clarity is almost wholly absent from contemporary discourse on the nature of health policy.

Managing for what?

In order to interpret the management task in any undertaking, it is desirable if not essential to have a notion of what the vision or ultimate goal of policy is. Often, however, this is lacking or exists only in rhetorical or symbolic form that bears little relationship to what actually happens in practice. If the vision or goal of policy is absent, fuzzy and impossible to discern, or riddled with ambiguity, then the management task will be messy or, at any rate, messier. Charles Webster, official historian for the NHS, has written:

> While the NHS claimed from the outset to give high priority to the promotion of health...in reality this aspect of the service was never more than weakly developed, notwithstanding claims to the contrary, habitually made in ministerial speeches. (Webster 1996)

One is tempted to add *plus ça change*.... Despite the numerous attempts reported in chapter 2 to nudge the focus of policy towards health and away from an exclusive concentration on health care, the bias towards treating illness has proved to be remarkably resistant to change. Spending on prevention is still less than 1 per cent of the overall NHS expenditure (Duggan 2001). Earlier chapters have offered explanations for this imbalance and for the mismatch between rhetoric and reality.

Persistent confusion over the management function has bedevilled the NHS since its birth (Hunter 1980; Harrison et al. 1992). This reflects a wider lack of clarity over the purpose and direction of the NHS in health policy as a whole. It often seems that the NHS and health policy are one and the same thing. In short, health has remained within the ghetto of, and has been eclipsed by, health care and the almost iconic position of the NHS.

Within the NHS itself, there is further confusion over the nature of the management task and the role of management in what has traditionally been regarded as a professionally dominated organization. Can professionals, notably clinicians, be managed in the same way as, say, cleaners or porters? Many would argue that, until recently, the question has been fudged or simply ducked. They would assert that the NHS has never truly been managed, as a significant proportion of its workforce – and certainly its most powerful group, the medical profession – has remained largely unmanaged despite its control over substantial resources (Klein 1989; Harrison et al. 1992). But there is then the matter of what is meant by management in this context, since, as was noted earlier, managing complex systems is not the same as managing a hospital laundry or catering service.

To put it another way, a convincing case can be made to support the contention that what the NHS has been subjected to almost continuously since its first major reorganization in 1974 is at best a sort of partial management which has left the core business of health care – that is, what clinicians do and how they contribute to improved health – virtually untouched. While the clinical core has continued to be largely administered, the infrastructure supporting the core has been progressively more heavily managed. Hardly any wonder, then, that managing *for* health has been eclipsed by a concentration on means (that is, the provision of health-care services).

The dilemma for managers is that, precisely because management as an activity is deemed so important, it is incumbent upon them, and their political masters, to ensure that the appropriate type of management is in place for any given activity or organization. Arguably, it is on this issue that problems have been encountered. Checkland (1995), for instance, is of the view that if we are serious about management then this means enlarging and enriching what we mean by it and getting away from the reductionist, rational, goal-seeking approach best represented by the scientific management school and subsequently adopted by new public management thinking. This type of management has its place in activities and tasks of an operational, routine, repetitive nature. But most of health care, and certainly health, is not like that, and therefore the type of management that has been imposed upon health systems is seriously flawed.

Government policy has also contributed to the confusion surrounding the management role and, indeed, the very purpose of the NHS. Appleby and Coote (2002: 123) blame a 'lack of definition and top-level leadership' for a confused policy over which the government appears to have little control. To its credit, the government has done much to stimulate local activities aimed at strengthening communities and enhancing the quality of life, all of which help to narrow the 'health gap' – though even here there is evidence that the local implementation of national policy on health inequalities has been hampered by deficiencies in performance management, ineffective integration between policy sectors, and contradictions between health inequalities and other policy imperatives (Exworthy et al. 2002). Some of these difficulties exist because the government has allowed the media to set the health policy agenda and has become trapped by its own rhetoric, reacting to events rather than taking the initiative and helping to shape them. Appleby and Coote again:

> the more the government promises to 'save' the NHS and signals that this is what it really cares about, the harder it becomes for it to capture the public imagination for a different agenda aimed at reducing inequalities, improving health and, ultimately, checking demands on the NHS that are triggered or exacerbated by social and economic factors. . . . [H]ealth inequalities still appear to be a second-order issue, liable to be elbowed out by the more pressing problems presented by a massive provider of treatment and care. That is potentially bad news for health. . . . It is ultimately bad news for the NHS as well. (Appleby and Coote 2002: 123)

The new rationalism and health

The arrival of new public management (NPM) in the 1980s constituted 'one of the most striking international trends in public administration' (Hood 1991). The principal doctrinal components of NPM are set out in box 3.1. NPM derived its theoretical origins from two sources: the new institutional economics and business-type managerialism. The former has helped to generate a set of related reform doctrines built on notions of contestability, user choice, transparency, and incentive structures. Such doctrines are markedly different from traditional notions, with their emphasis on orderly hierarchies and the elimination of overlap. The business-type managerialism is merely the latest in a succession of waves of this type which began in the 1970s. It is in the tradition of the scientific management movement, although it has undergone a facelift and image change and in the process has acquired a new jargon. Central to this type of managerialism is a set of common beliefs. Professional management

- is generic and portable
- is paramount over technical expertise
- requires high discretionary power to achieve results
- is central and indispensable to better organizational performance.

Box 3.1 Elements of the new public management

- Hands-on professional management in the public sector
- Standard-setting, performance measurement, and target-setting, particularly where professionals are involved
- Emphasis on output controls linked to resource allocation
- The disaggregation or 'unbundling' of previously monolithic units into purchaser/provider functions, and the introduction of contracting
- The shift to competition as the key to cutting costs and raising standards
- Stress on private-sector management style and a move away from the public service ethic
- Discipline and parsimony in resource use: cost-cutting, doing more with less, controlling workforce demands

---

Source: Hood (1991: 4–5)

There is no single accepted explanation for the considerable and continuing appeal of NPM. It would appear to be a response to global socio-economic changes with an abhorrence of 'statist' and uniform approaches in public policy, and a perception that public services seem to be run more for the convenience of those providing them than for those paying for and using them. In short, they are not customer- (or patient-)centred.

An emphasis on health sector reform adopting a particular managerial approach based on new public management principles and a pro-market, pro-business ethos has been encouraged by the World Bank (1993; 1996) and more recently by members of its senior staff (see, for example, Preker and Harding 2002). The thrust of the bank's approach, which has not gone uncriticized, has been to promote markets, diversity and competition (Stiglitz 2002). A system of 'managed competition' is seen to offer a number of advantages, although its limitations and disadvantages are acknowledged in passing. Managed competition or care pursues cost-effective health spending, universal insurance coverage, and cost containment through tightly regulated competition among companies that provide a specified package of health care for a fixed annual fee. Evaluations of it show mixed results, but Light (1993; 2000) regards competing managed care systems as unlikely to tackle the great health-care needs of the twenty-first century and the diseases of chronicity and preventable morbidities.

Growing concern among centre-left governments elected in the latter half of the 1990s that the application of market-style mechanisms may have resulted in various dysfunctional aspects in organizational design and management practice, notably greater fragmentation and rising management costs, has resulted in new waves of reform aimed at acknowledging that connected problems require 'joined-up' solutions. Therefore, and this is crucial, without abandoning the core features of NPM thinking, governments have sought to modify some of its more extreme market-style features. Yet, those same governments have not retreated as far from those market-style principles as they would have their electorates believe. In the case of the UK, for instance, it has been a case of 'back to the future', with the government actively reintroducing competitive principles and privatizing the delivery of care in ways that appear to go far beyond anything they inherited from their Conservative predecessors, who flirted briefly with an internal market in the NHS between 1990 and 1996 but, at the end of the day, shied away from letting it rip and allowing it to develop in an uncontrolled manner. Arguably, these various twists and turns and retreats in health-care policy have given rise to emerging tensions over the style of management that is most appropriate for health care.

As Hood describes it, NPM is a loose shorthand label for a set of broadly similar doctrines which dominated the management reform agenda in many of the OECD countries from the late 1970s (Pollitt 1990). It sought to replace 'old' public management which, with its complex bureaucratic structures and centralizing ethos, had failed spectacularly to improve the performance of services. Some observers saw NPM as nothing more than 'a gratuitous and philistine destruction of more than a century's work in developing a distinctive public service ethos and culture' (Hood 1991). Moreover, a contradiction was seen to lie at the heart of NPM thinking. Despite talk of the need for innovation and flexibility, this was to be achieved through a series of instruments, notably purchaser–provider separation, contracts and targets, all of which had proved themselves to be more than capable of limiting both innovation and flexibility, that is, bringing about precisely the opposite of what was intended (Stewart 1998).

The rise of managerialism in health policy

As noted already, a preoccupation with management is nothing new within UK health-care policy. The NHS has been subjected since the early 1970s to successive waves of reform, all of which have had as a common theme running through them the shift of the frontier of management further into territory traditionally occupied by the medical profession. The new managerialism has been directed towards the reform of the public sector, including health care. Significantly, there has never been any discussion of what it might mean to manage *for* health rather than to manage medicine. Health-care management has concentrated on hospitals, buildings, beds and clinical work. Managers are judged on their ability to manage institutions or facilities, not to manage the health of their communities or populations (Evans 1995; Hunter 1999).

There are four 'world views', or doctrines, about the management of organizations (Moore 1996). These are:

- *traditional bureaucracy* – with an emphasis on clear structures, hierarchical chains of command, clear accountability for performance
- *new public management* – with an emphasis on making organizations more like firms operating in markets through the introduction of competition to improve performance (see box 3.1)
- *'Japanese' organization model* – or 'clan', 'solidarity' model of organization in which a sense of identity with, and pride in, the organization itself is the main source of motivation
- *professionalism* – shares the 'Japanese' model's assumption that people work better when they are trusted and their performance is not closely monitored: the sense of identity is with the profession rather than with the organization, or possibly dual loyalty to both exists.

The central point about these world views, or doctrines, is that management is not purely, or even principally, a technical enterprise. Ideas, culture and ideologies make a real difference, and we ignore them at our peril.

Within many health-care systems undergoing reform, there has been a shift from models of traditional bureaucracy and professionalism to a model of new public management where, as the previous section showed, the emphasis is on encouraging public bureaucracies to mimic some of the 'successful' features of private-sector management practices (Harding and Preker 2002). These include government and public services steering more and rowing less, being mission driven rather than rule bound, and being more responsive to the customer and to quality (Osborne and Gaebler 1993). They also entail a preoccupation with notions of 'quality', such as total quality management (TQM) and continuous quality improvement (CQI), and other such processes and techniques.

In his critique of what he terms 'the new management thinking' and 'pseudo-science of management', Loughlin (2002: 65) is disturbed by the way this creed has 'continued to colonise human society, taking hold of public institutions and even the rhetoric of public debate.' The language of this management thinking originated in the world of business and is capable of application to every organized human activity. Loughlin asserts that the attempt to apply principles of good management derived from one context (business) to a very different one (the health service) represents 'a philosophical error'. Slogans and buzzwords dominate the debate, with little substance and clarity. Management fads and fashions appear to pass for sound management practice (Marmor 2001; Collins 2000). As Marmor suggests, expressions such as 'joined-up' government are persuasive terms 'that imply success by their very use' (Marmor 2001: 13). But their overall effect is one of alienating those providing health services who subscribe to a different ethos of public service. As Loughlin puts it, 'lurking in the hollow foundations of Qualispeak are the forces of the market' (Loughlin 2002: 109). Health is construed as a 'product' and the caring process as a 'production process' governed by the same principles as a commercial venture. Managers are encouraged to be 'leaders' in a venture intended 'to make every aspect of professional life comprehensible in terms of the same free market ideology' (ibid.: xix). Little wonder that many professionals and some managers feel alienated from such a view of management when applied to health and health care.

Managing doctors

It is not the purpose of this chapter to provide a study of the management of doctors. However, a brief review of the management–medicine interface is important because it is the preoccupation with health-care systems and their improved management that has dominated health policy in recent decades and, arguably, has contributed to the capture of public health medicine by health services at the expense of its core public health work. These dynamics need to be fully understood if they are to be modified in favour of a less restrictive view of health management. They are also relevant to Loughlin's dismissal of claims that there is a management science derived from business practice. As was pointed out at the start of the chapter, 'management is not a "science" in the sense that engineering is: what it means for a building to stand up does not change in accordance with the purposes for which it is used but what it means for an organisation to be "successful" does' (Loughlin 2002: xviii).

One of the most difficult issues in any health-care system that claims to be managed is how to manage professionals (Harrison and Pollitt 1994; Hunter 2002c). This theme has dominated UK health-care policy since the 1970s and lies at the heart of the concept of clinical governance introduced in the late 1990s. Clinical governance is not simply about improving the quality of care offered but is also about corralling professionals so that they become rather more corporate and accountable players in the NHS 'family'. The same reasoning underlies the creation in England of Primary Care Trusts, since, at one level, they represent a means of weakening general practitioners' independence as solo contractors and strengthening the degree of corporate management across practitioners and practices in a locality (Marks and Hunter 2001).

The health sector is characterized by the special position occupied by the medical profession, which functions largely outside the control of management. The notions of management and professionalism are in potential conflict with each other. As Harrison and Pollitt (1994: 34) note, management is about 'getting other people to do things' while professionalism is about 'employing one's own judgement about what to do and how to do it'. This notion of professionalism originates from the special private relationship between professionals and clients in which professionals are relatively autonomous in order to be able to exercise their independent judgement. In these circumstances, their expertise is not readily or easily managed by a third party. Hence, subordinating professional autonomy to managerial will is not really a feasible option.

Nonetheless, the replacement of consensus management, which survived in the NHS until the early 1980s, with general management and the notion of a single chief executive nicely illustrates the tension between management and medicine and the struggle for supremacy among managers in order that they may increase their influence within an essentially producer-dominated setting. Despite the acknowledgement that successfully managed companies relied on effective teams rather than single heroic chief executives, this was lost on the NHS as it sought to shed its allegedly outmoded consensus management team structure (Drucker 1955). Despite the management changes introduced in the 1980s, research showed that doctors' influence remained largely undiminished (Harrison et al. 1992). As Harrison and Pollitt observe, and recalling the discussion of power in chapter 1, 'it seems that doctors retained a good deal of *covert* influence; many general managers expected doctors to be difficult, and therefore refrained from raising issues that might arouse opposition, preferring instead to leave matters to be dealt with by peer pressure' (1994: 50). Having in place a cadre of general managers who owed their allegiance to the government of the day represented a powerful and efficient vehicle for implementing centrally imposed reforms. It also marked a turning point in the previous rather collusive relationship between managers (or administrators, as they were known up until the arrival of the cult of managerialism in the 1970s) and doctors and opened up a rift between them that has remained evident through subsequent management changes during the 1990s.

The Labour government's modernization of the NHS set out in its *NHS Plan* (Department of Health 2000) carries profound implications for the doctrine of professionalism, seeking to bring it within a new public management doctrine which was sweeping through other public services, notably education. At the heart of the government's reform programme is its desire to shift the nature of clinical work and subject it to the rigours of externally imposed performance management. In particular, there is a wish to modify the way in which clinical work is undertaken so that role boundaries between professional groups are blurred and there is a greater emphasis placed on integrated care pathways, thereby enabling easier transitions across the interface between primary and secondary prevention and acute care interventions. Too much health care, in the government's view, remains fragmented and conducted in silos with an absence of effective linkage between the component parts. Not that there is anything new about this discovery. The first NHS reorganization in 1974 was in part intended to address the problem of fragmentation in the delivery of care.

Probably most health policy commentators would accept the government's diagnosis of the problem confronting health-care systems, such as the NHS, where there exists an imbalance in favour of acute care over primary prevention and promotion. A reason for this appears to be the power of the medical profession to determine where resources are allocated and which services should receive investment. But if there is agreement on the diagnosis, the means for addressing the problems are viewed with rather less support, principally because they have failed so far to win over those they are supposed to influence and whose practices they are aimed at changing. Unless the medical profession engages with the management changes being imposed on them, it seems unlikely that the latter can ever succeed or work as intended. Reforming the way clinicians work, and seeking a better balance between 'upstream' and 'downstream' interventions, will continue to remain an elusive goal.

Compounding the management dilemma in health systems globally is the degree of rapid change that has characterized them in recent years. The UK NHS has been in a state of near constant flux ever since its first reorganization in 1974. In virtually every instance of reorganization, change has been driven by policy shifts at national level which are often riddled with confusion and ambiguity. Most managers are being compelled (and propelled) by complex forces over which they have minimal control. In such circumstances, few are able to develop coherent visions that are likely to generate long-term commitment. Little wonder, then, that the credibility of management and managers has become seriously eroded with each successive wave of change that they are largely powerless to direct or shape. Far from management being strengthened under such circumstances, as intended, its role is in fact being progressively diminished.

The paradox in health policy is that, at precisely the same time as the management task is being unintentionally undermined, government is looking to managers to take on greater responsibility and be held accountable for the performance of public services. But what chance of success is there when managers who feel disempowered must confront professionals who may be significantly empowered and who resent any significant erosion of this, especially if it means strengthening the hand of managers for whom generally they have little respect (Allen 1997)?

One way of getting round these tensions is to shift the burden of clinical accountability and other management functions onto clinicians (Degeling et al. 2001; 2003). Hence the rapid growth of clinical directorates in recent years. They can work effectively, but only if seen as compatible with professional values. If these collide, and substantial compromise with professional values is called for to achieve budgetary objectives, then clinicians are likely to lose their power and legitimacy and become subject to the top-down dictates of senior managers. Little wonder, then, that the role of clinical directors is proving highly problematic (Degeling et al. 1998).

The management task poses a dilemma for doctors. Is their role to attend to the needs of individual patients more efficiently and effectively, or to consolidate the needs of the wider community in order to reach a view on how to use limited resources prudently? Most discourses on management in medicine cite the latter conception, but the dilemma, or tension, nevertheless exists and probably always will. The challenge is not so much one of seeking to remove the tension but of managing it more effectively. There is no easy resolution of such difficulties and tensions, although moves to emphasize professional leadership that is separate from, but co-operative with, general management may offer a way forward (Comack et al. 1997).

The point to stress here is that, for all the reasons just mentioned, it is perhaps not so surprising that NHS managers should be suffering from a deep malaise rather than feeling enthused and energized by the changes thrust upon them. Overcoming this malaise is going to be possible only if serious attention is given to the concerns expressed above and, in particular, to the style and type of management that is appropriate for both a professionally dominated organization and one whose mission is to improve health.

If it is the case that professionals work best in networks rather than in hierarchies, and that it makes little sense to attempt to manage professionals and their intellect and expertise in any formal, top-down, restrictive way, then the management challenge is how most appropriately to support professionals and help them to develop in new ways. Successful strategies based on such a view require a more subtle and sophisticated management response than is implied by much new public management thinking.

Criticisms of new public management

Critics of NPM accuse it of being all hype and no substance (Rhodes 1995; Stewart 1998). Scratch away the trendy jargon and fashionable packaging and a fairly orthodox approach to management is all too evident. The language spoken may have changed, but beneath it all the old problems and weaknesses remain. Other critics claim that NPM has led to a rapid growth in the number and cost of managers without real evidence of effectiveness in terms of improving health.

Wider criticisms of NPM centre on the inappropriate importation of business-sector practices into a public service culture. Especially in health care, notions of competition and markets are viewed as anathema and as ultimately leading to the corrosion, or outright destruction, of a public service ethos. The idea that a pure market is possible in health care is akin to the naïvety of those who subscribe to the 'scientific management' school of thought, with its simplistic beliefs about rationality and human behaviour. If organizations are political constructs in which various interests jostle for supremacy then markets can be (and are) similarly manipulated and subject to the interplay of power between stakeholders.

Underpinning NPM is a belief in a 'consumer-led' model of health care which carries with it dangers for the wider public health. There is a risk, in the words of one public health doctor, that

> the power of individual demand will override considerations of community benefit, reducing commissioning of care to the sum of individual patient transactions. If personal needs take precedence over those of the population then not only will the public health perspective have been marginalised but the opportunity to improve health status will have been severely restricted. (McCallum 1997: 101)

The potential conflict between public health and market/business approaches may be illustrated in relation to exercise (Sallis and McKenzie 1991). Whereas the public health view supports initiatives aimed at reducing inequality of access to sport and leisure facilities and developing enjoyment and lifelong participation in physical activity for the collective and personal benefits it brings, the competitive team ethos of the market emphasizes the identification of a winning elite at the expense of the many. In short, the collaborative philosophy illustrated by public health programmes sits uncomfortably with a competition-focused health service. 'Effective public health programmes require co-operation between agencies which are now expected to compete to maintain their share of resources' (McCallum 1997: 101).

These words were written before the Labour government's modernization reforms had even been invented. But, despite the government's alleged abandonment of the internal market and competitive ethos, these remain alive as the government seeks to reintroduce competitive principles through the emergence of 'foundation hospitals', with the prospect of a two-tier NHS, and to encourage increasing diversity of provision through new types of public–private partnership. None of these developments in themselves need marginalize public health initiatives, but collectively they are likely to do so if the experience from the early 1990s is anything to go by. This is one of the findings from a study of the experience of the fifteen EU member states in introducing market forces into their health-care systems (European Health Management Association 2000).

Perhaps the most serious charge levelled against NPM is its inability to comprehend 'wicked issues'. As Stewart puts it,

> generally there is a tendency to simplify management tasks in the belief that clear targets and separation of roles can clarify responsibility and release management initiative. Simplification has been achieved by the separation of policy from implementation, the development of contracts, quasi-contracts or targets governing relationships, and their enforcement by performance management. (Stewart 1998: 16)

NPM, as mentioned, is based on a mistaken belief that there exists a generic model of management and that it is assumed to be a private-sector model based on the public as customers or consumers. But in public life, the position is rather more complex. There is not a single relationship but rather a diversity of relationships that require a diversity of management approaches. In particular, a focus on the public as customers ignores the relationship with the public as citizens. To caricature the position, whereas health-care services may be seen as customer-focused, public health services tend to be seen as citizen-focused. Each may be valid in its own terms, but they require different management approaches.

NPM thinking has also added to the problem of fragmentation within public services such as the NHS. This has resulted from a plethora of new semi-autonomous agencies set up to improve the efficiency of government and its responsiveness to users. Splitting problems and functions up into separate units each focused on a specific, limited task with its own targets and performance measures is seen as good management because it becomes possible to create manageable tasks. However, the downside of such fragmentation is a failure to ensure that sufficient capacity is in place to work across units or departments. It is in the public domain where 'wicked issues' such as social exclusion, the environment and so on can require action not by one unit, but across units in ways that cannot be predetermined. The government appears to recognize this at a conceptual level: hence its preoccupation with 'joined-up' government. However, its chosen means to realize the end are ill-suited to the task. Indeed, NPM is at risk of reinforcing a silo-based mentality when it comes to managing health care.

Such differentiation seems likely to develop further as a result of awarding hospitals foundation or self-governing status, which the government is anxious to do in the spirit of encouraging greater devolution and 'localism' in the NHS (Milburn 2003). Where this fits with the notion of partnership across the local health community so that primary and secondary care work in a closer, more integrated fashion is hard to comprehend. It is certainly likely to make the process more complex than it already is.

In short, NPM remains rooted in an industrial/mechanistic/top-down model of organization and management, as do many of the institutions and structures that operate in everyday life in modern societies (Kickbusch 2002).

Target-setting

Target-setting is a particular manifestation of NPM-type thinking. When governments adopt a target-based approach to health policy they generally have two purposes in mind. These may be pursued separately or jointly. First, they might want to ensure that policy is directed towards the achievement of health outcomes. Second, they might want to monitor progress in order to ensure that health policy objectives are being achieved. A target-based approach to policy implementation is predicated on a rational model of policy-making which many analysts acknowledge to be flawed and oversimplistic (Kickert et al. 1997). It is an imperfect process in an imperfect environment. It cannot be, as is often mistakenly assumed, a rational linear process. In practice, the construction and implementation of targets is a messy affair. Targets may have multiple purposes and meanings for the various stakeholders affected by them. For example, they may be seen as a source of aspiration rather than a management tool. They may achieve more as symbols of policy than as precise instruments designed to implement policy to the letter. Under the *Health of the Nation* strategy, described in chapter 2, targets were seen largely in symbolic terms. In contrast, under its successor, *Our Healthier Nation*, the government's strong managerial and technocratic bias may dominate unless the effort involved in modernizing the NHS overwhelms all other policy considerations – a not inconceivable possibility (Hunter 2002a).

Health targets have undoubted strengths. These include: targets being purposeful, achievable, realistic, owned by those they will most affect, and, as far as possible, evidence-based. But they can also possess, or give rise to, a number of undesirable features, including:

- perverse incentives – a disease-oriented, target-based approach may achieve quicker results but be less effective in reducing inequalities as well as ignoring the main determinants of health
- distortion of data, leading to goal displacement and manipulation of results
- target-setting in the absence of power and resources to bring about change
- too many targets – priorities become meaningless if they include everything
- measurability – there is a risk that what gets measured gets done.

Targets are also subject to abuse and misuse. What has happened to them in the UK is a good example of this danger. As Kickbusch (2002: 215) points out, 'while targets at first seem to be an ideal approach to monitor accountability and performance at various levels of the health system, their "overuse" can become counterproductive and unmanageable as time is spent on reporting rather than on implementing policy.' As the House of Commons Health Committee (2001a) heard from a succession of witnesses in the course of its inquiry into the public health function, the emphasis in the NHS on top-down targets has served to stifle innovation and creativity. This has, in turn, led to managers doing what was expected of them rather than what was most desirable locally. Arguably, the fixation with targets as a tool of performance management has resulted in considerable 'gaming' in order to appear to be meeting the targets. It has also tilted the balance in favour of holding front-line practitioners to account at the expense of allowing them sufficient freedom and space to lead and devise local solutions for local problems.

Kickbusch asserts that target-setting has been hampered by the marriage of epidemiology and 'managerialism', which, in turn, has led to an 'epidemiological-rationalist approach' that has been

plagued by two realities: first, that any order is always incomplete and imperfect and in the final analysis there is ordering but no order because new risks emerge, and, second, that even some of

the most straightforward epidemiological risks need a very complex political and social process in order to address them adequately. (2002: 214)

As a consequence of these realities, and the tensions associated
with them, 'increasingly target-setting has become a technocratic/
professional/managerial enterprise rather than a process to set in
motion the acceptance of new political priorities for health policy,
in order to define and ensure the new health territory' (ibid.: 215).

This analysis of the drawbacks and disadvantages of targeting
is not confined to outside commentators. A little noticed report
from the Cabinet Office's Performance and Innovation Unit, at the
heart of government, puts forward a strikingly similar critique
(Cabinet Office 2001a).

New forms of public health organization are needed if there is
to be a paradigm shift from managerial/instrumental issues
around better service delivery to meeting the central challenge of
postmodern society, namely, 'how do we want to live?' (Beck
1992). Addressing this question goes to the heart of stewardship
and good governance.

Implications for health policy

The implications of the critique of NPM for health policy and the
call within public health to move beyond the epidemiological/
managerial risk model based on disease categories are all too
clear even if they have proved elusive. The various attempts in
the UK, Canada and elsewhere to address the underlying factors
that promote health and turn attention away from setting targets
that measure symptoms proved short-lived. As Kickbusch recalls,
'during the 1990s health policy moved increasingly back into its
original domain, that of providing health services, and the political debate in most countries was dominated by finance driven
issues of healthcare provision, rather than issues of production of
health in the broader societal domain' (2002: 217).

If a way is to be found of rekindling the approach to thinking
about targets in societal and broad population terms, then there is
a simultaneous need to move away from a narrow, myopic managerial approach to health policy that takes as its starting point
the health-care delivery system as being at the epicentre of health

policy, whereby the only targets that count are those for which the health-care system is responsible. New territory needs to be claimed in order to rediscover the truth at the core of public health that the primary determinants of disease are mainly economic, social and political.

Complex adaptive systems

To start with, the assumption that there are universal ways of managing needs to be challenged. This is especially true in respect of complex public-sector policy challenges dealing with messes or 'wicked issues'. Indeed, this self-evident fact is understood by many managers working in a public sector that is highly varied in respect of the functions and services it undertakes. For instance, the Society of Local Authority Chief Executives (1995) distinguished between spotlights and lighthouse beams to make their point. Complex social problems that cross organizational boundaries require a lighthouse beam to illuminate the terrain; in contrast, spotlights tend to focus on particular parts of a problem and fail to see the interconnections. The danger with much NPM thinking is its spotlight orientation and tendency to concentrate on the parts rather than the whole. The model resembles Newton's 'clockwork universe' in which big problems are broken down into smaller ones, analysed, and solved by rational deduction (Plsek and Greenhalgh 2001). Chapman makes the same point when he argues that 'the current model of public policy making, based on the reduction of complex problems into separate, rationally manageable components, is no longer appropriate to the challenges faced by governments' (Chapman 2002: 11). Writers on NPM, such as McNulty and Ferlie, claim that a concern with 'joined-up' government, with its focus on laterally based principles of organization, conflicts with the strong vertical lines and functions that are a defining feature of NPM (McNulty and Ferlie 2002). At the same time, what Ferlie and Fitzgerald term 'the hegemony or underlying logic of a NPM' (2002: 352) will survive any challenge to it as 'the NPM archetype is in a mature state within the UK health care sector' (ibid.: 343). Perhaps. It is also possible that we may advance beyond NPM to another 'archetypal shift', a post-NPM archetype (ibid.: 345).

Complex adaptive systems demand a different management approach from that indicated by NPM, with its reductionist, mechanistic, scientific management overtones. As Plsek and Greenhalgh (2001: 625) point out:

> not so long ago public health was the science of controlling infectious diseases by identifying the 'cause' (an alien organism) and taking steps to remove or contain it. Today's epidemics have fuzzier boundaries...: they are the result of the interplay of genetic predisposition, environmental context, and lifestyle choices.

The growing frustration over a seeming inability to tackle, or successfully resolve, complex problems, coupled with implementation failure in respect of achieving stated policy goals, may suggest that the management models and approaches to which we have traditionally looked are simply no longer appropriate.

To make the point, the definition of a complex adaptive system offered by Plsek and Greenhalgh (2001: 626) is apt. Such a system 'is a collection of individual agents with freedom to act in ways that are not always totally predictable, and whose actions are interconnected so that one agent's actions changes [sic] the context for other agents.' Complex systems usually have fuzzy boundaries, with changing membership as well as members who may belong to several systems simultaneously. In such systems, tension and paradox are natural phenomena and will not necessarily be resolved. Rather, they need to be acknowledged and managed.

One major tension that springs to mind in the context of health policy is over evidence-based policy and practice. Whereas conventional reductionist scientific thinking assumes that we shall eventually be able to cite evidence as to what works and does not work according to certain scientific tests of what constitutes valid evidence, complexity science assumes no such thing and is comfortable with issues which cannot be resolved. It is likely that effective health interventions may never be evaluated according to the tenets of evidence-based practice because they are not appropriate to capture how behaviour is changed. We will require different methodologies and even reliance from time to time on hunch or the precautionary principle rather than assuming that it is only a matter of time and resources before we have the reliable hard evidence that we need to make an informed decision. The principal reason for this is that the effectiveness of interventions is highly context-specific and therefore cannot simply be deduced from randomized controlled trials or other experimental approaches that deliberately exclude contextual influences.

In short, treating organizations as complex adaptive systems allows a more realistic management style to emerge in health policy and one that challenges traditional mechanistic, linear thinking of the type evident in NPM doctrines. Managing *for* health requires such a management style if it is to succeed in shifting the paradigm from a 'downstream' to an 'upstream' focus on the factors and influences that determine improved health for individuals and whole communities. It has profound implications for the content and conduct of the public health function. These issues are the subject of the next chapter.

Last word: medicine, management and health

Before proceeding to the next chapter, a last word on the relationship between medicine, management and health is in order. As was argued earlier, although there has been an encroachment by management into territory traditionally colonized by doctors, who have enjoyed more or less untrammelled freedom to make decisions and allocate resources since the inception of the NHS, it has occurred within an overall context that shows no lessening of medical dominance in respect of the growing medicalization of social and personal problems, whether in regard to mental health, obesity or whatever.

As Mechanic (1991) and Harrison (1999) have pointed out, the changes occurring at the medicine–management interface 'all fall within a continuing medical paradigm and therefore perpetuate its intellectual dominance even if the autonomy of particular groups is under challenge' (Harrison 1999: 64). It is an example of Lukes's third face of power we encountered in chapter 1 (see p. 20). Managers' values and preferences are shaped by doctors whose autonomy is being challenged by those very same managers. The challenge to what might be termed the medicalization of life (and death) will come not from management but from alternative paradigms, although management will remain an important instrument by which any particular new paradigm can be realized. Hence the relevance of the thinking that has recently resurfaced around complex adaptive systems noted above. One of these alternative paradigms has been at the core of this book, namely, putting the health of the public first rather than disease and ill health. For this to happen, there needs to be a wholesale change in how health and management is conceived. The issues are principally political ones involving a reconfiguration of vested interests and a redistribution of power in favour of those forces advocating healthy public policy. It represents the major challenge for those seeking to manage *for* health rather than just managing.

4 Managing *for* Health

Introduction

Advancing the public's health has always been the stated goal of health policy, even if in practice a systemic bias in favour of responding to ill health and tackling disease has remained all-pervasive and remarkably impervious to change.

Previous chapters have presented some of the reasons why this is so. In this chapter, this policy paradox is explored more directly from the viewpoint of the public health function. Traditionally, public health has been charged with the task of promoting, and providing leadership for, the public's health. But the function has acquired, and embraced with more or less enthusiasm, a broad range of responsibilities, not all of which are compatible with each other or strictly belong to the core business of public health as perceived by many of its practitioners. Moreover, each function requires particular expertise and knowledge. Too often, in the view of both its supporters and critics, the practice of public health within the NHS has allowed itself to be captured by a narrow health-care management agenda centred latterly on clinical governance and evidence-based medicine. Elsewhere, notably in local government, the public health function lacks legitimacy and focus – although this may be changing now that local authorities have both a responsibility for improving the social well-being of their communities and a new scrutiny function over not just the NHS but the health needs of their populations. Furthermore, often the term 'public health' is a handicap, since it is not recognized outside the NHS and is imbued with medical over-tones.

Despite all the obstacles, and as previous chapters have indicated, the government appears committed to tackling the wider determin-ants of health through a 'whole systems' approach and a belief in 'joined-up' government. Partnership working has a long, and mostly unimpressive, history in health policy. Undaunted, the government has shown renewed energy in its endeavours to secure effective joint working. Among the many initiatives launched have been Health Action Zones, Health Improvement and Modernization Programmes and, more recently, Local Strategic Partnerships. Their progress will be assessed in terms of the available evidence. If the intention is to shift health policy from managing for health care to managing for health then a number of prerequisites need to be in place. Above all, a new model of decision-making and implementation is urgently needed to help realize the government's stated aspirations. Along-side it are a particular set of skills and competencies which will need to be imparted to those practising public health in the new model. They do not currently exist in sufficient abundance for us to be confident that the new model can be fully realized. Indeed, this deficit lies at the heart of the so-called crisis in public health.

Public health has historically been one of the key drivers leading to effective collective action for improved health and well-being (Frenk 1992). But recent years have witnessed a weakening of public health's leading role. Julio Frenk, now Minister for Health in Mexico and formerly director-general of the National Institute of Public Health in Mexico and a senior official in WHO, has written that 'public health is experiencing a severe identity crisis, *as well as a crisis of organisation and accomplishment*' (1992: 68; my italics). It is the issue of organizational weakness and the absence of effective impact that is the primary concern of this book, and in this chapter an attempt is made to explain this state of affairs in respect of the public health function. Frenk cites a US Institute of Medicine (IoM) report which opens with an indictment of public health: 'In recent years, there has been a growing sense that public health, as a pro-fession, as a governmental activity, and as a commitment of society is neither clearly defined, adequately supported nor fully under-stood' (Institute of Medicine 1988). A new report from the IoM concludes that fourteen years later public health in the USA remains 'in serious disarray' (Institute of Medicine 2002). Similar conclusions apply in respect of public health policy in the UK, in Canada and throughout most of Europe.

Frenk believes the challenge is to put public health once again at the centre of scientific and political debate on the future course of health. Later sections of this chapter consider what might be done to meet the challenge in the UK.

What is public health?

Definitions of the term 'public health' abound. Frenk asserts that it is 'charged with ambiguous meanings' and goes on to specify the five connotations that have been particularly prominent in public health's history (Frenk 1992: 69). First, use of the term 'public' equates with governmental action, that is, the public sector. Second, more broadly, 'public' embraces the community as a whole – the public – and not only government. Third, public health is directed towards non-personal health services, that is, services affecting the environment or the community. Fourth, preventive services are part of public health when directed at particular groups, such as children. Finally, the term 'public health problem' is sometimes used to refer to illnesses that are particularly dangerous, such as the epidemics associated with tuberculosis or HIV/AIDS. Part of the problem in clarifying the nature of the public health function is its very breadth and amoeba-like nature. It is hardly surprising, therefore, to find that the practice of public health has 'shifted uneasily between the analysis of health problems and the administration of health services' (Berridge 1999: 45). Giving the sixteenth Duncan Memorial Lecture in Liverpool, the Chief Medical Officer for England, Sir Liam Donaldson, reaffirmed this uneasy mix of tasks and responsibilities (Donaldson 2002). He noted the many key interfaces between public health and health services as follows:

- delivering population public health goals
- improving the outcome of care
- reducing inequity
- practising public health in a health service environment
- evaluating health services. (Ibid.: 836)

It is interesting to note that, of these five interfaces, two and possibly three are directed towards health-care services.

In 1988 the Acheson committee, set up to restore confidence in the specialty of public health medicine and set it on the right track after years of confusion and lack of role clarity, defined public health as 'the science and art of preventing disease, prolonging life and promoting health through the organised efforts of society' (Acheson 1988). The definition has appeal because it reflects what modern public health is all about, namely,

> a population perspective, an emphasis on collective responsibility for health and on prevention, the key role of the state linked to a concern for the underlying socio-economic determinants of health as well as disease, a multi-disciplinary basis which incorporates quantitative as well as qualitative methods and an emphasis on partnership with the populations served. (Beaglehole and Bonita 1997)

Holland and Stewart believe it to be 'a clear and acceptable definition' which should be at the forefront of all policy affecting public health (Holland and Stewart 1998: 189). It is reflected in the Chief Medical Officer's (and others') conception of the function as falling into three broad parts:

- promotion of health, including tackling health inequalities
- quality and clinical standards, i.e., clinical governance
- protection of public health and the management of risk.

Despite Acheson's attempt to refocus public health on its core business, the specialty has continued to be buffeted by successive NHS reorganizations and has found itself more and more at the mercy of managers, who have strengthened their grip on the service and on its priorities. Few managers have been advocates for public health and have sought instead to use expensive public health professionals to pursue their own, or their political masters', agendas around evidence-based medicine, contracting, commissioning, and clinical governance. For the most part, public health specialists have been willing accomplices. No one would deny the importance of such functions or the need for clinicians to be involved in at least some of them. But whether public health physicians should see their role and purpose largely along these lines is questionable. Contributing to the problematic nature of public health and its tasks is the fact that the three parts of the role of public health listed above entail sizeable and complex chunks of activity that are not easily invested in a single specialty or individual. The same conclusion can be drawn from the list of five key interfaces between health services and public health cited above. Yet, the CMO in describing these tasks makes no mention of whether it is reasonable or feasible for a single team or specialty to discharge such a diverse range of functions. There is only a passing reference to the fact that meeting these challenges 'will require a full assessment of the capacity and capability of the public health workforce' (Donaldson 2002: 838). On the face of it, this seems a rather curious recommendation because the CMO presided over the closing stages of a major review of the public health function published after a lengthy delay in 2001 (Department of Health 1998b). The review is described in chapter 2. An outcome from it was the production of a workforce development plan which, although getting to an advanced stage of completion, has never been published. The reason for the delay, and presumably ultimately the burial of the plan, was allegedly the cost of implementation and a failure within government to agree on this.

As this brief section has sought to demonstrate, the reasons for the mess in which public health medicine has found itself are complex and have persisted over time. They are not easily resolved, and passions can quickly be stirred which often hamper reform.

The evolution of the public health function

The history of the specialty of public health can be briefly told. 'Whereas public health doctors in 1948 started out demoralised but grew in confidence during the 1950s and early 1960s..., community physicians [introduced in 1974] began optimistically but rapidly became disillusioned' (Lewis 1986: 162). Since that time, and notwithstanding several hopeful fresh (though, as they turned out, false) starts, public health has never really regained its former confidence.

Until 1974, public health practitioners were located in local government. Many commentators regarded that location as more appropriate for the pursuit of the health of a population or community than a place in the NHS that was dominated by service and management considerations. As Holland and Stewart note, even if there is a consensus about the skills and concerns of public health, 'there remains confusion between its role in the management of clinical services and its primary role in the management of public health services' (Holland and Stewart 1998: 208). They argue that, as part of the corporate body responsible for allocating resources and developing services, public health is well placed to develop policies and services to improve health rather than simply clinical care. Unfortunately, public health concerns are always in competition with the needs of clinical services, and these nearly always take precedence. 'Treatment of individual patients seems far more immediate a priority than changes in health status for the future' (ibid.: 209).

By the mid-1970s there was a growing belief that public health had to be reformed and set on a new course. The 1974 NHS reorganization resulted in public health changing its name to 'community medicine' and becoming integrated within the NHS, and from then on the leadership role for public health resided with the health-care system. By changing the name to 'community medicine', the hope was that a new specialty based on epidemiology and population medicine would emerge that was distinctive in much the same way that general practice and hospital medicine were distinctive. Reforming public health involved significantly extending its remit. The Faculty of Community Medicine envisaged community physicians analysing patterns of health and illness, assessing needs, and evaluating services. All this was at some remove from the previous job of those in public health, which was to co-ordinate and administer community health services.

But the attempt to broaden the remit of community medicine carried with it costs. For a start, the task of analysing patterns of health and illness and health needs involved factors and agencies far beyond the scope of the NHS. These included work, environment, income and housing, which are not normally viewed as health problems (see figure 2.1). Second, taking a holistic view of the NHS and its responsibilities, including the balance between 'upstream' and 'downstream' activities, carried the risk of public health practitioners coming into conflict with those in other medical specialties. In particular, public health's concern with the health of the collective runs counter to the medical profession's focus on the individual. It is hardly surprising, therefore, that this ambitious vision for community medicine failed to materialize.

Possibly of greater concern was that, paradoxically, public health became 'more remote from the community' at this time 'and more closely identified with hospital-based medicine' (Berridge 1999: 48). Moreover, in contrast to the vision set for it, the whole nature of public health underwent a redefinition that can be characterized 'as a move away from environmentalism

towards a greater degree of individual responsibility for the maintenance of health' (ibid.).

This narrowing of the public health function resulted in a
number of perverse consequences. Principal among them has
been a tendency for public health to become part of the NHS
management agenda in respect of issues such as contracting for
services under the former internal market, developing long-
term service agreements following the demise of the market, clinical governance, and evidence-based medicine. None of these
issues is unimportant, but it is questionable whether public health
specialists are the obvious or exclusive choice to assume responsibility for them. There was unease within the public health profession about its loss of contact with the local community and about
managing health services rather than analysing broader health
problems (Berridge 1999). The loss is echoed in Donaldson's reference to public health and community development, which has its
roots in the establishment of a health centre in Peckham in the
1930s (Donaldson 2002). But sustaining a community development approach has proved difficult, as a later section of this chapter shows when describing the lessons from the community
development project carried out in the 1960s and 1970s. In future,
as Donaldson puts it, local public health partnerships will be required to rediscover a community development agenda. It 'will
entail a strategic shift away from the management contracts for
services to the management of skills, influence and networks'
(ibid.: 837).

As Lewis points out in her history of public health since World
War I, because little attention was paid to the practice of community medicine in the reorganized NHS in 1974, it was little wonder
that

> the position of community physicians was subject to serious con-
> flicts in terms both of their relationship with other members of the
> medical profession, and the nature of their primary responsibility,
> whether for the management of health services or for the analysis
> of health problems and health needs. (Lewis 1986: 135)

She goes on:

> community physicians experienced considerable tension in recon-
> ciling first their responsibility for the management of health ser-
> vices with that of analysing health problems and, second, their
> formal accountability to the NHS bureaucracy with their ethical

accountability to their communities. Their role was very much determined by their place in the new NHS structure. (Ibid.: 162)

With the NHS reorganization's focus on management and major structural changes, community medicine became associated with that agenda. It did not help it find its niche in the new system. If anything, being associated with such developments severely contaminated the new specialty and contributed to the role confusion its practitioners experienced both then and since. Subsequent NHS reorganizations have been similarly focused on structural and management issues and have always put the needs of clinical services and the acute sector ahead of population health and improvements in health status which do not depend on medical care.

Lewis suggests that the specialty of community medicine could be called to account over a failure to define its goals. 'In practice, the community physician tended to be preoccupied with his [sic] responsibility to the health services rather than to health' (Lewis 1986: 154). It is hardly surprising, therefore, that the position of community physician, and public health specialist subsequently, has been at the mercy of, and largely determined by, the ever-changing structure of the NHS.

By the 1980s, attempts were being made to revive what Berridge terms 'formal' public health, although they did little to resolve some of the tensions identified by Lewis. The impetus for a fresh look at public health was a traditional concern with the threat of communicable disease following outbreaks of salmonella at Stanley Royd Hospital in 1984 and legionnaires' disease at Stafford in the following year. The advent of AIDS in the mid-1980s, with its threat of an epidemic, added renewed urgency to the review of public health. An inquiry was duly set up chaired by Sir Donald Acheson, then Chief Medical Officer for England. As mentioned earlier, much of the review was concerned with upgrading the status of public health and restoring its former authority.

As Berridge comments, the review followed an orthodox path as far as the public health function was concerned. 'The strong medical emphasis precluded the likelihood of an effective intersectoral approach. The importance of epidemiology in giving the specialty scientific legitimacy was emphasised' (Berridge 1999: 87). Consequently, public health failed to perform the public watchdog role many had envisaged for it and became more embedded in the NHS management agenda.

At around this time – the 1980s – the broader public health/ health promotion constituency began to flourish. Known as 'the new public health', it sought 'to marry the twin objectives of personal prevention and a growing reawakening of interest in environmental matters' (Berridge 1999: 91). This led to greater interest in the international, and especially European, dimension to public health policy issues (see chapter 5 for a discussion of the European public health agenda).

With contemporary health systems facing major public health challenges that are increasing in both scope and complexity, a false dichotomy has emerged between public health specialists (usually, though not always, medically qualified) and managers. It is sometimes suggested that public health specialists are 'dreamers' while, in contrast, managers are 'pragmatists' (Richardson et al. 1994). They are the 'doers', while public health specialists dream up unworkable schemes and comment on how difficult it all is. Of course such a polarization risks being oversimplistic, but there remains some truth in the assertion. Public health medicine has been concerned more with knowledge acquisition than with its application to change practice (Hunter and Berman 1997; Nutbeam and Wise 2002).

There are other differences, too, between the two camps. Whereas public health specialists have generally looked outwards towards society and the health needs of the population – at least when they are not being sucked into managing health services – health service managers have tended to focus either upwards, in order to do their political masters' and mistresses' bidding, or inwards on the organization, and to become captured by the pressures, and seemingly insatiable demands, of the acute sector. The difference between these groups is neatly captured in the title of a lecture in 1987 delivered by Marc Lalonde, the former Canadian Minister for Health responsible for the Lalonde report described in chapter 2. The title of his lecture was 'Health Service Managers or Managers of Health?' (Evans 1995).

That public health practitioners feel daunted, if not overwhelmed, by the enormity of the agenda facing them cannot be doubted or denied. There is a sense in which the high expectations of public health specialists and the burden of responsibility weighing upon them are impossible and unacceptable. At the same time, the cost of failure to deliver will be high and likely to result in a further loss of credibility in public health specialists. They are already vulnerable in such circumstances, as history has shown (Lewis 1986). Indeed, it is precisely their vulnerability and fragile confidence that has allowed them to become so easily diverted from their core business and drawn into a narrow health service management agenda. In becoming indispensable to managers they may improve their chances of survival in a climate which puts the pursuit of health in second place to improving health-care services. But many now believe that it is perhaps too heavy a price to pay.

Most discussions of the public health function have centred on finding an optimal location for those practising it within the specialty of public health (which does not include many other practitioners of public health, who would not necessarily see themselves as such). This move is predicated on the widespread belief that the present structure and powers do not serve public health practitioners well. Holland and Stewart (1998) put forward three possible options for a better structure: the return of the medical officer of health, a national commission of public health, or re-creating the institutes of public health within the existing structure.

Return of the medical officer of health

There is an almost nostalgic hankering after the former medical officer of health (MOH) model in the belief that local government offers a more appropriate location for the pursuit of community health. For example, the House of Commons Health Committee during its inquiry into public health took the view that much was lost in the transition from MOH to community medicine. In particular, the MOH was able to influence, as an officer of the local authority, social and environmental aspects of health. These functions were lost with the transformation of the MOH into a community medicine specialist.

As a result, the specialty lost its way and failed to meet expectations. The Acheson inquiry, mentioned above, found that community medicine had failed to deliver as a result of blurred definitions of roles, while the need for community physicians to take a long-term view of events 'often conflicted with short-term pressures on health authority management' (Acheson 1988). Advocates of a return to the MOH view local government as more fertile territory for those engaged in public health, since many of the factors that influence the health of the population are administered by local government. But Holland and Stewart (1998) warn against such a move on two counts. First, access to reliable and accurate information might be difficult since it is held by the NHS. Second, the role and authority of doctors is vital in understanding, knowledge and communication. 'If public health were not considered as a mainstream health activity, it is likely that the status of the subject and its attraction for medical graduates would diminish and public health and the health service in general would be the poorer' (Holland and Stewart 1998: 211–12). This is a somewhat curious argument and is akin to that of the battered wife who, despite all the evidence, is unable to leave the person responsible for her beatings and constantly returns to the source of the problem. All available evidence suggests that the NHS, essentially a 'sickness' service, will never take the wider public health seriously. But the fear of marginalization or being sidelined appears to count for more. Being at the centre of the health scene is regarded as important for the survival of the specialty of public health medicine, regardless of cost.

National commission of public health

The option of setting up a national commission of public health would seek to remove public health from the contaminating influence of the NHS and enable it to retain its independence. The option has many attractions. It would establish a clear distinction between clinical services and public health services. But there are disadvantages with this option, too, in particular being vulnerable to government shifts in support. The risk of a free-standing agency is that it gets ignored and is unable to influence the agenda because it is removed from 'where the action is'. Such a commission could become vulnerable to spending cutbacks as well, especially if it were to be outspoken and a critic of government policy. The experience of such a body in New Zealand was not encouraging, and it proved short-lived (Beaglehole and Bonita 1997).

However, the model clearly retains appeal. The US Congress has recently been told by the Institute of Medicine (IoM) that it needs to establish a national public health council to advise the government on public health issues and to review the policies of other agencies for their impact on the national health (Institute of Medicine 2002). The hope is that such a council would address the serious disarray in which public health finds itself. The IoM report cites a long list of inadequacies in the health systems, including an insufficient and inadequately trained public health workforce and an outdated health information system.

Re-creation of institutes of public health

Re-creating the institutes of public health is the option favoured by Holland and Stewart. It is essentially a modest modification of the existing structure of public health with the addition of re-creating expert regional institutes with a national institute. Such a structure would allow public health to focus on its own issues rather than be preoccupied with clinical service management and contracting, thereby reducing or removing many of the conflicts which have beset public health over the years.

Public health: a specialty or an arena?

The problem with all the above solutions to the dilemma of how best to organize public health is that they fail to address more fundamental questions in regard to the nature of public health and who should undertake it. Only then is it reasonable to consider possible options for locating public health and agreeing a structure for it.

Despite public health acquiring a broader remit at both the national and international levels through the 1980s and 1990s, there remain what Berridge terms 'long-standing tensions in the remit of public health' (Berridge 1999: 92). It is certainly true that the public health community is now accepted as being much broader than the specialty of public health medicine, and for the first time the government has accepted that not all senior appointments in public health, at least within the new primary care trusts (PCTs), need be filled by clinically qualified public health practitioners. PCTs, according to the Minister for Public Health,

> are at the heart of the health improvement agenda...I see the appointments of PCT Directors of Public Health as a huge opportunity. They are a crucial new lever in the new system – and one that can advance the cause of public health....I welcome the fact that this generation of DsPH come from a variety of backgrounds –

both medical and non-medical, and including some former Health
Action Zone directors and an economist. Some are joint appointments with local government and that is good news. It gives cause
for optimism that multi-disciplinary public health will become a
reality while, at the same time, recognising that doctors remain a
crucial part of this new world. (Blears 2002)

Are we witnessing the erosion of the hegemony of the speciality
of public health medicine over the development of public health?
Or, at the risk of appearing cynical, is the Faculty of Public
Health Medicine intent upon retaining its overall power and authority by appearing to accommodate the inevitable need to make
concessions at the margins? After all, not only are the key public
health posts at health authority and regional levels remaining
clinical posts but the faculty has provided assessors to assist with
the appointment of directors of public health (DsPH) within
PCTs. And the government has assured all public health specialists with medical qualifications that there will be no redundan-
cies, although this does not mean that the posts on offer will
always appeal to those displaced following the latest restructuring of the NHS. Moreover, PCTs are fledgling organizations, and
no one can predict with any certainty what their future will be or
even if they are likely to have one at all. To be sure, they have
been accorded a pivotal role in improving the health of their
populations, but will they be allowed to do so by a central
government desperate to see improvements in health-care services? And even if they are allowed, will they possess the requisite capacity and capability? There cannot be answers to these
questions at this time, but the responses to them will determine
the direction taken by public health in future and the extent to
which the function does in practice manage to shed its medical
shackles and break free from the dominance of its clinical heri-
tage.

Closely related to the issue of how far public health remains
medicalized, and how far, under the government's NHS changes,
it can break out of its medical ghetto, is another tension which
has been the subject of heated, and largely inconclusive, debate
over the years. Arguments have raged over whether the lead for
public health should remain with the NHS or be relocated to local
government. Holland and Stewart argue that the issue of relocation requires wider discussion between key stakeholders.
Although the NHS is not a perfect place for public health, local

authorities, in their view, 'have little interest in health affairs' and do not have budgets to fulfil health requirements (Holland and Stewart 1998: 217). There is also a need to retain medical expertise in, for instance, the control, surveillance and prevention of disease. Given their comments about the MOH being sidelined in local government, it seems that Holland and Stewart would prefer the NHS as a location for medical expertise. However, they acknowledge that the interdisciplinary nature and working of public health is crucial and should be established more firmly than at present.

In its evidence to the House of Commons Health Committee's inquiry into public health, the Royal College of Nursing commented that, despite the 'welcome renewed focus on public health amongst policy-makers', confusion remained concerning the central function of public health (House of Commons 2001b: 211). In particular, the RCN believed a distinction should be made between public health *science* and public health *practice*. Both were essential to improving health, but public health practice 'is still a much neglected area of the public health function'. Public health departments had become too preoccupied with health service delivery, which precluded any real engagement with agencies outside the NHS. This view is echoed by the Local Government Association (LGA) which, in its evidence to the Health Committee, accused public health of being 'unhelpfully dominated by medical thinking' (ibid.: 142). Far from showing little interest in public health, the LGA asserted that, 'through their community leadership role and their power for social, economic and environmental well-being', local authorities 'should be required to lead the public health agenda' (ibid.). A similar view is taken by the Society of Local Authority Chief Executives (SOLACE) in its assessment of the role of 'modern local authorities' in 'creating healthy communities' (Duggan 2001). In his introduction to the report, the president of SOLACE admits that 'local government is not very good at talking about health and the role it plays in achieving good health for its citizens' (ibid.: 4). This is partly explained by the fact that local authorities do not necessarily use the term 'health' to define their activities, often preferring, or being more comfortable with, concepts such as 'well-being' or 'quality of life'. The goal, however, remains the same: 'the overall improvement of local population health and the reduction of health inequalities and social exclusion' (ibid.: 2). To this end, the new health policy context provides 'opportunities for local authorities to reclaim their original role as champions of the health of local communities' (ibid.).

And it is not only local government adopting this stance. The first joint Director of Public Health to be appointed in England, Dr Andrew Richards, giving evidence to the Health Committee, commented that 'it is irrational that most of the interest, skills and resources to improve public health are outside the NHS while the DPH is locked into it' (House of Commons 2001b: 442). He claimed that an ideal solution over where best to locate public health may not exist, 'but there are strong arguments that DsPH have to be eased out of the NHS box' (ibid.). Whether placing DsPH into PCTs is sufficient to free public health from the yoke of the NHS is, as I have already suggested, far too early to judge.

The House of Commons Health Committee had intended that one of its recommendations might be a proposal that public health departments be relocated from health authorities to local authorities. Indeed, there were some innovative developments in this direction to which the committee were exposed, such as that being implemented in Manchester by the health authority and city council.[1] However, many of those organizations giving evidence to the committee, even those most likely to favour such a move, resisted the temptation to go down the structural reorganization route. Typical of the responses forthcoming was that of the RCN, which believed that 'relocation of public health departments is not the key issue', since 'it is likely that neither health authorities nor local authorities as single organisations have all the appropriate pre-conditions and structures in place for this at present' (House of Commons 2001b: 213). The RCN's favoured solution was the 'creation of public health teams for a given locality which would be multi-agency and multi-disciplinary and bring together key NHS and local authority staff and other local stakeholders' (ibid.).

The notion that local government might play a more prominent role in an explicit health agenda is not new. Clarke, Hunter and Wistow, writing in 1997 at the time the health strategy *Health of the Nation* was beginning to lose its position and influence, urged

[1]   As a joint venture, Manchester Health Authority and Manchester City Council agreed to the creation of a joint health unit to be located within the local authority but incorporating public health expertise from the health authority. The move was designed to demonstrate the local authority's leadership role of the wider public health agenda as well as to minimize the risk of the public health function being constantly diverted into NHS management concerns.

local authorities to play their full role in developing a strategic view of health (Clarke et al. 1997). More recently, the Institute for Public Policy Research, a left-of-centre policy think tank that is held in high regard by the government, has proposed that local government could take responsibility for commissioning both health and social services, with the NHS becoming the main provider (but not purchaser) on the health side (Kendall and Harker 2002).

Given that the challenges facing public health are beyond the resources or competence of any single group or specialty or any single agency, it may be more appropriate, therefore, to conceive of 'public health' as a way of thinking and working for professionals located in many sectors and agencies rather than as a wholly separate profession (Hunter and Goodwin 2001). Moreover, if the three tasks noted near the start of the chapter put forward by the CMO and others are separated out, it becomes clearer which require clinical input and which do not and therefore those functions that might require to be located within the health service and those that need not be.

Reconceptualizing public health as an arena rather than a specialty is helpful in addressing the government's desire for 'joined-up' policy and management. At present there is very little of either in evidence. As Caulkin puts it: 'although New Labour may have come to power talking of "joined-up government", in practice it has approached policy from exactly the opposite, "reductionist" point of view – breaking a problem down into its component parts and then attempting to solve them in a linear fashion' (Caulkin 2002). The last chapter described the rise of managerialism, with its attendant preoccupation with targets, performance indicators, and performance measurement. Such instruments may not be entirely inappropriate in themselves – it is the manner in which they have been designed and applied that is being questioned. A similar message about the absence of 'joined-up' policy is evident in an Audit Commission study of the government's neighbourhood renewal strategy. The study reports 'the absence of a common message across Government' as 'one of the clearest signals to emerge from the first phase of the project' (Audit Commission 2002: 11). The study makes particular mention of the setting of performance targets by different government departments as reinforcing the absence of a 'joined-up' approach.

As we saw in chapter 1, 'wicked issues' transcend organizational and professional boundaries and levels of government. They cannot easily be broken down into bite-sized problems that can be conveniently disposed of. They are complex and messy and therefore require a style of management very different from the reductionist, mechanistic approach that is in vogue in government.

What other approaches or paradigms might be available and provide a more meaningful way of making sustainable progress in addressing the wider public health challenge that lies at the heart of so much of the government's social policy? The final sections of the last chapter introduced the notion of a complex adaptive system as offering a more appropriate way of tackling public health issues, and this is pursued further below.

Responding to implementation failure

It has been argued (see especially chapter 1) that, despite its reasonably clear articulation, health policy largely fails to get implemented and often gets overshadowed by an overriding concern with health-care policy and delivery. The government takes a somewhat naïve view of the dilemma and asserts that the policy is clear and that any problems must reside at the delivery end. It falls into the trap identified by the Cabinet Office report on policy-making, which states that most policy-makers concentrate on policy analysis and advising ministers, leaving little time for developing implementation strategies and reflecting on previous policy decisions and their impact (Cabinet Office 1999).

Unfortunately, the transmission of policy into practice is more complex than perhaps the government appreciates or is yet prepared to acknowledge, despite the efforts of its own officials and advisers in the Cabinet Office's Performance and Innovation Unit and, more recently, the Policy Strategy Unit. There are serious, and often neglected, issues about whether, and how, national policy can be effectively implemented locally and what needs to be in place for this to occur; about whether a plethora of national initiatives from various departments which appear disconnected rather than joined up are dysfunctional or disabling rather than productive and empowering; and about who should be taking action locally to implement national policy – the NHS, local government, regional agencies, or some combination of these organizations. These concerns are brought into sharp focus in the sphere of health policy.

Effecting sustainable policy implementation is destined to become an even greater challenge in future both for national policy-makers and for those locally who have been charged with the task of securing change. Sustainability is of particular concern for addressing inequalities in health, given the accumulation of disadvantage across the life course and the time required to demonstrate changes in health outcomes.

From rationality to complexity

The complexity and breadth of the public health agenda at both national and local levels are not in doubt. It may therefore be useful to start from this point and to view the various moves to tackle health, as distinct from ill health, as resembling a complex adaptive system (see also chapter 3). In complex systems, unpredictability and paradox are ever present, and some things will remain unknowable. Such systems also interact in ways whereby small changes can have huge effects. In many ways complex systems are self-organizing – changes arise, the system adapts and a new order emerges spontaneously. But, as Glouberman (2000: 54) observes, 'the state of flux and constant evolution to new kinds of organisation pose a challenge to most "clean" and orderly conceptualisations of the policy process.' A better appreciation of complex adaptive systems can allow us to tolerate the underlying 'mess' and accept the order that emerges from it. But it means adopting a political perspective in place of one that pretends policy and its implementation is a rational, value-free activity.

Furthermore, the interactions within a complex adaptive system are often more important than the discrete actions of the individual parts (Plsek and Wilson 2001). Complexity-based organizational thinking is concerned with the whole system rather than with artificially viewing the system in discrete parts or sectors. However, developing a common vision becomes more difficult in an increasingly heterogeneous organizational environment. Moreover, allocating resources according to a whole system is rendered difficult by the existence of separate budgets, many of them tightly controlled by central government for a specific purpose or initiative. For example, pooling budgets to tackle inequalities would entail drawing together resources from across the NHS, local government, regional agencies and possibly the private sector. The mechanisms and systems for such pooling to achieve the desired outcomes are not well developed.

Studies of implementation became more common from the 1970s on as efforts were made to explain the 'implementation gap' that had been detected (Dunsire 1978). The notion of policy failure is of interest to social scientists but does not seem unduly to concern policy-makers, who often equate proposing a policy with its effective disposal. Yet, as the work by Pressman and Wildavsky (1979), Lipsky (1980), Pfeffer (1992) and Gunn (1978), among others, has amply demonstrated, nothing could be further from the truth. The inability to get things done, to have ideas and decisions implemented, is widespread in organizations today, regardless of whether they are public or private. Some observers consider it a problem that seems to be getting worse (Pfeffer 1992; Chapman 2002). Indeed, the ability to get policies and/or decisions implemented is becoming increasingly rare.

Policy failure can result from *non-implementation* or from *unsuccessful implementation*. In the former case, a policy is not put into effect as intended (as seemed to be the case in respect of the central finding of the independent evaluation of the English health strategy, *The Health of the Nation*, which was operational from 1992 to 1997 (Department of Health 1998a; Hunter, Fulop and Warner 2000)). Unsuccessful implementation, on the other hand, occurs when a policy is carried out in full and external circumstances are not unfavourable, but the policy still fails to produce the intended results or outcomes.

Policy failure can occur as a result of bad execution, bad policy or bad luck. Ineffective implementation will be viewed by policy-makers as bad execution. Or external circumstances may be so adverse that bad luck is identified as the reason for failure. In other words, it was no one's fault. The reason that is less commonly advanced to explain policy failure is that the policy itself was defective in the sense of being based on inadequate information, poor reasoning, or hopelessly unrealistic assumptions.

The point about policy failure is that it suggests there can be no sharp distinction between formulating a policy and implementing it. Yet a naïve assumption persists in government that precisely such a distinction does exist. The line adopted is that the government has produced the policies and it is now up to those working at the periphery to implement them. Policy failure will therefore be regarded as bad execution and not bad policy. But studies show that it is more likely that what happens at the implementation stage will influence the actual policy outcome in ways that might not have been anticipated or foreseen (Lipsky 1980). Conversely, the likelihood of a successful outcome (defined as that outcome desired by the policy initiators) will be increased if thought is given at the policy design stage to potential problems of implementation. This might suggest the need for a policy impact statement or audit of some kind to identify possible implementation problems or barriers to success. Instead of these being picked up after the event, possibly through evaluation research, an attempt would be made to have some prior warning and understanding of these constraints so that the policy could be modified or adapted in advance of its implementation.

'Top-down' versus 'bottom-up' perspectives on policy and action are at the heart of discourses on policy implementation (Barrett and Fudge 1981). Policy failure or an implementation gap can occur when policy is imposed from the centre with no thought given to how it might be perceived or received at local level. It is not a case of bottom-up approaches to policy and action being superior to top-down ones. Arguably, a balance between the two is necessary (Harrison 1998). After all, it could be argued that one reason why progress in tackling health inequalities is slower than it perhaps should be is that central policy-makers refuse for whatever reason to take a stronger line, thereby allowing local decision-makers to redirect resources to other activities.

Reflecting policy commitment at a national level to address 'upstream' health issues, an empirical body of knowledge is emerging on local decision-making in this area (Marks 2002). In devising local strategies, decision-makers have to decide, for example, which of the many possible interventions related to specific aspects of the inequalities agenda are to be prioritized; the relative emphasis on disadvantaged groups, areas, and services likely to narrow the health gap or make effective inroads into the wider determinants of health; and the combination of measures most likely to narrow the health gap and over what period of time.

Gunn (1978) identified ten reasons why implementation is so difficult. Despite the passage of some twenty-five years, they have withstood the test of time. The reasons he gives are:

- the circumstances external to the implementing agency impose crippling constraints

- adequate time and sufficient resources are not made available to the programme or policy
- the required combination of resources is not available
- the policy to be implemented is not based on a valid theory of cause and effect
- the relationship between cause and effect is indirect and there are multiple intervening links
- dependency relationships are multiple
- there is poor understanding of, and disagreement on, objectives
- tasks are not fully specified in correct sequence
- there is imperfect communication and co-ordination
- those in authority are unable to demand or obtain perfect or total compliance.

A key insight from systems theory, and political science before it, and reflected in Gunn's list above, is that different individuals and organizations within a problem domain, such as health, will have significantly different perspectives, based on different histories, cultures and goals. Such diversity is a feature within health-care systems as well as between health-care systems and other professions and agencies whose activities impact on health (Degeling et al. 2001). These different perspectives have to be integrated and accommodated if effective action is to be taken by all the relevant agents. This insight conflicts with the command-and-control culture that dominates government but which is entirely inappropriate within complex systems.

How far does the local implementation agenda for tackling public health reflect these implementation difficulties? Marks undertook a study of thirty-six key decision-makers across the Northern and Yorkshire region in order to find out how they were responding to the health inequalities agenda (Marks 2002). Her findings largely confirm the continuing salience of Gunn's list of impediments to effective implementation.

First, the health inequalities agenda is being pursued in the context of competing priorities arising from a modernization process which focuses on speed and ease of access (rather than on structured variation in access) and a performance management agenda which does not prioritize inequalities in health. There would seem to be a clear mismatch here between what the policy calls for and what the management agenda actually demands. There are echoes, too, of what happened in respect of the earlier health strategy *The Health of the Nation*, where a failure of the performance management system to accord priority to progress in tackling health targets was in large part responsible for poor implementation and ultimately for a loss of confidence in the strategy (Department of Health 1998a).

Second, integration of resources in relation to joint targeting of mainstream funds is proving difficult. In particular, targeting mainstream resources towards some disadvantaged areas (and away from others) over a long period of time can be difficult to argue for and sustain within local political systems.

Third, outcomes in relation to interventions for tackling inequalities are typically long term and difficult to attribute to any specific intervention. Process and intermediate indicators or milestones are therefore needed, but these may be difficult to measure and their relationship to outcomes uncertain. As one example of this, how are area-based projects to assess their effectiveness in relation to long-term health outcomes, when both areas and the populations within them change over time? In addition, decision support systems for those accorded the task of allocating resources across the four kinds of capital (human, economic, social and environmental) and in balancing long- and short-term goals are poorly developed.

Fourth, while objectives in relation to specific disadvantaged groups, areas or services may be clear, strategic clarity in relation to narrowing the health gap is hampered by the wide range of priorities seen as relevant to the inequalities agenda. For example, the thirty-six local decision-makers in the Northern and Yorkshire region interviewed for the study identified no fewer than thirty-five different priority areas for tackling inequalities in health. Moreover, the potential conflict between utilitarian and egalitarian approaches is often fudged in the commonly expressed twin aims of improving health and tackling inequalities in health.

Finally, the emerging evidence base is perceived as difficult to access, research studies are difficult to synthesize, and there are concerns over the relevance of research to the local context in which change must take place. Innovative and context-sensitive approaches, along with local rolling evaluations, and 'executive friendly' research summaries are also important for local decision-makers.

Understanding implementation, as well as securing its effectiveness, is likely to entail a number of approaches: structural, procedural/managerial, and behavioural. A fourth approach, and perhaps the most fundamental, though often ignored or under-stated, is political. Even when carefully planned in terms of appropriate organization, management and influences on behaviour, if implementation of a policy takes insufficient account of the realities of power then the policy is unlikely to succeed. A polit-ical approach may also challenge the assumptions on which other approaches are based, for example, those of behavioural analysts or management consultants. For instance, implementation failure often results in laments about the absence of leadership. But it could be that problems of implementation are in many cases problems in developing political will and expertise (Pfeffer 1992). Problems of performance and effectiveness are problems of power and politics, notably power imbalances, powerlessness, and the inability of some groups or causes to get their ideas or policies taken seriously.

A political approach to implementing policies to tackle health inequalities would seem intrinsic to the complex reality of changing practice and perhaps challenging vested or entrenched interests. Implementation in this policy area is by definition multi-levelled, multi-organizational and multi-professional. It involves political bargaining and conflict, or at least the potential for such. Therefore, a political strategy for implementation is as im-portant as a strategy for agreeing more technical factors. 'Unless and until we are willing to come to terms with organisational power and influence, and *admit that the skills of getting things done are as important as the skills of figuring out what to do*, our organisa-tions will fall further and further behind' (Pfeffer 1992: 12; my italics).

Implementation should involve a process of interaction between organizations whose members may have different values, per-spectives and priorities from each other and from those advocat-ing the policy (Hogwood and Gunn 1984). There exists some expertise about effective management within specific public ser-vice organizations. However, less is known about

> good ways to manage initiatives which cross boundaries between public, voluntary and private sectors, about initiatives which are based in communities and involve networks of different agencies, or about management outside the rules. The skills required to bal-ance stakeholders' interests, understand complex accountabilities, and manage for social outcomes are as necessary outside the formal public sector organisation as within it. (Parston and Timmins 1998: 14–15)

Approaches to joined-up policy and practice

Attempts to improve the capacity of policy-making and implementation in respect of complex problems or 'wicked issues' are
not confined to New Labour and the late 1990s when it entered
government with a vigour and determination to do things differently. In fact, there had been a well-documented experiment in
the mid-1970s, now largely forgotten it seems, to modify the way
in which cross-cutting policy issues were handled at the centre.
Known as the joint approach to social policy, or JASP, the initiative was the work of the Central Policy Review Staff (CPRS), set
up in 1970 to improve policy capacity at the centre with particular
reference to the interdepartmental aspects of social policy. As two
of its architects, Tessa Blackstone and William Plowden, concluded:

> [JASP] perhaps came closest to an attempt to apply an ideal model
> of rational and co-ordinated policy-making to the untidy processes
> prevalent within Whitehall; it was an ambitious, schematic, and
> completely unsuccessful attempt to devise a comprehensive system
> for doing this. (Blackstone and Plowden 1988: 102)

In 1977, a decision was taken by the CPRS to shut off JASP's life-
support system. This was on the advice of the JASP team, who had
concluded that the time had probably come to redeploy CPRS staff
to other work since JASP was absorbing a substantial amount of
staff time. Moreover, JASP no longer seemed to arouse much ministerial interest; nor did it seem to be having much impact on the
real world. JASP formally died in 1978 with the publication of its
last report, but as an ideal it survived for much longer. As Blackstone and Plowden note, 'the clearer it became during the late
1970s that public spending on social problems was having little
impact on those problems, the stronger seemed to be the case for
systematic thinking about priorities and for better co-ordinated
action' (ibid.: 116). But 'the difficulties, formidable even when
public spending was growing, of co-ordinating the thinking and
the actions of different agencies, proved in a period of cut-backs to
be politically and managerially almost impossible' (ibid.). In their
independent study of policy co-ordination in central government,
Challis and her colleagues found that a major difficulty facing JASP
was the 'all-too familiar problem of developing a sense of collective

purpose strong enough to overcome the inevitable pressures towards departmentalism' (Challis et al. 1988: 97). Loss of interest
among ministers was another factor in JASP's demise. Once the
initial initiative had been taken and announced, 'ministers found it
hard to keep their interest in the details of the inevitable long grind
that followed. Few ministers saw the point of JASP-type approaches', regarding them as an intrusion into their own departmental fiefdoms (ibid.: 98). Importantly, JASP was seen by some
officials as 'too rational, too a-political', and might have achieved
more had it sought to engage ministers more directly on a small
number of problems in which they were interested (ibid.). Indeed,
ministers' interest could be secured only if they were to see some
direct gain to themselves from being involved in JASP. Hence, in
Huxham's (1996) terms, 'collaborative advantage' could be secured
in place of what actually happened, namely, 'collaborative inertia'.

Whatever JASP's defects, it was widely agreed that 'these
lessened its ability to survive in the face of ministerial indifference
and departmental obstruction – two mutually reinforcing problems' (Challis et al. 1988: 100). On the other hand, a few officials
believed that JASP should have continued despite the opposition
to it. In particular, the CPRS should not have allowed it to wither
but should have been tougher with obstructive departments on
the grounds that it could take at least ten years to develop a
genuine and workable joint approach. Sustainability should have
been the aim of JASP in order to ensure its institutionalization.

The JASP experiment contains many lessons for those who care
to heed them. A problem for New Labour in the late 1990s,
some twenty years after JASP took its last gasp, was that it seemed
to believe that history ended in 1997 when it entered office. Yet
there were things from the past from which it might have benefited
had it chosen to take the time to listen to those, such as William
Plowden, an architect of JASP, who saw clear parallels between the
government's emphasis on 'joined-up' policy and JASP. The importance of winning political commitment and building a consensus is no less important today than it was over a quarter of a
century ago.

There were other lessons to learn at local level from the community development project (CDP) carried out in the 1960s and 1970s
under the auspices of the Home Office to tackle poverty (Higgins
1978). Among the lessons were that the sums allotted were quite
inadequate to tackle the task given the CDP teams; expectations
were unreasonably high; and there were limits on how far local

action could be effective as a strategy of social reform when many of the forces at work had their origins in national, if not global, policy and should therefore be dealt with at those levels. Significantly, too, the experience of the CDP demonstration projects showed 'how research is often offered as a substitute for action rather than an accompaniment to it' (Higgins 1978: 133). John Mays, in referring to 'the research smokescreen', makes the point powerfully:

> Research is seen as an excuse to do ameliorative work on a minor scale while the political and basic moral dilemma remains unsolved and hardly touched. The bureaucratic machine goes on its way untouched by radical questions and the social researchers and academics collaborate. It is yet another illustration of the well-known *trahison des clercs*. (Quoted in Higgins 1978)

History shows that most of these and other lessons were not heeded in subsequent attempts to deploy area-based initiatives, such as Health Action Zones, with the consequence that many of the same mistakes were simply recycled. Government learning is not a priority for administrations impatient to put their own imprint on new initiatives and anxious to secure their place in history. Yet, without that learning it is almost certain that little useful progress will be made or that successful interventions will be 'mainstreamed' rather than remaining isolated beacons of good practice with little future or, ultimately, value.

Since 1997, the government has introduced various mechanisms to encourage cross-sector policy, planning and action. Principal among these are Health Action Zones (HAZs), Health Improvement Programmes (HImPs) – known since 2002 as Health Improvement and Modernization Plans (HIMPs) – and, more recently, Local Strategic Partnerships (LSPs). Each of these initiatives is commented upon in a little more detail below, but a general criticism of them is that they have not linked well, partly because, with the exception of LSPs, they were all introduced separately. Moreover, as will be discussed, HIMPs have all but disappeared from the scene, to be replaced by local delivery plans.

Health Action Zones

One of the government's early actions in 1998, following its 1997 white paper on the NHS, was to establish Health Action Zones

(HAZs). These are seven-year multi-agency programmes between the NHS, local government, the voluntary and private sectors, and local communities. Forty-one bids were received in the first round and eleven areas were successful in achieving HAZ status in April 1998, and a further fifteen were announced following a second round in April 1999. Together these twenty-six areas cover thirteen million people in England and include some of the most disadvantaged areas of the country.

HAZ projects have concentrated on those whose needs are greatest and aim to reduce health inequalities. Their strategic framework emphasizes the importance of public involvement in activities that meet these needs. Projects have included plans to provide integrated services to meet the health needs of specific client groups, such as elderly people, parents and children, ethnic minorities and so on. Baggott (2000) mentions some examples, among them a project focusing on the health needs of Asian women, a community-based diabetes service and a scheme to improve the health of elderly people through services such as transport and housing. Judge et al. (1999), responsible for the national evaluation of HAZs, note that the kind of activities that HAZs have funded vary considerably.

> Some have chosen to focus very specifically on reducing inequalities in access to health services, because it is something they feel they can achieve in the short term. Others have very much taken a lifestyle/settings approach, whereas others have focused on some of the social and economic determinants of health such as unemployment, low incomes, social isolation and poor neighbourhood infrastructures. (Judge and Mackenzie 2002: 306)

HAZs were set up to provide action and be different, while contributing to achieving the overall aims of the government's programme to reduce health inequalities and modernize services, by giving additional financial and other support to some of the most deprived areas in the country. They were expressly intended to do two things: find new, innovative ways of meeting local health needs, and operate so as to cut through prevailing bureaucracy that might otherwise have prevented them from giving full expression to such ways of working. Specifically, HAZs were 'to explore mechanisms for breaking through current organisational boundaries to tackle inequalities and to deliver better services' (Department of Health 1997).

However, although freed from some aspects of performance management, new ways of monitoring their activities were devised, and after their first year or two of relative 'independence' HAZs, ironically, became among the most scrutinized bits of machinery within the NHS. From the outset, expectations were high and probably unrealistic. Ministers saw HAZs as being in the 'vanguard' or 'frontline of the war on health inequalities'. Furthermore, ministers were keen to get 'early wins' from the work of HAZs and to do so before they had had sufficient time to prove themselves. In its evidence to the Health Committee's inquiry into public health, Health First, the specialist health promotion unit for Lambeth, Southwark and Lewisham, claimed that 'the pressure to have early wins by the Government is in contrast to the long-term development of innovation and sustainability which is supposed to be at the heart of the HAZ' (House of Commons 2001b: 520).

As noted in earlier chapters, there are few quick fixes to the problems of poverty and poor health, and the expectation of early results from HAZs put them under unreasonable pressure to deliver. There was also criticism that ministers and their officials were distorting HAZ priorities by looking for evidence of success in respect of improved access to health services, especially where cancer and coronary heart disease services were concerned. While not unimportant, HAZs had other priorities in relation to the wider public health where the focus was not on medical, health service concerns. A problem with concentrating attention on health service considerations was that it only confirmed to other partners, especially local authorities, that HAZs were an invention of the NHS and, at the end of the day, had to dance to its tune.

It is also hard to see how those running or actively involved in HAZs could be expected to function differently and adopt new ways of working when the HAZ might be tagged onto their full remit rather than constitute their main responsibility. Although HAZs attracted modest additional funding, the key to their success is their catalytic role designed to reorientate mainstream services to work in new and more effective ways.

The area-based approach to alleviating poverty has come in for much criticism following its failure to succeed in earlier attempts in the 1960s. The Health Committee made this point in its report on public health. In its response, the government rejected the claim that area-based initiatives had usually failed to engage their communities (Department of Health 2001e). It claimed that many innovative and effective initiatives to engage communities had occurred and that the lessons being learned from areas such as Bradford, Tyne and Wear, Manchester, Salford and Trafford were being disseminated.

HAZs were subject to a national evaluation in addition to several local evaluations (Judge et al. 1999). Early lessons showed that in the early days there was tremendous enthusiasm and commitment among those involved in operating HAZs. However, despite some innovative plans and effective ways of tackling obstacles to effective access to health services, progress proved frustratingly slow. Among the reasons for this were the following:

- establishing effective partnerships takes time
- HAZs were not the only partnership in an area – they sometimes had to compete with others, each with its own goals and structures
- many HAZs failed to develop coherent strategies – plans were strong on identifying problems and articulating long-term objectives, but short on linking the two; early interventions were often 'leaps of faith' rather than clear and logical steps in the pathway between their problems and desired outcomes.

It was felt that these factors hampering the progress of HAZs were by no means unique to them. However, 'promoting and achieving change in pursuit of ambitious goals will be possible only if HAZs are encouraged to invest in the planning process, to take risks, and to adapt to changing circumstances' (Judge and Mackenzie 2002: 305). Such encouragement was not forthcoming from ministers. By the end of the government's first term in office, HAZs had for the most part failed to impress sufficiently and fell out of favour with ministers. While they have not entirely disappeared, their funding has been curtailed and they are being integrated with other initiatives, notably Local Strategic Partnerships (LSPs).

The NHS Plan mentions HAZs only once in the context of the new LSPs that the government has established. It is intended that HAZs will in the medium term 'be integrated' with LSPs 'to strengthen links between health, education, employment and other causes of social exclusion. In the meantime *effective* health action zones will continue' (Department of Health 2000: §13.24; my italics). This reference to HAZs hardly amounts to a vote of confidence in them.

A two-year research project undertaken for the then Department of Environment, Transport and the Regions on collaboration and co-ordination in relation to area-based regeneration initiatives, including HAZs, found that 'most ABIs represent a distraction from mainstreaming rather than a contribution to new ways of thinking about and responding to core problems in mainstream services' (Neighbourhood Renewal Unit and Regional Co-ordination Unit 2002).

From Health Improvement Programmes (HImPs) to Health Improvement and Modernization Plans (HIMPs)

Health Improvement Programmes (HImPs) were another new initiative announced in the first flush of the government's commitment to stress the importance of health rather than simply health care. Of all the policy initiatives surrounding the modernization of the NHS, the HImP was one of the most important. It was the means by which the government intended, and still intends, to achieve its principal objective, namely, to tackle health inequalities and narrow the health gap between rich and poor. It offered an opportunity to put health, and not only health care, at the top of the policy agenda.

HImPs have been subject to some research aiming to analyse their impact (Marks and Hunter 1999; Hamer 2000; Hunter, Marks and Sykes 2000; Health Development Agency 2000 and 2001). There was great variety in HImPs – in presentation, length, accessibility, the degree of involvement of partner agencies, the breadth of the agenda, the degree of partnership with the local authority in relation to wider determinants of health, and in relation to involvement by the public. The Health Development Agency's (HDA) national review of HImPs between 1999 and 2000 concluded that, while HImPs were generally perceived as a positive vehicle for local health improvement planning, 'they need to place greater emphasis on reducing inequalities and tackling the wider determinants of health' (Health Development Agency 2000: 2). In particular, HImPs failed to tackle 'upstream' public health issues such as housing and transport. To do so would mean having to focus more on the determinants of health.

Hunter, Marks and Sykes (2000) found that many primary care groups and trusts (PCG/Ts) were rather puzzled by HImPs and did not fully understand their purpose or what was required in their development. Nor were they seen as central to the work of PCG/Ts. There was also a feeling that they could appear as abstract and insufficiently action-oriented. A balance was needed between strategic content and specific action plans if HImPs were to be truly useful. Another concern was the lack of opportunity to specify local priorities and needs, since so much of the policy agenda had already been predetermined by national demands and targets. Moreover, since national policy placed the emphasis on acute care, it tended to skew the HImP in this direction also. A common complaint was that the HImP had been hijacked by the acute sector. As a result, public health got sidelined. In the first couple of years or so, therefore, the impact of HImPs on the wider health agenda was minimal. It did not help that, during the early phase of HImP development, the NHS, and primary care in particular, was going through major change. As a result, the HImP slipped down the agenda both locally and nationally.

Inevitably, the HImP built on what had gone before in respect of joint plans between the NHS and local government, although the agenda for improving health and tackling health inequalities pointed to the need for new partnerships, new approaches to integrating local resources, and new ways of using shared information.

HImPs were intended to be joint plans between all the agencies whose activities impacted on health. The NHS was accorded the lead role in co-ordinating the plans, but these were to be owned by all relevant local stakeholders. The problem was that HImPs were not the only plans of importance for the wider public health. In particular, there were separate community plans drawn up by local government. The relationship between HImPs and community plans was not always clear, and many observers recommended that community plans be regarded as the principal strategy for a local area, with the local HImP being seen as part of the community plan. For example, one local authority chief executive told the Health Committee:

> At the moment we are bedevilled by far too many planning processes – we have more than 40 statutory plans which local authorities have to produce and they are all driven by separate sets of guidance and separate government departments requiring separate presentational styles. (House of Commons 2001a: xlv)

Not only does the available research examining the impact of HImPs show that it was limited, but the plans themselves varied greatly across the country. Even within a region, HImPs 'vary in size, detail and scope, acting as filters of local activity in order to provide manageable documents' (Marks 2001: 7). It is also the case that, 'as rolling programmes of health improvements, HImPs are not comprehensive, but may focus on selected priorities in any one year' (ibid.). The HDA's national review of HImPs concluded that the main problem at the start was the 'limited time available to establish a meaningful consultation and involvement process during production of the HImP' (2000: 13).

Before their transmogrification into Health Improvement and Modernization Plans (see below) after their third round, HImPs were not given sufficient time to mature. They were originally conceived as rolling programmes which would take some time to develop. Early assessments of their progress and impact concluded that ownership of the HImP process, involvement of PCG/Ts and clarity over individual responsibility for implementation still had some way to go (Hunter, Marks and Sykes 2000). It was also claimed that the link between the HImP and resource allocation was tenuous so that, despite the priority for public health clearly set out in the HImP, in practice resources were allocated to quite different, and low-ranking, priorities. Following publication of *The NHS Plan*, it was felt that the identification and pursuit of local objectives and priorities, a major thrust of the first-round HImPs, risked becoming swamped by central targets emanating from the national service frameworks and other centrally determined and imposed initiatives. The tension between national and local priorities, and between clinical and social/environmental priorities, was also identified by the HDA national review of HImPs as putting a brake on progress.

Following the third round of HImPs, a major reorganization of the NHS was announced in April 2001, ostensibly to allow for a greater measure of devolution in response to critics that the NHS was overcentralized and that ministers exercised too much command and control. This began to be implemented in April 2002. Its focus was on developing new primary care organizations, which meant fewer health authorities, which had previously taken the lead role on HImPs. The government therefore sought to develop and reposition HImPs as Health Improvement and Modernization Plans (HIMPs) in order to ensure that they set the strategic framework for improving health and tackling health inequalities for a local population. This included setting out for partners in the local health system high-level objectives, measurable targets for improvement, and expected outcomes.

HIMPs are seen as the key strategic document for local health communities to reflect local approaches to health improvements, health inequalities and the NHS modernization agenda. They are to be developed in partnership between NHS bodies, local government and the community. From April 2002, primary care trusts had lead responsibility for the process. In future HIMPs will be linked to the activities of Local Strategic Partnerships (LSPs). For example, the Health Committee in its report on the public health function concluded:

> We see great potential for health inequality targets to give real bite to the HIMP/Community Plan and to provide a yardstick for Directors of Public Health, local authorities and health authorities. (House of Commons 2001a: xx)

Elsewhere, the committee recommended that health should be a key element of the local authority community plan. Aligning HIMPs with community strategies is likely to gather pace with the arrival of LSPs. As Marks comments in her review of HImPs and tackling inequalities in the Northern and Yorkshire region:

> the emergence of community strategies and LSPs has led to reflection about the remit of HImPs, increasingly described as the strategic health input into community strategies developed through LSPs and building on existing locality work across health and local authorities. (Marks 2001: 22)

A number of health authorities, such as Gateshead, were already moving in the direction of 'seeing the community strategy as the overarching strategy into which other strategies will fit'. Added impetus is likely to come from the Minister for Public Health, who believes that the HIMP does not have as high a profile as she would like. 'It needs to be much more closely aligned with the community plan if it is to be effective. Otherwise the community will have little sense of the NHS making progress in meeting their needs' (Blears 2002).

Far from having a higher profile, it seems that HIMPs have been abandoned altogether, just when they were beginning to become embedded in NHS organizations. Or, if one was being charitable, they have been subsumed within the local delivery plans introduced in 2003. Local delivery plans are intended to be different from previous planning approaches. In particular they will not be annual plans but cover a three-year period from 2003 to 2006. Reducing health inequalities is one of the stated national health and social care priorities to be observed in the plans. Nevertheless, it is striking that, in the guidance document, little mention is made of health as distinct from health care, and the term HIMPs does not appear at all (Department of Health 2002c). Whereas the process involved in producing HIMPs stressed the community health needs of local populations, such notions, while not wholly absent from local delivery plans, are no longer high priority. Local delivery plans are clearly intended to deliver on the goals and targets of the NHS plan. Whereas HIMPs were intended to take account of, and be linked to, local authorities' community plans, with perhaps in time a single community plan being envisaged (already achieved in some areas), the local delivery plans make no mention of local authorities in the round, focusing solely on social services, presumably because of their importance in both preventing access to hospital beds and allowing prompt discharge of NHS patients.

Local Strategic Partnerships

Local authorities are required under the Local Government Act (2000) to produce a community strategy to promote the economic, social and environmental well-being of their communities. It was this new responsibility bestowed upon local authorities, together with the 2002 reorganization of the NHS, that prompted a reassessment of links between HImPs and wider community strategies, with increasing convergence between the two. Local Strategic Partnerships (LSPs) are to be seen as the motor of local regeneration. In the words of a (then) Department of Environment, Transport and the Regions consultative document (2000):

> An LSP is a cross sectoral, cross agency, umbrella partnership which is focused and committed to improving the quality of life and governance in a particular locality. LSPs will therefore bring together the public, private, voluntary and community sectors to provide a single overarching local co-ordination framework within which other, more specific local partnerships can operate.

The government has not prescribed how LSPs should work, what geographical areas they should cover or when they should be established. An incentive for authorities to establish an LSP is that having such a partnership is a condition of access to the Neighbourhood Renewal Fund.

LSPs have a number of tasks, the most important of which is the co-ordination and rationalization of local partnership and delivery arrangements across a range of different local and central government initiatives. The Audit Commission study on neighbourhood renewal comments that, so far, few LSPs 'appear to have set about reducing the number of partnerships locally' (Audit Commission 2002: 18–19). LSPs are intended to bring together area-based initiatives and develop action plans to tackle poverty and disadvantage at a local level (Marks 2001). LSPs work with local authorities to help meet their duty to produce a community strategy. Some HImPs, such as that of the East Riding and Hull, saw this development as a 'major opportunity to address root causes of ill health, bringing together community involvement, wider public health and the service planning focus of the HImP' (quoted in Marks 2001: 10). In Bradford, LSPs were seen as an opportunity to mainstream HAZ principles. The HAZ chair is also chair of the emerging LSP executive, and the HAZ director is acting as an adviser to the emerging LSP.

The fieldwork for the Audit Commission study indicated that LSPs had different ambitions. Three broad groups are clear: one group wants an operational focus, another wants a hands-off strategic approach, and a third wants to adopt a network approach (Audit Commission 2002: 21).

The NHS Plan mentions the development of LSPs and the NHS's role in these, but subsequent guidance on LSPs is silent on the connection between them and HImPs and says little about the role of NHS organizations or about the value that active public health involvement might accord LSPs.

LSPs offer a way out of the structural debate about where to locate public health. As Tony Elson, chief executive of Kirklees Metropolitan Council, told the Health Committee, 'there are functions in LSPs which need to be supported by a team of people with expertise, and public health is one of the key elements of that' (House of Commons 2001a: §1.33, xliii). But, as research on area-based initiatives shows, while LSPs have the potential to make a real contribution to co-ordination and collaboration at area level, they do not offer 'quick fix' solutions (Neighbourhood Renewal Unit and Regional Co-ordination Unit 2002: 28). Rather, they offer 'the possibility of sustained change over many years.

The greatest danger would be if they were over-burdened too early with a proliferation of administrative or programme tasks.' Also, LSPs must maintain the sense of equal 'collaborative advantage' and not be seen 'as dominated by a central, or a local government agenda' (ibid.: 27). So far, 'central government has not successfully resolved the tensions between regional, strategic and neighbourhood activities' (ibid.). Above all, LSP working is complex and demands the existence of 'relationships of trust' between partners.

Conclusion

This chapter has reviewed the public health function and its failure to drive the health policy agenda in a way that might have redressed the imbalance in policy-making. Despite this, there remains a commitment on the part of policy-makers to do something about the deteriorating state of the public's health and, in particular, the growing health gap between social groups.

Various initiatives and structures have been introduced at local level in recent years in an effort to make progress. But many of these, such as HImPs and HAZs, have not been allowed time to settle and deliver before being subjected to the next round of change, management fashion or political whim. As a consequence, there is a feeling of insecurity and a sense of impermanence which is both unsettling and damaging to making sustained progress on a complex agenda.

A recurring theme of the book has been the competing pressures on local agencies arising from government policy. The commitment to tackling poor health and health inequalities may be genuine but the energy and resources appear to be devoted to other more immediate and pressing concerns, thereby dashing hopes of implementing national policy locally (Exworthy et al. 2002).

The focus on new initiatives and structures appears misplaced when the attempts at 'joined-up' policy and management depend *a priori* for their success on changing mindsets among those occupying the various roles. Do structures determine how people behave or do people shape structures? The truth probably lies somewhere in between, but, as I shall argue in chapter 6, perhaps it is time to pay more attention to changing mindsets and rather less to structures and systems.

Before setting out the nature of the challenge, there is one further set of issues to explore. The UK is now less monolithic than it was following the devolution settlement after New Labour came into office in 1997. Health is a devolved policy sector, so it seems reasonable to look at what is happening in Wales and Scotland to see if they are proving any more successful than England in giving higher priority to health. Northern Ireland has not been included in the review because of the special circumstances prevailing. It is also fair to say that, post-devolution, there has been less activity there in respect of health policy than in Wales or Scotland. For example, a major review of the public health function in Northern Ireland has been mooted but has yet to be undertaken.

There is also the likelihood of regionalism taking root in at least some parts of England, and this is likely to have implications for public health that need to be considered. Finally, it is no longer possible to ignore Europe and its growing influence on health policy. The EU has recently adopted a new public health strategy, as the next chapter will describe.

5 Health Policy in a Devolved Polity within Europe

Introduction

This chapter is concerned with two developments involving the governance of the UK and the making of health policy that are of fairly recent origin and growing importance: the emergence of devolution in the governance of the UK, and the rise of Europe. Their relevance to health is potentially considerable.

The UK is no longer, if it ever truly was, a unitary state. The degree of administrative devolution traditionally enjoyed by Wales, Scotland and Northern Ireland was overlaid with a raft of devolved political institutions and new powers in the closing years of the twentieth century. While public health issues know no boundaries, whether geographical, professional or organizational, and are often global in character, there remains merit in looking across the UK to see how the health/health-care tension in policy has been, and is being, addressed in the new post-devolution arrangements and structures. Devolution in the UK has created a laboratory in which a naturally occurring experiment in devising new forms of governance and tackling 'wicked issues' and policy dilemmas is under way. The potential for learning lessons from this experiment should not be missed. These become more important when a by-product from devolution has been the mounting pressure within England to establish elected regional assemblies in those areas where a clear majority of the local population wishes to see them established.

The other development of fairly recent origin is the growing presence of Europe and its impact on domestic policy. Increasingly, policy-making in the UK is inextricably linked to the European Union and its growing influence on the lives of its citizens. Until recently, domestic social policy matters were strictly off limits and, under the principle of subsidiarity, remained the strict preserve of national governments. After all, the EU was created principally to develop a single economic market and not to harmonize social, including health, policy across member states. But recent public concern over food safety and other issues, such as the environment, has raised the importance of public health on the EU agenda. Concern over public health cannot be separated from the development of the single market.

So, as regions and other subnational governmental structures assume greater importance within countries *below* the level of the nation state, so European institutions are assuming greater importance *above* the level of the nation state. Whether there is a concerted move towards a Europe of regions, as seems to be happening, is not the concern of this book. However, such a development cannot be altogether ignored either.

The impact of devolution

The arrival of political devolution in 2000 has given rise to a potentially and increasingly dis-United Kingdom. Indeed, it would be surprising if this were not so, since growing diversity is a consequence of devolution – it is even one of its purposes – and the experience from other countries with devolved systems of government confirms this to be the case. Administrative devolution has long existed in the UK, with important differences evident in the way in which the NHS was run in England, Wales, Scotland and Northern Ireland respectively (Hunter 1982 and 1983; Hunter and Wistow 1987a; Hunter and Williamson 1991). Policy differences have been less in evidence though not wholly absent (Hunter and Wistow 1987b). In what follows, the focus is on devolution to Wales and Scotland. Northern Ireland represents a rather special case in the light of the troubles there and the religious divide. Moreover, developments in health policy post-devolution have lagged behind those in the rest of the UK. Therefore, Northern Ireland is not included in the following discussion of devolution.

Political devolution brings with it an expectation that intra-UK policy differences will grow over time, especially in areas such as health policy (Hazell and Jervis 1998). Such a conclusion is directed particularly at Scotland, where the devolved parliament has powers of primary legislation. Of course, greater policy divergence does not necessarily imply good or better policies. What it ought to mean is policy that reflects more sensitively the wishes and preferences of the different countries making up the UK and their respective populations and communities.

Following the lead from England, both Wales and Scotland produced their own plans for their health services. Each plan is briefly reviewed below.

Wales

The title of the Welsh plan for the NHS is an indication of where the emphasis lies. Called *Improving Health in Wales*, it is, according to the Minister for Health and Social Services, 'based on an understanding that the NHS, though vitally important, is but one part of the drive to improve the nation's health' (National Assembly for Wales 2001: 5). It is well understood that improving the health of the people of Wales poses challenges that no one organization in isolation can meet. Strong partnerships among the key stakeholders lie at the heart of 'our new and inclusive approach to health' (ibid.).

Chapter 1 of the plan sets out a vision for care and states that, 'though development of primary, secondary and tertiary services are vitally important, the prevention of illness and the promotion of health are among our primary objectives' (National Assembly for Wales 2001: 18). Making comparisons with the Canadian health-care system, which it is by no means certain the Canadians would recognize or accept, the plan mentions its commitment to investment in prevention through a strategy of lifelong investment in health. 'The NHS will develop further into a *health* service and away from a primary focus on illness' (ibid.). As part of this endeavour, the NHS has an important advocacy role and must therefore lead by example 'in the way it manages and carries out its business and through its contribution to the social, economic and environmental development of Wales' (ibid.). Echoing the Wanless report in England conducted for the Treasury (see chapter 2), the Welsh NHS plan points out that investment in health makes the population healthier and contributes in the long term to overall economic and social development.

To achieve its goal of realizing the full health potential for all the people of Wales, the plan focuses on four main areas for action:

- multi-sectoral strategies to tackle the determinants of health, ensuring the use of health impact assessment
- health-outcome-driven programmes and investments for health development and clinical care
- integrated family- and community-oriented primary health care supported by a flexible hospital system
- a participatory health development process that involves relevant partners for health at home, school and work and at local community and national levels (National Assembly for Wales 2001: 19).

The plan acknowledges that none of these actions is new but that they must now be applied to decision-making about improving health. For them to be taken seriously and lead to action it will be necessary for structures, habits and thinking to change. New skills will be required. The plan shows awareness of the barriers to progress when 'the forces of inertia are strong'. Central to the new approach is the concept of *Lifelong Investment for Health* – 'a pragmatic approach for a credible and sustainable plan for the promotion of health' (ibid.).

Scotland

The Scottish NHS plan follows a similar approach to the Welsh one. Its title is *Our National Health*, which directs attention to a focus on health rather than health care (Scottish Executive 2001). Section 2 (out of nine sections) is devoted to the theme of improving health. A core aim is to 'build a national effort to improve health'. The challenge is especially acute in Scotland, with its reputation as the 'sick man [*sic*] of Europe'. The plan concedes that much of it is about the NHS, but it points out that 'improving people's health comes first. The organisation of health care comes next' (ibid.: section 2).

The plan admits that, 'for too long, health policy and health services have focused on the treatment of ill health rather than on its prevention. We are now working to shift that emphasis. Other countries have done so' (Scottish Executive 2001: section 2). The goal is to transform Scotland from 'a case study in ill health' to 'a showcase for good health'. The Scottish Executive's commitment to a health improvement agenda was reinforced when in late 2002 the health minister announced a four-point plan backed by £173 million over three years, 2003–6, to improve public health (*Health Service Journal* 2002: 8–9). The focus is on the health of children from conception through childhood, better life circumstances for teenagers, workplace health initiatives, and community-based health projects.

To assist with public health capacity-building and to provide evidence about what works, the plan mentions the creation of a public health institute for Scotland. This followed a high-level review of the public health function in Scotland set up by the former Chief Medical Officer for Scotland (Scottish Executive 2000). The review believes that current Scottish Executive policy provides 'an outstanding opportunity' to improve health and that public health and the reduction of health inequalities is one of the executive's key cross-cutting programmes. Among its recommendations, the review wanted health boards to become known as 'public health organizations' working closely with local authorities and others. They would have the central role in improving population health, since that is the *raison d'être* of boards. Each board would provide high-profile leadership for public health, developing well-managed multi-agency partnerships for health. The board's organizational development will reflect public health values and methods, and many of its resources will be devoted to the public health function. Its decision-making will be driven by public health principles.

The review identified several threats to a policy for health becoming a reality:

- health improvement is not seen as a 'long game' but is subject to short-term gains
- the importance of a good 'sickness' service continues to overshadow the need for a 'health improvement service'
- an inadequate response by all stakeholders to the new public health agenda could limit demonstrable health improvement, thereby leading some to question the 'added value' of the public health function.

The review identified as a problem the absence of a national forum. Of the many possible options considered, the proposal for a public health institute for Scotland attracted most appeal. Such an institute 'would serve as a centre of excellence, a source of authoritative advice to the Scottish Executive, a focus for multi-disciplinary working and as a real force that could help to implement policy that would improve the health of the people of Scotland' (Scottish Executive 2000: §350).

The English regions

The development of regionalism within England has rumbled on for many years without any clear progress or sense of direction. Various regional agencies – government offices, regional development agencies, regional chambers – exist, but these have few powers and only limited accountability to local people. Devolution to Wales, Scotland and Northern Ireland has rekindled interest in English regional government, especially in areas such as the north-east and north-west which border Scotland and feel especially acutely that the advantages available to Scotland are denied them.

Devolution as a general concept, according to Greer and Sandford (2001: 5), offers the 'integration of public services, the development of innovative regional strategies, the democratisation of policy and the adaptation of policy to place.' Moreover, devolution to the English regions would offer all these advantages, too. The government has struggled over recent years to design an English regional settlement that would provide for the advantages while retaining the integrity of England as a country. Unlike Scotland, Wales or Northern Ireland, where administrative devolution existed for many years prior to political devolution, there is no route map to follow. As Greer and Sandford put it, 'thus the process of political devolution must go with the process of constructing the region as a political unit' (ibid.). Given England's history as a highly centralized political unit, establishing regional identities that have real meaning is a major challenge for the Whitehall-Westminster political culture that remains dominant. Otherwise, it is hard to see the purpose or relevance of regions.

The link between regionalism and public health is widely supported by those working in public health, but it has not developed particularly vigorously. To a degree, regional government has discovered public health, and there have been recent moves to strengthen its capability and capacity in this area. *The NHS Plan* began the process in earnest by stating that:

> by 2002 there will be new single, integrated, public health groups across NHS regional offices and government offices of the regions. Accountable through the regional director of public health jointly to the director of the government office for the region and the NHS regional director, they will enable regeneration of regions to embrace health as well as environment, transport and inward investment. (Department of Health 2000: §13.25)

The move was widely welcomed, especially by those concerned with the wider public health and keen to remove its sole locus from within the NHS. It was greeted less enthusiastically by some of those in public health who tended to operate within narrower parameters derived from a medical model of health rather than a social model.

As was pointed out in chapter 2, the NHS plan rather unexpectedly got overtaken by a major reorganization of the service under the banner *Shifting the Balance of Power*, designed to devolve responsibilities to the lowest possible level. The changes were not foreseen, especially their ambitious scope, which resulted in a wholesale restructuring of the service of a kind not witnessed since its birth. Part of the thrust towards encouraging local responsibility was the demise of the eight NHS regions, to be replaced by four directorates of health and social care that were arms of the Department of Health. These, too, were abolished in a further round of reform designed to reduce the Department of Health by at least one-third by October 2004.

Despite the hiatus arising from continual reorganization, the regional public health function as articulated in the NHS plan has remained more or less intact. In its implementation strategy for *Shifting the Balance of Power*, the government restated its commitment to relocating the Regional Directors of Public Health (RDsPH) plus support teams to each of the nine regional offices of government to provide the public health function. The RDsPH would have a wide-ranging role:

> They will manage and co-ordinate the health protection and emergency planning functions in their regions; they will design, develop and maintain public health networks; they will tackle the root causes of ill health and inequalities through the health component of cross-government policies in the regions (eg transport, environment and urban regeneration), deal with major health service incidents and provide overall leadership. (Department of Health 2002a: §3.2.3, 15)

It is the third of these tasks that is potentially the most exciting. As the implementation report from the Department of Health acknowledges:

> For the first time, [RDsPH] and their teams will be uniquely positioned to work with other Government Departments in the regions to build a strong health component into regional programmes.... Tackling the fundamental root causes of poor health and inequalities is vital to underpin effective local public health action. (Department of Health 2002a, Appendix C, §18b, 40)

To fulfil this function, RDsPH will be required to work closely with the regional offices of government directors on 'jointly agreed work programmes' and will be expected 'to contribute fully to the corporate business of the Regional Offices of Government' (ibid.: §18d, 40).

In one of her first major speeches as the new Minister for Public Health, Hazel Blears told the Faculty of Public Health Medicine's annual scientific meeting in June 2002 that the new regional arrangements 'will help spread the influence of public health across the business of the regions. It is a new world of relationships' (Blears 2002). She continued: 'The co-location between public health and the other regional functions is a very exciting prospect.'

A note of caution needs to be sounded, however. Looking at the remit of the regional public health role outlined above, it is notable for its wide-ranging and comprehensive nature. It is questionable, as was argued in chapter 4, whether it is reasonable to expect one person and a small support team truly to be able to perform such a role in a balanced and equally committed way. Would it not have been better to break the role down into its component parts and retain the more medical, health service elements within the NHS while confining the new regional public health function, involving the work of the regional offices of government, to a dedicated senior post? At least one senior public health practitioner has expressed concern over the requirements stated by the Department of Health that the RDPH will continue to be 'the point of contact for any clinical governance issues that are likely to give rise to grave public concern' (Department of Health 2002a: §18c, 40). Such a focus, in this person's view, not only perpetuates the present role of the RDPH but is not consistent with the potential offered by co-location of the RDPH with the

regional government office for effective cross-governmental working to tackle the wider public health agenda. Such a role, in his
view, should not have any responsibility for managing clinical
performance in the NHS.

Apart from the influence of devolution, there has also been
mounting dissatisfaction within government about the highly centralized nature of government policy-making and the weaknesses
arising from this in respect of effective implementation. An influential report produced by the Cabinet Office's Performance and
Innovation Unit (PIU) in early 2000 sought better integration at
regional and local levels in order to improve the delivery of government objectives, especially in areas such as health (Cabinet
Office 2000). The report was critical of the fragmented nature of
much government policy, despite a commitment to joining it up.
The problem was compounded by the absence of effective regional networks of government departments. The solution lay in
strengthening regional government offices, giving them a higher
profile, and making them accountable for the delivery of cross-
cutting outcomes. The move to strengthen public health at a regional level within the government offices can therefore be seen
as a response to the PIU's report. But it is only a beginning and is
unlikely to come to much unless elected regional assemblies
emerge.

After considerable delay, the government produced a white
paper on regional government in May 2002. It is described as 'a
cautious document' produced against a background of little interest in the issue of elected regional assemblies, and the wonder is
that it appeared at all (Sandford 2002: 4). It remains the case that
the concept of regional government is an alien one to Whitehall
mandarins and Labour Party traditionalists, and this should not
be underestimated. Public health is not to be an executive function of elected assemblies but an 'influencing' function.

Integrating public health with regional activities in social and
economic development and inclusion is a welcome and overdue
move to those advocating such a shift in order to wrest public
health from what is perceived as the crippling and distracting
embrace of the NHS. But the obstacles should not be underestimated. There are three in particular, and these are in addition to
the note of caution sounded earlier, although it overlaps with
these. First is a strong assumption that health is what the NHS
does. This is already a problem within local government and is
likely to be even more deeply entrenched within regional agen-

cies, where traditionally there is even less evidence of an interest in health. Second, 'an atmosphere of deep suspicion and dislike' pervades relations between the NHS and other parts of local and national government (Greer and Sandford 2001). Public health, as we have seen from earlier chapters, is a victim of this negative context. The core of the NHS is seen to reside in health services and not in public health, and this has left public health marginal-ized except where its practitioners have 'gone over' to the NHS. Only recently has there been a concerted, if at times fragile and unstable, effort on the government's part to encourage support for attention to health beyond the health service. Third, the pressure for short-term delivery sits uneasily with a public health agenda whose pay-off is by definition long term. This makes public health vulnerable to sacrifice and to having its budget raided in pursuit of short-term delivery. A strong regional presence may offer a defence against such behaviour, but only if the RDsPH and their teams regard this as one of their primary functions, if not *the* primary function.

Some observers are confident that the regions can rise to the challenge because of the 'development of strong regional policy networks and webs of secondments with slack resources and shielding from central pressure' (Greer and Sandford 2001: 22). In their view, an elected regional assembly would enhance all of this. Most important, public health would be removed from the con-stant pressure on waiting lists that damages NHS public health working. But this will happen only if RDsPH NHS functions are not allowed to overwhelm, or squeeze out, their new role in put-ting public health onto the agendas of regional government offices. To succeed, public health may need to become a regional function. Under present government proposals this would not be the case, since public health is listed as an influencing and not an executive function. However, as the Greater London Authority has shown, it is possible to make progress in the area of public health even when it is not a core function, and things can only happen through influence and negotiation. The vehicle con-structed for this purpose is the London Health Commission.

The London Health Commission is an advocacy coalition for public health. It predated the election in May 2000 of the London mayor but was able to provide a health policy for him when he took office. The commission's most important contribution has been to carry out health impact assessments on various of the mayor's strategies, including transport, although their impact in practice has been questioned when recommendations have not been conveyed to the mayor by his advisers (Greer and Sandford 2001). The commission cannot continue forever since, once the policies have been agreed and accepted, implementation of them will take over. The commission's role will have to change accordingly or give way to a new organization.

Assessing intra-UK health policy differences

From the above brief review of the health components of the NHS plans for Wales and Scotland respectively, it is evident that both share a similar thrust in respect of putting health before health care. In this regard, they are different in tone and focus from the English NHS plan which, as was suggested in chapter 2, tended to bury the health agenda by retaining a strong emphasis on the NHS. In contrast, the Welsh and Scottish plans both opened with a firm commitment to putting health first. However, it is not clear if the strong rhetoric is, or will be, matched by developments on the ground (see below). Greer (2001: 21) is sceptical: England is 'primarily focused on health care services organisations', Scotland is 'speaking of public health but still focusing on health care services', and Wales is 'focusing on integrated public health activities and promotion'. But there is a long history in the struggle within the pre-devolution Scottish Office over the tension between health care and health. The first secretary of the Scottish Health Service Planning Council, a product of the 1974 NHS reorganization, argued that Scotland had not suffered to the same degree from the managerial ethos which had permeated the English NHS and that this afforded an opportunity for 'planning for health' to go to the 'top of the agenda' (T. D. Hunter 1989: 215). He went on: '*health service* planning is dead – long live planning for health!' (ibid.: 219). It remains to be seen whether, this time round, policymakers in Scotland can fulfil Scotland's historic, innovatory role (McLachlan 1987).

In presentational terms, Scotland in its NHS plan appeared to give a higher priority to public health through the establishment of a new public health institute, but substantively this has not resulted in a significant difference in policy or approach. Perhaps Wales has shown the most distinctive, though hardly novel, approach. Whereas England and Scotland relied somewhat vaguely on selecting leaders at national and local levels to take forward the cause of public health, the Welsh approach focused on better planning aimed at taking advantage of the common boundaries shared by health and local authorities (Greer 2001). These organizations were to be compelled to work together on local public health needs. Such a commitment to planning is in keeping with a Welsh tradition which developed during the early 1990s, when planning was eschewed in favour of the NHS internal market (Welsh Health Planning Forum 1989a and 1989b).

The Welsh plan also shows a strong focus on health outcomes in contrast to the English document's concentration on health care. As Greer (2001: 26) puts it, 'if the English NHS Plan is a strategy to use investment in health care in order to rebuild and reform the NHS, the Welsh Plan proposes to use public funds to alter health outcomes.'

It is still early days as far as devolution is concerned and as to whether it will lead to marked divergence in health policy as distinct from what happened in the past, when policies and reforms varied at the margin but rarely in substance or in principle (Hunter and Wistow 1987b; Hazell and Jervis 1998; Pollock 1999). Greer (2001: 19) makes the interesting point that 'a key to understanding devolved politics is not taking England as a baseline', tempting though this might be. While this made sense under the pre-1998 unitary system, when there was a UK policy with marginal adjustments in each of the three administratively devolved countries, political devolution changed all that. 'There are now four policy arenas with four health policies in the UK' (ibid.). Within these arenas there is likely to be a mix of convergence and divergence. So, for example, although all three NHS plans in respect of England, Wales and Scotland stress the need to modernize services and for health-care organizations to be smarter, each differs in respect of the commitment to putting health before care. Wales and Scotland, as noted above, place a greater emphasis on health while still seeing the NHS as taking the lead role.

One of the more interesting features of devolution to Wales and Scotland is the impact it is likely to have on English regionalism. Although regional government across England is some way off, and there is in general little enthusiasm for it, this belies local differences. Where there is a strong regional identity, as in the north-east for example, then it could well be the case that an elected regional assembly could be operational within two years or so. With the abolition of NHS regions, the regional public health function has been co-located with the regional government offices. While in theory this could lead to new and innovative ways of thinking about and developing public health, in contrast to its ghetto-like existence in the NHS for the past thirty years or so, in practice considerable obstacles remain. These particularly concern the remit of the regional role and the human resources available. We will return to the twin issues of capacity and capability and how these might be strengthened in the final chapter.

Much of the day-to-day activity in respect of the NHS, and health policy more generally, is likely to remain essentially the same for some time across the UK because policy developments take time to build up and have an effect. In any case, if the thesis of this book has any salience, the doubtless sincere commitment to shift the policy paradigm upstream in favour of health is likely to prove short-lived as it gives way to a familiar retreat into the NHS as a sickness service. It is, at any rate, an empirical question, and it is unfortunate that at the time of writing it is not possible to provide any convincing evidence either way. The opportunity to do so and take full advantage of the potential for intra-UK policy learning should not be lost.

Perhaps the influence of Europe will, in time, act as a spur to give public health policies and interventions a higher priority in terms of sustainable development. It is to the role of the European Union in health policy that we now turn. Whereas devolution within the UK is about looking down, the role of the EU in health means looking up. It could be that member states are moving towards a Europe of regions where the emphasis in on 'thinking big and acting small'.

The impact of Europe

The public health directorate in Bradford Health Authority, in a memorandum submitted to the Health Committee's inquiry into public health, claimed that it was 'illogical and impractical' to examine public health policy in the UK without including 'its European and global partners' (House of Commons 2001b: 323). The memorandum went on to cite the WHO's estimate that only about 25 per cent of public health issues fall within the jurisdiction or sole influence of the UK acting alone. Nonetheless, for many engaged in health policy in the UK, Europe exists in a remote, rather shadowy form. It remains a complete mystery and a source of considerable ignorance. If it figures at all on anyone's radar it is viewed with mild academic interest. It is rarely taken seriously or regarded as central to anyone's business. As Mossialos and McKee (2002: 991) observe, the UK was for many years 'in a state of active denial about the influence of Europe'. Such a myopic view is no longer tenable and may already be changing in the light of BSE, foot and mouth and other public health issues that transcend national borders.

Within the European Union public health has remained somewhat marginal, although this situation, too, is changing rapidly. This is entirely understandable given the history of the EU and its origins in achieving greater economic stability. Public health issues were never accorded much prominence. But then if they receive scant attention within member states, as a recent study conducted by the European Health Management Association for the European Commission discovered, why should the position be so different at a supranational level (European Health Management Association 2000)? As Holland, Mossialos and Permanand (1999) point out, all EU countries face difficulties in the allocation of resources to different strategies, for example, prevention versus cure, and many of the current health-related problems in European countries are related to lifestyle behaviour and political/ economic issues such as smoking and unemployment. The situation has begun to change recently in the aftermath of crises in respect of food safety (BSE, foot and mouth, GM crops) and environmental hazards. After much delay over its budget, a new public health programme has been adopted by the Health Council.

There are also the implications of the operation of a single market on health policy. These have been the subject of study by the European Health Management Association (Busse et al. 2002). They are considered further below.

The EU and health policy

The European Commission concluded recently that 'health policy at EU level is still in its infancy and it has not yet been given the priority it requires in policy-making within EU institutions' (European Commission 2001: 22). And an independent study conducted for the European Commission by the European Health

Management Association concluded that 'Health policy has always played a subordinate role in the course of European integration' (Wismar et al. 2002: 17). The EU has no formal role in health-care services, in contrast to public health, which has a specific provision in the European Treaty under Article 152 (Article 129 prior to the Amsterdam Treaty). But this is slowly changing, and health care is not a complete no-go area for the EU (Belcher 1999). In fact, the EU has a very real and increasing influence on the way health care is delivered at national level (Duncan 2002). As a report of the High Level Committee on Health observed, a wide range of community-level legislation impacts on health systems, albeit in an unsystematic way (European Commission 2001). However, it remains the case that health care is a very sensitive political issue at EU level, since member states jealously guard their competence to make health policy and provide health services – the principle of 'subsidiarity' applies.

This principle, enshrined in Article 3B of the Maastricht Treaty, is often cited as a basis for defending national sovereignty over health services. It states:

> The Community shall act within the limits of the power conferred upon it by this Treaty and of the objectives assigned to it therein. In areas which do not fall within its exclusive competence, the Community shall take action, in accordance with the principle of subsidiarity, only if and so far as the objectives of the proposed action cannot be sufficiently achieved by the Member States and can therefore, by reason of the scale of the effects of the proposed action, be better achieved by the Community.

Member states invoke the principle when they believe that they are capable of achieving the same policy goals without intervention by the EU. However, its precise interpretation is as much, if not more, a matter of politics as it is of law (Belcher 1999).

Public health   Until recently, the EU has shown little interest in health, and there is certainly nothing that can be described as a comprehensive health policy framework. This is principally because the union is concerned primarily with economic matters. The most significant provision in health policy was introduced in the 1992 treaty on European Union agreed at the Maastricht summit. The treaty granted the commission a new and specific competence in public health in the form of Article 129. Its main focus was on health promotion and disease prevention.

At the June 1997 Intergovernmental Conference in Amsterdam, there was a revision of Article 129, partly as a result of the concern over food safety arising from the BSE crisis in the UK. There was criticism that Article 129 was being revised in an over-hasty manner and that such changes should occur only after a careful review of the EU's health competencies. In the end, the revised Article 129 (which became Article 152 in the new treaty) did not represent a comprehensive overhaul of its predecessor and disappointed those lobbying for a stronger statement of public health policy. As a consequence, the revised treaty represented 'a missed opportunity for policy-makers to consolidate the EU's competencies in the public health field' (Holland, Mossialos and Permanand 1999: 8).

There are some good things about the revised treaty and Article 152, in particular its acknowledgement of a broader definition of health to include 'improving public health' rather than simply 'the prevention of disease'. But the treaty does not consider the broader determinants of health necessary for a comprehensive definition of health along the lines of WHO's statement that 'health is a state of complete physical, mental and social well-being and not merely the absence of disease or infirmity.' According to Holland, Mossialos and Permanand, 'by neglecting the questions of the EU's role in poverty alleviation, transport, the environment, education and housing, etc., the EU has not been able to identify a clear definition (in intersectoral terms such as WHO) as to what public health is' (ibid.). Once again, as at Maastricht, the subsidiarity principle applied, thereby reaffirming that community action in the field of public health shall fully respect the responsibilities of the member states for the organization and delivery of health services and health care. Critics of the weak public health provisions consider the application of the subsidiarity principle could 'limit the potential scope for co-ordinating the European public health activities' (ibid.: 9). Despite much promise and high expectations, in practice the new treaty 'failed to address the basic issues of institutional reform requisite for the easier development and integration of health policies' (ibid.: 11).

However, the emphasis in the Amsterdam discussions on a broader view of public health did reflect a growing recognition that the EU lacked a single definition of public health. A unifying focus on the outcome 'health' would obviate viewing 'public health' and 'health care' as separate policy fields (Belcher 1999). The focus on health as an EU policy objective was supported by the European Parliament in its discussion on future EU health policy. In May 2000, the commission put forward a communication on the health strategy of the community together with a proposal for a programme of community action in the field of public health between 2001 and 2006 (Commission of the European Communities 2000). The new programme will replace the eight existing action programmes in the field of public health.

The European Parliament adopted a large number of amendments in April 2001. In the light of these, the commission drafted an amended proposal (Commission of the European Communities 2001). The amended public health programme 'takes a horizontal and policy-driven approach on the basis of a broad view of public health' (ibid.: 2). It focuses on three strands of action:

- *Improving information and knowledge for the development of public health* – while health systems of the member states are distinct, they all face common problems, and the potential for exchanging ideas about how to address these is considerable
- *Responding rapidly to health threats* – at present there is no effective community mechanism to deal with emerging health threats such as those arising from communicable diseases and bio-terrorism attacks following the events of 11 September 2001
- *Addressing health determinants* – improving the health status of the population by tackling the underlying causes of ill health through health promotion and disease-prevention measures.

The commission's public health programme was finally adopted in September 2002 by the European Parliament and the Council of Ministers. The delay was caused by the failure to agree the budget for the programme and concerns over the commission's lack of expertise and institutional capacity to deliver the new programme. The programme will run from 2003 until 2008 and represents a significant departure from the EU's approach to public health hitherto, with a decisive move away from public health as a series of separate action programmes, largely disease-oriented, to a more structured approach linked to clearer policy objectives (Merkel and Hubel 1999). The amended version produced in June 2001 strengthens the community's commitment to 'an integrated and coherent approach to health' – a primary objective of its health strategy (ibid.: 3). The commission also takes a broad view of public health that embraces issues in relation to health determinants, health status and health systems rather than focusing on specific diseases or conditions.

Health systems As mentioned, responsibility for financing and operating health systems remains the prerogative of each individual country in the EU. There exists no political will within the community to harmonize the delivery of health care in member states. At the same time, there is growing interest in health systems across Europe, reinforced by increased travel and European citizens looking at experiences in other countries in respect of how and to what standard health services are delivered. In the case of the UK, patients who are unable to gain treatment within a reasonable time-limit in Britain are able to travel overseas to obtain it. Many of the destinations are within Europe. This move, initially resisted by the government, follows on from rulings by the European Court of Justice concerning the ability to receive treatment 'without undue delay'. There have also been several rulings by the European Court of Justice which appear to challenge the subsidiarity principle. In the case of the individuals concerned who sought treatment in another country and wished to be reimbursed by their own country, the court upheld the claimants' cases under existing treaty provisions governing the free movement of goods and services.

There is also recognition that the single or internal market has an impact on health systems – an issue that has tended to be ignored or downplayed. The whole basis of the EU is the freeing up of markets to obtain the economic benefits associated with free competition and reduced barriers to trade. Health is not a typical market and is therefore not easily subject to the competitive model. Nevertheless, most of the actions taken in other areas do have an impact – intended or otherwise – on health systems (European Commission 2001). Most of the community legislation which impacts on health systems has been developed in the general context of the completion of the internal market. This comprises a wide range of actions targeted at ensuring free movement of persons, goods, services and capital within the EU. Indeed, the European Health Management Association in a study has concluded that 233 regulations, directives, decisions, recommendations and rulings of the European Court of Justice related to the internal market issued between 1958 and 1998 have the potential to affect member states' health systems.

A range of EU measures in the area of social policy can also be seen in this general context. For example, the working time direct-ive contains provisions fixing maximum working time in a given period. An initial exemption for junior hospital doctors has now been abolished. This has had extensive repercussions in member states' health systems.

But none of the measures has been developed 'in the context of a clear and coherent health policy' (European Commission 2001: 21). It is this realization that has led the commission to press for a more coherent and comprehensive community approach to health. So far there is no dedicated directorate for health, although a commissioner and corresponding directorate-general are respon-sible for health and consumer policy. However, other commission services deal with health-related matters. Until the impact of the EU on health policy is recognized, community measures which impact on health will continue to be largely influenced and dom-inated by economic considerations and factors, and not by health policy matters. Compounding the problem is the lack of interest showed by health ministries in member states. Inaction at a polit-ical level means that decision-making in this area has effectively been transferred to the European Court of Justice.

To overcome these problems, the commission wants to raise the profile of health policy at EU level by developing a health policy framework including health-care issues. It has called for a debate on the issues, perhaps to be led by the newly created European Health Forum. Significantly, the EU Council of Ministers – the decision-making body of the union – at its meeting in June 2002 took the unusual step of agreeing that 'there is added value in examining certain health issues from a perspective that goes beyond national borders' (council conclusions on patient mobility and health care, quoted in European Health Management Associ-ation 2002). The council noted that health-care systems in the EU share common principles of solidarity, equity and universality, despite their diversity. It also recognized 'the emerging inter-action between health systems within the EU particularly as a result of the free movement of citizens, and their desire to have access to high quality health services' (ibid.).

The momentum around developing an EU approach to health policy is gathering pace. Reflecting the growing interdependence of health policies and health systems, the Health Commissioner, David Byrne, speaking at the European Policy Centre in Brussels in October 2002, announced that he would be publishing a communication on how EU health policy should develop to meet the challenges posed by enlargement of the EU and the impact of globalization on health and health services. A key priority would be to achieve progress on improving co-operation between national health systems across Europe. Among the key questions to be addressed are the following:

- What powers does the community need to address health problems that transcend borders, such as communicable diseases and environmental threats?
- How can we ensure a proper balance between the operation of the single market and the functioning of national health systems?
- How can we ensure clarity about what the EU can and should do to protect and improve health?

With health policy issues rapidly rising up the EU agenda as a result of landmark judgements by the European Court of Justice, it is only a matter of time before the politicians begin to reassert their control over the direction of European health policy.

Conclusion

This chapter has reviewed developments in the governance of health systems which are likely to have a growing impact on their shape and content in future years. On the one hand, the UK, having laid claim to being the most centralized state in Europe following the fall of the Soviet Union, has entered into uncharted waters in respect of political devolution to the countries making up the Celtic fringe. No one knows where these developments will end up or what their impact will be on the future integrity of the union. There is also uncertainty about what may happen in England in respect of regionalism. Suffice to say that the bonds of a United Kingdom have been loosened with consequences that remain to be determined both for health policy and other sectors.

On the other hand, beyond the UK's borders is the European Union. It, too, is beginning to flex its muscles over health policy and is creating pressures for a more coherent approach to member states' health systems. Public health has for long been a responsibility of the EU, although many believe it has not had much impact and could have been a more vigorous force for sustainable public health policy-making across Europe. But the EU is primarily about economic integration and a single market, and anything which might interfere with its smooth running is not given priority. However, this may be changing, as the EU, mainly through its parliament, is beginning to see the importance of public health across Europe. At the same time there is growing interest in the development of health-care services across Europe, and the subsidiarity principle, while unlikely to disappear, is being slowly eroded.

There is a risk in the EU becoming more involved in health-care systems, and it reflects on a transnational scale the problem that has dogged individual countries. It is this: the more policy-makers' attention becomes focused on health-care services, the greater the tendency to ignore or give short shrift to public health. Up until now, the EU has not been distracted by the concerns of health-care systems and has been able to focus on public health issues and threats. Whether this focus can be maintained and, more important, strengthened in future will be a test of the EU's resolve to take public health seriously and give it the attention it requires. In particular, the recommendation put forward by Holland, Mossialos and Permanand (1999: 44) is well made: 'Public health must be forthright in the advocacy of programmes that improve health and be able to state clearly and openly the dangers and consequences of some actions – whether clinical, environmental or political.'

The next few years in health policy-making promise to be interesting ones within a European context. Certainly no one either with an interest in, or affected by, it can afford to ignore Europe. It is no longer an option, and that, perhaps, is the greatest change in the climate since the UK joined the community.

6 Moving out of the Ghetto

Introduction

The purpose of this final chapter is twofold: to reflect on the various key issues and arguments reviewed in previous chapters, and to suggest what might need to be done if progress is to be made on delivering the wider health agenda. In particular, how realistic is it to imagine an 'upstream' health policy that is not constantly eclipsed, sidelined or derailed by a preoccupation with a narrow 'downstream' agenda in which health-care delivery issues take precedence over health improvement?

In chapter 2, mention was made of the Health Secretary's LSE lecture delivered in 2000, in which he claimed the time had come 'to take public health out of the ghetto' (Milburn 2000). He meant by this that public health's marginal status both within the NHS and apropos its partners had to be challenged as well as the assumption that public health could be delivered only by professionals trained in medicine. It seemed at the time that the speech marked a turning point in the priority to be attached to public health. This was reaffirmed in a speech delivered by the Secretary of State for Health in November 2002, when he stated that 'the health debate in our country has for too long been focused on the state of the nation's health service and not enough on the state of the nation's health' (Milburn 2002).

However, as preceding chapters have shown, government attempts to give public health policy a higher priority over health-care policy have failed; have been eclipsed by the NHS reforms started in 1997, but pursued in a frenzy from 2001 following the NHS plan; or have simply fizzled out having made little impact (possibly because they have not been given a chance). Part of this sorry state of affairs may be the result of the challenge itself and the complex nature of health. It is, after all, an imprecise concept embracing virtually all aspects of public and private life. For something with so few fixed boundaries and lacking a simple, clear focus in respect of what policy instruments to introduce in order to achieve results, it is hardly surprising that progress has been unimpressive and that governments struggle to keep the issue in their sights. Combined with the simple truths set out in chapter 1 governing the dynamics of all health systems, more surprising perhaps is the fact that policy-makers show any interest at all in health as opposed to health care.

And yet that interest does persist, because policy-makers are mindful of the limitations of health-care services and their increasing cost. They are also aware, if at times dimly, of the evidence which shows unequivocally that the major killer diseases such as cancer and stroke are largely preventable and that resources could be better spent on 'upstream' rather than on 'downstream' interventions. The obstacles to making the shift in attention are not entirely, or even primarily, due to poor or no evidence in regard to what works, although this is certainly a contributing factor. However, the argument is not really sustainable as a major cause of lack of progress when one considers that a great deal of modern medical practice has not been subjected to rigorous evaluation. Yet this has not prevented these treatments or interventions from being resourced or undertaken or persisted with when the evidence has challenged their efficacy. 'Custom and practice' and experiential knowledge remain more important guides to medical practice than evidence-based decisions. Moreover, EBM does not obviate the need for clinical judgement in respect of individual cases. Indeed, it makes the importance of such judgement even more critical. In any event, in the fields of health care and more especially health, there are no unequivocal answers to the question 'what works?' (Macintyre et al. 2001: 225).

As I have argued, there appear to be other forces at work to account for the imbalance in policy even where policy-makers appreciate that it makes sense to invest in improving the public's health. From the earlier discussion, three of these forces are worth singling out for particular comment:

- the time lag between resource outlay and impact in terms of measurable change is too long for most policy-makers to contemplate with equanimity when they operate according to a four- to five-year electoral cycle – waiting for changes to occur in ten years plus is difficult when political survival may be at stake
- the powerful vested interests clamouring for resources and investment are well entrenched in health-care services and represent a significant constraint on shifting priorities and investment; they may not be utterly opposed to investment in health policies but they would not wish to see such investment occur if it was at the expense of 'their' services and interests; the battle for improved health is therefore also a matter of politics and power rather than being solely, or even principally, a technical issue to be resolved through rational debate and the application of hard evidence to practice
- the notion of health is diffuse and plural and its pursuit does not sit neatly within the confines of a single agency, policy sector, or level of government; health is everywhere and therefore risks being nowhere; in recent decades in the UK the lead for health has been accorded the NHS, although its primary concern is with ill health.

Chapter 2 demonstrated that these constraints are evident not only in the UK. The pursuit of health is a global concern. Other countries which have struggled to raise the priority attached to health policy have encountered similar obstacles and have found surmounting them to be exceedingly difficult.

Considering why this might be so has been the central theme of this book. In seeking explanations for this state of affairs, and for why things have gone wrong or not quite worked out, at least as far as the UK is concerned, we then proceeded to consider where, in particular, the public health function appears to have lost its way. Rather like the concept of health itself, the public health function has become too diffuse and all-embracing, combining activities that might better be separated and undertaken independently by different groups with relevant skills. I concluded that a preoccupation with the NHS management agenda from the 1970s on appears to have been a major factor in accounting for public health remaining trapped in a ghetto that has done its cause little good in terms of impacting on the public's health.

Indeed, a former NHS manager who not so long ago moved to become chief executive of a major local authority reckoned that he had achieved more for the health of the local population in nine months as a local government manager than he had done as an NHS manager over a fifteen-year period.

Part of the problem appears to have been the conception of the management task in public services. The managerial revolution and 'new rationalism' underpinning it has been largely imported from the business sector and is based rather crudely on traditional scientific management, or Fordist, principles that make little allowance for the complexity of health care and especially of health. A preoccupation with the health-care 'product' and the means of production through numerous quality initiatives, including the notion of clinical governance, has further sidelined wider health issues, since they are less susceptible to the application of business or industrial processes.

Paradoxically, the government over the past few years appears to have acknowledged the limitations of an approach to management which breaks problems, or 'wicked issues', down into segments or chunks that can be picked off and tackled separately. It has adopted the language of 'whole systems' thinking, 'joined-up' policy and management, and has sought to emphasize the interconnectedness of problems and their solutions. 'Complex problems demand complex solutions', has been the mantra. Yet there remains a serious, and growing, gap between the diagnosis of the problem and its prescription. Indeed the prescription adopted so far has remained a stubborn adherence to 'new public management' concepts, including traditional notions of top-down command and control, and of setting targets which organizations and professionals operating in their individual silos are required to meet. Such an approach is failing badly, and yet, despite this system failure, recognized at the heart of government within the Cabinet Office, politicians remain slow to adapt to the analysis. It is not enough to shift the policy paradigm in favour of health; the management model also needs to change to enable a new 'upstream' policy focus to occur. Arguably, it is a failure to align the two that lies at the root of the government's difficulties and explains many of the criticisms of its policy. As Barnard (2000) argues, we must emphasize the importance of the health *system* in its widest sense over and above the health *sector*. To this end, policy-making must be based on recognition of complexity and interdependence and of 'emergence', that is, the unanticipated effects of decisions and other happenings which can neither be anticipated nor foreseen. A reflective response is unavoidable, yet rarely acknowledged as the appropriate response by governments trapped in a macho mode of action management (Schon 1991).

But there are glimmers of light – mainly to be found in the Cabinet Office and some of the policy 'think tanks' that have influence on the government. But more recently the Department of Health has shown a readiness to embrace the notion of complexity, and the NHS Modernization Agency's Leadership Centre has employed Paul Plsek, a US consultant on complexity science, to assist with the development of its leadership programmes (with Trisha Greenhalgh he co-produced a series of articles on the subject, published by the *British Medical Journal* in 2001). There is more open discussion of health systems as complex adaptive entities that require to be managed in quite different ways which entails a paradigm shift in respect of how governments and managers think and operate. There is also the evidence now accumulating that the government will not improve the delivery of public services if it continues to apply the tools it has so far deployed. In his guidance on managing for excellence, the NHS chief executive, Nigel Crisp, acknowledges the need to embrace 'modern ways of working through teams and networks rather than through hierarchies and formal systems' (Department of Health 2002d: 1). Furthermore, there is a need to recognize the complexity of the environment 'with pulls in different directions and apparent contradictions'. Much of this approach to the management task in health and elsewhere in the public sector was first articulated in government through the work of the Cabinet Office's Performance and Innovation Unit.

In its report *Better Policy Delivery and Design*, the Performance and Innovation Unit (PIU) is critical of the linear model of policy delivery which has dominated thinking in central government (Cabinet Office 2001a). While it may work in some fields some of the time, in important respects it does not describe the real world that governments inhabit, and its application often leads to failure and frustration. Why this should be so is the purpose of the report to investigate. It states that policy delivery involves at least three related, though distinct, elements:

- *implementation* of policy
- achievement of *targets*
- achievement of better *outcomes*.

While these can reinforce each other as sequential stages in a single process, often they are in tension. So, effective implementation of a flawed policy can worsen outcomes, as can too great an emphasis on the wrong targets. The report, in a comment directly critical of much of the government's approach to improved policy delivery, notes that 'too many new policies and initiatives can wreck delivery by diverting management time – carrying out instructions gets in the way of better outcomes' (ibid.: 6). It also points to the limited control central government has over many of the agencies and people responsible for delivery. Consequently, 'excessively directive methods of government that appear to treat front-line deliverers as unable to think for themselves, untrustworthy or incompetent, undermine the very motivation and adaptability on which real-world success depends' (ibid.).

Importantly for the purposes of this discussion of health policy, and why it is so difficult to achieve, the PIU report points to the fact that in practice few policies are implemented fully formed. While the traditional rational linear model assumes that policy-makers possess complete knowledge about what will work and is possible, the ideal of policy being fully informed by an evidence base is rarely attainable. 'Not all the evidence is holy, pure, or perfect' (Law 2001: 560). In the real world it can be interpreted in different ways, depending not only on its content and method but also on the values and beliefs of the interpreter. Moreover, it is not easy to predict how institutions and people will respond. Policies have to be adapted in the light of experience, drawing lessons from the front line. They are then more likely to succeed.

In a companion report, *Strengthening Leadership in the Public Sector*, the PIU considers the state of leadership in the public sector and finds it wanting (Cabinet Office 2001b). In contrast to the naïvety evident in many ministerial pronouncements on management and leadership, the report acknowledges the critical role of context. The more complex environment in which public-sector organizations operate, and the increased demands on them, 'create a need for highly effective leadership and a requirement for new leadership skills' (ibid.: §2.10, 9). Aside from delivering improved 'vertical' services (e.g., shorter waiting lists), 'there is a greater demand for "horizontal" leadership within and across sectors . . . Above all, there is a need for leaders who are able to see the whole picture, and create a common vision with other agencies' (ibid.: §§2.10–2.11, 9). In a comment remarkable for its candour and directly critical of the government's own management style, the report claims that effective leadership is constrained by various structural and cultural barriers, including the lack of space given leaders to lead. 'Excessively tight control, and the coexistence of multiple levers of central control, can easily corrode the capacity to lead' (ibid.: §2.13, 10). Elsewhere, the report is critical of detailed external control over process. 'Government must be sparing in the number of frameworks that it sets. Leaders who are overburdened with directions will be unable to function effectively' (ibid.: §4.12, 27).

The report makes mention of the criticisms by public-sector managers of many of the instruments adopted by the government in its pursuit of improved policy and service delivery. In particular, targets can stifle innovation and initiative, with leaders concentrating on centrally set targets rather than working across boundaries or considering the long-term development of their organization. Targets can also have unintended consequences and distort organizational activity towards the measurable. Similar criticisms were reviewed in chapter 4 (see also Hunter 2002a). The report is careful not to dismiss the value and importance of 'well-set' targets, while agreeing that at worst they can have damaging effects.

Of course, it is necessary to ask why the government persists with what many commentators and researchers consider to be a flawed approach when confronted with this authoritative analysis challenging the whole basis of its modernization programme. The nub of the problem is that the government does not trust those managers charged with implementing its reform programme, especially when its own electoral fortunes are tied so directly to the success of this programme. If it did it would not seek to maintain such a tight grip of reform at the centre. It is never publicly admitted, or only rarely so, but privately ministers do not rate many public-sector managers. One may question on what grounds they make this claim, particularly given their own lack of management expertise and experience and that of the majority of those advising them. To compound the problem their suspicions may not be entirely unfounded – the quality of management may indeed be part of the problem rather than the solution (Caulkin 2002).

Whatever the true position, an unspoken belief that failure in the public sector can be explained to a large extent by poor and incompetent management goes far to explain why there is a mismatch between much government policy and the instruments chosen to realize it. If complex problems demand complex responses, then these cannot be reduced to simple mechanistic management nostrums. But to allow front-line managers space to explore options and find creative solutions demands high-trust relationships and letting go. This is something the government cannot bring itself to countenance – at least not so far – despite the rhetoric (or mask) of devolution. But something may have to change. For front-line managers to succeed also demands practical management and leadership skills which are lacking, as the PIU report demonstrates. Part of the responsibility for this sorry state of affairs must rest with the government and civil service, which have consistently undervalued management, probably because they do not really understand or appreciate its nature or what is required to ensure the right people with the right skills are appointed to key positions. As the PIU report states, 'magic solutions – such as wholesale import of leaders from the private sector or big increases in pay – will not address the public sector's leadership problems' (Cabinet Office 2001b).

Given the poor state of management in the UK, it is hardly surprising that policy failure, from which is emerging a growing implementation gap, is staring the government in the face. It is not a question only, or even primarily, of resources – important though these are. Nor, most important, is it a case of applying traditional management thinking to the problem. 'More of the same' is not going to work, especially if there is to be a real push on promoting the public's health. If the ambition is simply to improve health-care services then one possibility is for government to continue with its current policies and mechanistic management reforms. They won't work, but neither will the NHS collapse completely, although it will function less and less as a healthy or integrated organization. But if the ambition is to do something to 'break the mould' and give serious and sustained attention to health policy, then progress will prove impossible without a different approach being found to implement the policy. That is the real nature of the challenge facing those who believe that rebalancing health systems in favour of health is overdue. It is also first and foremost a political challenge rather than a technical one. Until this simple truth is grasped progress will remain piecemeal and disappointing – as has been the case in the UK and elsewhere over many years.

What is to be done?

A Canadian deputy minister for health promotion claimed 'that facts alone are not enough to convince people to change their traditional ways of thinking, understanding, and acting. The process of developing and adopting a new paradigm takes time, and resistance to change is inevitable' (Potter 1998: 16). The reallocation issue is at the core of shifting the paradigm and of whether a population health approach can succeed. Potter is acutely aware of the challenge noted above, namely, how to contain the costs of a restructured health-care system while moving investments to other 'health creating' sectors. There is also a need to tackle the 'tensions and misunderstandings that exist between proponents of population health on the one hand, and the health care system and health promotion on the other' (ibid.). The tensions can in part be explained by the competition which exists between groups for research and programme funding, but they also stem from other factors relating to the nature of health and health care of a more political and cultural nature.

As we have seen in the UK, and elsewhere, although population health has begun to influence the thinking of policy-makers, with some progress to report, it is not yet embedded in the wide range of public policies that influence the health of the public. In part this is a reflection on the language employed. The words 'public health' are not widely understood outside the health-care or clinical domain. Certainly within the world of local government, public health is associated with the specialty of public health medicine and the work that goes on within the NHS. Other terms such as 'social responsibility', 'well-being' or 'living well' might therefore have greater impact in a non-NHS setting, although they have yet to find well-developed constituencies to support and drive them.

But underlying these linguistic niceties is a more deep-seated and enduring problem that has surfaced. The research base explaining the nature and source of poor health and the inequalities linked to this is now pretty impressive and robust. Yet there remains a 'logjam', as Glouberman (2000) puts it, about the policy consequences. These remain 'mired in a left–right debate and in issues about the social determinants of health' (ibid.: 59). There is nothing new about this debate, but it has remained stubbornly resistant to change. There is also an associated tension between individual and collective responsibilities. Recent health-care reforms have sought to 'empower' individuals, but critics argue that this has been at the expense of collective obligations which are the basis of a health-care system such as the NHS.

If health is 'a function of the dynamic non-linear interaction of many forces' (Glouberman 2000: 60) and has many characteristics

of complex adaptive systems, then what are the practical implications in respect of implementation? And what is the nature of the
skills required by the workforce that will be engaged on improving population health, however this is defined, and among all
those agencies with responsibilities for it?

Applying some ideas derived from complex adaptive systems to
health cases in Canada, Glouberman sought to draw out lessons
for policy-makers. Without reporting the details of the case studies
Glouberman cites, the important themes that emerge are as follows:

- complex systems are adaptive – a side effect of complexity
  and of managing messes is that such systems will self-
  organize to evolve and regain stability
- promoting the public's health is a proactive process, not a
  reactive one, as is the case of reducing ill health
- making decisions under conditions of uncertainty is unavoidable, since there are real limits to the amount of certainty that is possible; decisions need to be made with best
  available rather than perfect data – 'to wait for certainty in the
  outcomes of one's actions is to wait forever' (Glouberman
  2000: 74)
- reverting to rational planning remains a constant temptation
  to those raised or trained in such a culture; it often leads to
  decisions to streamlining systems, even though by doing so
  the risk can be increased
- resources need to be made available to engage people to
  think through and resolve issues of co-ordination across the
  boundaries that occur in a networked system – such boundaries are not dysfunctional and are important to give identity and legitimacy to those working in organizations, but
  the boundaries still require to be negotiated and made per-
  meable
- effective management does not hinge on a single individual
  or group – it is a collective enterprise
- promoting health needs more than education alone – attention must be given to community-building and strengthening
- policies to promote health need to be located within the
  wider context of policies aimed at fostering the well-being
  of the population
- most behavioural changes in respect of smoking cessation or
  taking up physical exercise occurred by interactions within

a changing social context; in particular, where groups had adequate resources and freedom to self-organize, members stopped smoking or began engaging in exercise

- changing behavioural patterns will not succeed in the absence of social supports to aid the change process; lifestyle behaviours are a product of complex interactions between biology, peer groups, educational achievement, employment opportunities and the type of work, urban sprawl, car culture and more
- interventions in complex environments must be multiple, pursuing different routes to the desired goal or health state; reliance on a single bullet option or on simple solutions is unlikely to bring about change.

The stewardship role of government

There is growing interest in the notion of stewardship as constituting the defining purpose of government (Hunter et al. 2004). In its *World Health Report 2000*, WHO identifies stewardship as 'arguably the most important' health system function, ranking above health service delivery, input production and financing (World Health Organization 2000). This is because 'the ultimate responsibility for the overall performance of a country's health system must always lie with government.' Stewardship makes possible the attainment of each health system goal, including improving health. Protection of the public is a key element of stewardship. It is therefore about collective rather than individual responsibility. In its *World Health Report 2002*, WHO asserts that governments, in their stewardship role for better health, need to invest in risk prevention in order to contribute significantly to avoidable mortality (World Health Organization 2002). The report claims that 'substantial agreement' on what needs to be done exists among the research community and those charged with improving public health. But progress can occur only if there is 'sustained policy action and commitment by governments and other partners'.

When it comes to health policy, most governments, in the shape of ministries of health and other central departments, are ill-equipped to act as effective steering organizations. Such organizations set policy, allocate resources to operational bodies, and evaluate performance. But, as Osborne and Gaebler (1993) point out, when governments separate policy management from service delivery they often find that they have neither the real policy management capacity nor the appropriate skills to hand. Whatever their pretensions to the contrary, government departments often become embroiled in service delivery or micro-management, with the consequence that policy management at a strategic level is done poorly or not at all. A key conclusion from the discourse presented in this book is that in the UK the government's early commitment to improved health (what might be termed a policy management responsibility) progressively gave way to a preoccupation with micro-managing service delivery.

Yet a core task of stewardship, as defined by WHO, is formulating health policy and defining the vision and direction. It is a matter of governments being clear about what it is they wish their health systems to achieve. Are they concerned simply with the means (e.g., the amount of resources allocated to health care, numbers of doctors and nurses, and so on) or also with the ends (e.g., health gain, narrowing the health gap between social groups, improving the health of populations)? Many governments seek to address both means and ends, although, as just noted, there is often a tendency for the means to overshadow the ends or even to become ends in themselves.

Having an explicit health policy serves several purposes. At a purely symbolic level it provides a rallying point for those seeking to change the health system. It can show the way forward to a different future and act as a route map for getting there. Health policy is therefore an important instrument of governments and, in WHO's words, 'an important role of governance'.

It is also common practice, as the discussion of developments in the UK in chapter 2 revealed, for countries to produce eloquent and usually highly ambitious strategies for their health systems. These are often long on rhetoric and good intentions but short on delivery. There are many reasons for this, as was reported earlier, including the absence of ownership of the strategies by those charged with their implementation. This was the fate that befell the first health strategy in England, *The Health of the Nation*, which was operational from 1992 to 1997 (Department of Health 1998a).

All too often, governments equate managing a health system with the provision of acute hospital care. In part, this preoccupation reflects public and media concern with rising demand, lengthening waiting lists, and problems of access to care. Either the fact is overlooked that these pressures might have deeper causes in respect of lifestyles and structural determinants of health or the pressures are viewed as making for 'wicked issues' that are just too difficult to confront. Or, as is almost certainly the case, the pay-off is seen as too distant and long term, with no immediate prospect of easing pressures on the health-care system. So, there is almost something inevitable about health systems focusing almost exclusively on 'downstream' pressures rather on tackling 'upstream' issues.

As was noted earlier, producing the vision or strategy is often the easy part. Much more problematic is ensuring effective implementation, because it involves time-consuming alliance-building among many potentially competing interests or, as Caulkin (2002: 8) puts it, 'the grubby business of getting things done'.

Towards implementing a policy for health

In the UK, the key elements of a policy for health are already in place. Indeed, the various developments in respect of the health strategy, neighbourhood renewal, Sure Start programme, efforts to redistribute resources to the poor, and so on, are all concerned with the same common goal, namely, to improve the social and economic context for people. Their improved health will follow from this concentration of effort on creating a favourable social and economic context. Obviously, achieving this goes far beyond the Department of Health. However, the problem or lack of action does not reside in a policy deficit or in gaps in research (Long 1998). As chapter 5 suggested, there may be some lessons to learn across the UK, where the countries making up the Celtic fringe appear to have put improving health higher up the agenda than is evident in England. There is also the growing interest in health matters being shown by the European Union with the announcement of a new public health programme.

But if there is a problem anywhere it resides in the area of implementation. Some of the reasons for difficulties here were offered in chapter 3, and ways forward were described in chapter 4. It seems appropriate to conclude this discourse by going a little further in pressing the case for changes in management, given the importance attached to it. It is also critical if effective implementation is to occur.

As has been argued, health has all too easily been subsumed within the management of health services (Coote and Hunter

1996). Some might say that this has been both the NHS's strength and its weakness. By pretending to be a health service concerned about health, rather than openly acknowledging its reality, which is, by and large, an ill-health or sickness service, the very existence of the NHS has helped to ensure the marginalization of a broader health agenda.

Evans (1995) favours the development of a 'managerial epidemiology'. He means by this a commitment to managing for health which would vest in managers responsibility not for institutions or collections of facilities but for the effective management of resources (human and financial) to promote and maintain the health of a defined population. The core task of managing for health is not about markets for products or services but about long-term collaborative planning in pursuit of public interest goals. As described above, it is a manifestation of stewardship.

The skills called for by a health system built around the concept of managing for health are very different from those required to run health-care institutions. Indeed, management focused on population health might well involve the transfer of resources away from institutions providing care towards other health-promoting activities outside the conventional health system. This sort of creativity is precisely what ought to be happening in areas selected to be Health Action Zones, although, as was pointed out in chapter 4, it has not occurred on a significant scale.

In seeking to prepare managers for managing for health, the notion of public health management may be helpful (Hunter 1999, 2002d and 2003; Hunter and Berman 1997; Alderslade and Hunter 1994). It is an issue which WHO has recognized as being of some importance. A working document on developing public health within the European region prepared for the Regional Committee for Europe in September 1998 states that:

> modern public health practice...includes not merely scientific technical practice but also the knowledge and skills to build effective coalitions and partnerships for health and collectively to manage actions for health improvement. This capacity to achieve positive change for health can be described as public health management. (World Health Organization 1998)

Public health management requires managers who understand the importance of population-based approaches to health and public health specialists who are not mere purveyors of knowledge. They are also change agents, skilled in managing change and in building coalitions of support for change, both within the health-care sector and across and into other sectors that have a significant, perhaps an even more significant, impact on health. As the WHO document on developing public health puts it, 'public health practice is always a dynamic combination of knowledge about health and the causes of ill health, and action towards health improvement' (ibid.).

Public health management is not concerned exclusively with the analysis of the health needs of the population, health promotion and prevention. It must also concern itself with the management of all resources provided from public funds intended to improve the health of populations, including acute care, which has an important contribution to make to secondary prevention. The essence of public health management is its commitment to link knowledge and action. As a former Chief Medical Officer for England, Sir Kenneth Calman, has expressed it:

> The practical implications of public health are an art and require special skills in themselves. These skills need emphasising and developing and include both management and political skills and skills in the communication of ideas and complex public health issues. (Calman 1998: 118)

There have been encouraging signs that the concept of public health management has moved beyond the realm of academic discourse and is being taken seriously at high levels in government. The CMO's project aimed at strengthening the public health function to ensure fitness for purpose was reported in chapter 2 (Department of Health 2001d). There is also the general commitment to a 'whole systems' approach to tackling complex public policy problems.

What are the prerequisites needed to ensure, or at any rate improve the chances of, success? Three come immediately to mind:

- the importance of trust relationships
- the need to experiment and evaluate different approaches to managing performance
- the value of 'government-as-network' model.

Trust

Trust is an essential ingredient if the shift of mindset required in managing for health is to become a reality and if managers are to collaborate rather than compete. Supporters of the quasi-market in health care contend that decentralized competitive environments axiomatically provide a more powerful stimulus than do centrally directed systems to change behaviour and improve outcomes (Harding and Preker 2002). The countervailing view is that the marketization of health-care policy has made it more difficult to manage for the achievement of public interest goals because it has seriously eroded trust and introduced dysfunctional competitive modes of behaviour.

Trust is increasingly acknowledged not just as a key component of good management but as a core ingredient of social capital thinking and notions of citizenship and civic responsibility (Halpern and Mikosz 1998). Trust implies mutual understanding and respect rather than dependency or any imbalance of power. Equally, being too hard nosed and rigid about audit and regulation may well erode trust or make it more difficult to achieve and sustain (Calman et al. 2002). This is certainly the view of the 2002 BBC Reith lecturer, Onora O'Neill, who explored the 'crisis of trust' in her series of lectures. Far from offering reassurance and strengthening trust, the impact of increased regulation has had precisely the opposite effect (O'Neill 2002). A paradox of public policy is that the more transparency there is, the less trust and confidence there is. O'Neill believes that currently fashionable methods of accountability 'damage rather than repair trust'.

In his seminal study of labour management issues, Fox (1974) argued that purely economic exchanges, and those relying on formal contracts, institutionalized the dynamics of low trust and low discretion. Social exchange, conversely, entails judgement in task performance and loyalty and sustains high-trust relationships and high levels of work discretion. With remarkable prescience, Fox went on to claim that, with markets and contractual relations permeating every sector of social and public life, the reciprocity and diffuse obligations essential for high-trust relationships were being progressively undermined. Such a development is a product, at least in part, of the managerial revolution in public policy over the past fifteen years or so which has borrowed heavily from the commercial sector as if that sector represented a benchmark for all managerial activity. Much of chapter 3 sought to challenge that assumption in the context of health policy.

Managing performance

Assessing performance in the area of achieving improved health through tackling health inequalities requires sensitive and contextualized approaches. Crude, broad-brush quantitative measures are unlikely to be sufficiently sensitive to capture the success factors operating within local areas. Strengthening local communities and individuals through the activities of HImPs (and their · successors) and HAZs, as well as through the efforts of the Social Exclusion Unit, requires local approaches, since what works and makes a difference is likely to vary enormously from place to place. There are a huge number of variables with which to contend. Micro-level work is essential in order to regenerate neighbourhoods and support individuals. Understandably, government departments and ministers want to be able to point to tangible, and preferably visible, progress being made, and there is a tendency, if not a temptation, to produce standardized approaches and indicators. This might work against the efforts of local agencies, the very essence of whose efforts is small, highly diverse, and not always visible. Process indicators may help, although identifiable change may be hard to pin down. There is a need to experiment with and evaluate different approaches. This is especially so in respect of 'joined-up' management, which demands an assessment of partnership working *across* organizations rather than treating each one separately as a discrete entity.

Developing networks

In preference to the government-as-machine model and the performance-control model of management, Mintzberg (1996) opts for the government-as-network model. This is the opposite of the new public management approach, which has more in common with the first two models. Government-as-network is loose rather than tight, free-flowing rather than controlled, interactive rather than sharply segmented. Governments, or subsets of governments, are viewed as single interconnected systems, complex networks of often temporary relationships fashioned to work out problems as they arise. Such an approach is well suited to 'wicked issues', such as improving population health, and to complex adaptive systems, described in chapter 4.

Networks and partnerships are not a free good or soft option. They incur significant transaction costs and can be justified only if seen to add value. They are invariably fragile and need careful nurturing (Neighbourhood Renewal Unit 2002). They cannot be commanded through instrumental devices which must place limits on the relevance of a statutory duty to enter into partnerships being imposed on prospective partners. Partnerships 'require shared insights, values, strategies, time and commitment' (Society of Local Authority Chief Executives 1995).

The obstacles to closer working across agency and professional boundaries are considerable, as the literature shows unequivocally (see, for example, Huxham 1996). They generally have less to do with flawed structures than with defective processes. Yet, improved population health will not be forthcoming unless the challenge of creating effective partnerships is met. As was pointed out earlier, it is not a case of getting rid of boundaries. They serve an important purpose. But what might be useful is the development of a new breed of what Glouberman (2000) terms a 'boundroid' in the health field – people who are adept at working in the interstices of organizations.

Managerial capacity-building

The managerial challenge arising from the foregoing is a considerable one. But it is also crucial that it be addressed because, without adequate capacity, there will be minimal chance of shifting the paradigm in favour of an upstream health policy agenda. That much has already been learned from the efforts of the government so far, although it may not be a case only of faulty or inappropriate management but also of an absence of political will to make the shift other than at a symbolic policy level. Such a conclusion is shared by the World Health Organization (2002). Its *World Health Report 2002* argues that most of the measures proposed to improve population health are proved approaches, such as taxing tobacco, encouraging safer sex, and fortifying food with vitamins and minerals. It is political will, not knowledge, that is lacking. Governments of all kinds are urged to adopt bold policies.

The managerial challenge has major implications for the recruitment, training and professional development of the new managers for health (Hunter 2002e). But before considering the requisite skills and competencies, it is essential to be clear about what sort of managers are wanted for the complex task they will confront.

Loughlin's uncompromising stand on the subject is both challenging and unsettling. He finds a great deal of the literature on management science 'nonsense' and is concerned that, in management, in the health service and elsewhere, 'dogmatism and formalism are in the ascendancy and good intuitive thinkers are rare on the ground' (Loughlin 2002: 232). He wants to see more reflective managers and is dismayed by those who take the view that, as 'servants of the state', managers exist to implement whatever the ruling political party of the day requires. The manager's primary moral duty is to think for themselves and to 'exercise the virtues of self-direction and solidarity' rather than appear as mouthpieces for the dominant political order (ibid.: 234).

A context in which managers feel unable to challenge the prevailing orthodoxy and assumptions made can only encourage cynicism and cowardice, in Loughlin's opinion. This occurs because managers seem all too content to issue forth pious utterances upon the world. 'They churn out documents full of talk about empowerment and honest dialogue, while allowing environments breeding fear and dishonesty to continue' (Loughlin 2002: 246). What Loughlin wants to see are more 'decent managers' who take control of the organizations which purport to represent them. It is important that managers can criticize nonsense wherever it is found and reconsider their moral relationships with their fellow-workers and society as a whole. If managers felt more passionate, for example, about the impact of their actions on health, and also those of their colleagues, then it is possible that they could help create a constituency for change, urging a rebalancing of priorities in favour of health. It is a matter of what Mintzberg calls 'soul' (Mintzberg 1996). Attitudes count, not numbers, and control is rooted not in hierarchy but in values and beliefs. This approach has implications for how managers are selected and then function. They should be chosen for their values and attitudes rather than just their credentials. And they should practise a craft style of management rooted in experience. Only in this way can management regain a sense of its own worth.

The draft *Code of Conduct for NHS Managers* was issued in May 2002 (Department of Health 2002e). The final version was published

in October 2002 alongside the report on strengthening management in the NHS, noted above (Department of Health 2002d).
The code sets out the duties and style of management and leadership required in the modern NHS. There are five key duties (see
box 6.1).

The code applies to all managers and is expected to be incorp-
orated in their contracts (Department of Health 2002e).

Strengthening management capacity is central to the achievement of the government's commitment to improved health. This
is not about listing competencies. One of the more acute criticisms
of competency-based approaches to management education, which
have been in vogue, is that the context within which management
occurs is overlooked (Edmonstone and Havergal 1998). Organizational context is a critical factor in management performance, as
has been stressed by various leading researchers in recent years
(Pettigrew and Whipp 1991; Pettigrew et al. 1992).

There are two further key shifts required to facilitate and support the development of managerial capacity in the pursuit of
improved health:

- from a hard- to soft-systems approach to problem-solving
- from managers as old-style bosses to conductors of the orchestra (though a jazz group might be a more appropriate
  metaphor in the context of health policy).

Box 6.1   *Code of Conduct for NHS Managers*

As an NHS manager, I will observe the following principles:

- make the care and safety of patients my first concern and act to
  protect them from risk
- respect the public, patients, relatives, carers, NHS staff, and partners in other agencies
- be honest and act with integrity
- accept responsibility for my own work and the proper performance
  of the people I manage
- show my commitment to working as a team member by working
  with all my colleagues in the NHS and the wider community.

Source: Department of Health (2002e)

Hard problems and soft systems

The position taken up by, and value base underpinning, much of the approach to management adopted here owes a great deal to soft-systems thinking. It may be contrasted with the hard-systems thinking prevalent in the 'scientific management' school and undergoing a revival under the term 'new public management' (NPM) (see chapter 3). NPM displays more hard-systems characteristics than soft-systems ones. What distinguishes them is that, whereas hard-systems thinking tackles well-defined problems (e.g., for optimizing the output of a hospital laundry), soft-systems thinking is more suitably directed to ill-defined, messy or 'wicked' issues of the kind with which this book has been concerned. But the distinction goes deeper.

According to the pioneer of soft-systems thinking, Peter Checkland, whereas hard-systems thinking assumes that the world is a made up of a set of systems which can be methodically engineered to achieve objectives, soft-systems thinking assumes that the world is problematic but that the process of inquiry into problematic situations can be organized as a system (Checkland 1995). In other words, what is systematic shifts, so that it is not the world which is systemic but the process of inquiry into that unsystemic world.

In our review of health policy and its implementation there is limited room for hard-systems thinking. This is because goals and measures of performance are not clear-cut and not contested, communication between people is diverse, and those responsible for acting on policy are spread across many organizations and professions, both vertically and horizontally. Organizational and managerial life is notable for its complex and varied nature.

Given this context, good management practice is not reducible to easily describable, testable, replicable techniques or stratagems derived from research (Schon 1991). Hence the serious limitations of a narrow, reductionist, evidence-based management approach predicated on a spurious quasi-science of management (Whitley 1988). Of course managers need to be equipped with a range of skills, whether in project management or health needs assessment. But managers at senior strategic and operational levels, rather like doctors (with whom they perhaps have more in common than is often appreciated), make numerous, and often complex, judgements which defy easy descriptions or procedures and rules.

It has been said that 'managers do not solve problems: they manage messes' (Ackoff 1979). Marmor recommends a return to realism. 'Sensible management requires modesty, not zeal' (Marmor 2001: 22). He asserts that management 'is not a solution to seemingly intractable stresses. Rather it is a means of coping with and sometimes improving only marginally tractable situations' (ibid.: 25). If managing complexity is beyond the skills and techniques imparted to managers on most training courses, then we need a new way of capturing the art and craft of management. Allowing managers to reflect in action could prove to be a powerful means of meeting this need and more meaningful than a misconceived attempt to apply evidence-based management (Schon 1991).

Managers as leaders / conductors of the jazz orchestra

Managers of health policy and its implementation are akin to leaders/conductors of the jazz orchestra rather than old-style bosses. This style of management is crucial in the formation and sustainability of interdependent networks, which are the principal means by which a 'whole systems' approach to problem-solving may be achieved. The notion of the manager as 'servant leader', whose ethic is a responsibility to guide and support the work of others rather than to seek status and assert power over them, is central to this shift in managerial authority. Servant leaders as managers 'will need not only technical training in essential competencies but also a creative, inquiring spirit, diplomatic skills, and an ability to relate to others in the building of trust' (Barnard 1998). Such a style of leadership contrasts sharply with the cult of the heroic leader which still holds sway in many circles, especially among politicians whose understanding of management is largely, and perhaps frighteningly, minimal and often crude and unsophisticated. As Wilkinson and Applebee (1999) put it in their important discussion of implementing holistic government,

> there is often a view that leaders need to be charismatic and perhaps aspire to hero status. This is mistaken. Effectiveness is more usually an outcome of determination, personal openness and the integrity and honesty experienced by others around them. Leaders communicate more by what they do, champion and support, than by what they say...It is important that leaders find their own styles and can act with a range of styles, contingent upon the situ-

ation. Above all, they need to be able to live and work with paradox, dilemmas and uncertainty – both their own and others.

Echoing the earlier discussion on public health management, which it is suggested here is what is required (though in short supply) to take the health agenda forward, a seasoned NHS manager, Ken Jarrold, advocates developing public leadership within a health system through genuine community development. This entails learning to work with all those who can influence health. He maintains that the most valued leaders of the future

> will not be the most effective managers of institutions – although that remains an essential skill. The most valued leaders will be those who are able to work with others to facilitate, to negotiate, to influence, to serve. The NHS needs to recognise that it will not always be in the lead. (Jarrold 1998)

Developing the new manager

When it comes to developing managers, a balance must be struck between 'how to' training, of a rather conventional standard type, and what Barnard terms 'a liberal education exploring ideas and alternative views of the world', which arguably has received less attention in the preparation of managers (Barnard 1998). Only if management development moves forward in such a direction may the deeply entrenched mistrust of managers and management – 'the enemy within', as Loughlin (2002) describes them – begin to disappear. A commitment to a genuine public health agenda, designed to improve the quality of people's lives in a community, stands a better chance of winning wide support for the management task than a continuing obsession with business-driven service 're-disorganizations' and restructurings (Smith et al. 2001).

Such an orientation has been referred to as comprising a 'public service ethic' (Barnard 2000). It may be out of fashion in an increasingly individualistic society, but it is nonetheless of critical importance for all that. There is a need for managers 'who are ready to act, to contribute, to participate without expecting or assuming an immediate return of personal benefit beyond fair reward and recognition' (ibid.).

As I, and the reader, approach the end of the book, it has to be said that there is nothing startlingly new or original in all this, even if the fashion is to invent new designer labels to describe old and/or familiar topics and processes. But if it is the price to pay for being listened to because what is being expressed is 'modern' and 'cutting edge' rather than dismissed as old-fashioned, then so be it. The point to make, however, is that history is important and is not to be lightly rejected as being of no consequence. There is much to borrow and learn from the management thinking alive in the 1960s and 1970s around inter-corporate planning and organized social complexity (Friend et al. 1974). Indeed, Chapman's recent and timely discourse on 'system failure' draws heavily on this literature (Chapman 2002). Working across organizational and professional boundaries was as alive then as it is now. It remains difficult work.

Last word

If the purpose of health policy, as a key component of governments' stewardship role, is to improve health and to do so in ways which reduce the health gap, then managing and leading *for* health, rather than health care, becomes the central management task and the one on which the performance of health systems should be judged. Unfortunately, we still have some way to go before governments take their responsibility for policies for health, and all that they entail, seriously. Too often they continue to indulge in 'decisionless decisions' (Bachrach and Baratz 1970). On the whole, as a WHO review of health policy development in Europe concluded, the health sector 'still appears to act largely alone, and tends to be dominated by medical models' (Ritsatakis 2000: 353). The review continues:

> even when attempts have been made to carry out more community-based programmes for health promotion, it is not unusual for this to be carried out almost as a sideline, parallel to actions in the traditional health care sector where it is 'business as usual'. (Ibid.)

This book has sought to provide an account of why this state of affairs persists despite attempts to disturb the status quo and shift the paradigm. At root, the impediments to change owe as much, if not more, to an analysis centred on politics and power as to one centred on technical or managerial defects or deficits. It is a view shared by the World Health Organization in its review of the state of global health (2002). As a respected American policy analyst concluded many years ago, 'the politics of medicine is just as much about the power of doctors as it is about the authority of politicians' (Wildavsky 1979: 294). Little of substance has changed over the years. But the more important point is one that Wildavsky goes on to make: 'if health is only minimally related to care, less expertise may be about as good as more professional training' (ibid.). It is a heretical thought at a time when the government, through its NHS plan, is seeking to strengthen capacity and increase the number of doctors and nurses when they are singularly lacking. But the questions remain: What is their link with improved health? And will their training and recruitment make it more or less likely that a shift to a focus on health will be possible?

I do not pretend to claim that the interplay between politics and power is the only, or even the most critical, impediment to change. But I do believe it has fallen out of favour as a credible and legitimate explanation for policy inaction in an age and a policy context where all the emphasis is on a misplaced scientism and a narrow managerialism pervades or, more precisely, passes for political discourse. The prevailing orthodoxy that lack of action or progress is a technical problem arising from poor or defective evidence cannot go unchallenged. The assumption underlying such thinking is that if we get the evidence 'right' then action will follow. This simplistic and naïve model of policy-making is not supported by history or by the 'mobilization of bias' in favour of health care. Such bias is the product not of evidence but of predominant values, beliefs, rituals and standard operating procedures (Bachrach and Baratz 1970). These are the key drivers of policy, and they largely determine both which issues get onto the policy agenda and which ones do not. My rather modest aim in this book has been to revisit a political explanation of why putting health before health care has proved so difficult and to restore its position as one that deserves to be taken seriously.

But, as I have also sought to show, the prognosis is perhaps not all gloomy. Even failed, or only partially successful, attempts to move 'upstream' and enact a policy for health have a value. Ritsatakis offers five reasons for why the experience of formulating and implementing a policy of health is in itself of value:

- it has led to an improvement in information for health policy development, particularly in the area of inequities
- mechanisms for wider participation have been put in place
- cross-sectoral attempts at collaboration have been articulated and even tried, and our knowledge and understanding of partnerships has increased as a result
- even where implementation has not been successful, the attempt to do so while working with others has provided important lessons and identified possible opportunities for change
- the work on policy formation has raised the profile and importance of a health agenda, thereby making possible incremental progress towards the fulfilment of health goals.

Equally, there is no room for complacency. Acute health-care services everywhere are creaking under the weight of growing demand and buckling from the pressure to deliver more with less. New, ill-thought-through gimmicks such as the creation of NHS foundation hospitals (the first wave is expected to come on stream in 2004) with new freedoms from central control only serve to reinforce an outdated model of hospital care. It is one that not only risks marginalizing primary care, at a time when it is supposed to have a critical role in shaping future health and health care, but also fails completely to make a reality of the 'whole systems', 'joined-up' approach to policy and management to which the government was committed on entering office in 1997.

There is a sense of a system running like mad to stay in the same place – a classic example of the phenomenon known as 'dynamic conservatism' (Schon 1973). Tinkering with such arrangements is not going to solve the underlying 'wicked issues' with which they are seeking to deal. Hence the growing evidence of 'system failure'.

What is to be done? As one policy analyst has put it,

> health policy is pathological because we are neurotic, and we insist on making our government psychotic. Our neurosis consists in knowing what is required for good health (Mother was right: Eat a good breakfast! Sleep eight hours a day! Don't drink! Don't smoke! Keep clean! And don't worry!) but not being willing to do it. Government's ambivalence consists of paying both coming and going: once for telling citizens how to be healthy, and once for paying people's bills when this goes unheeded. Psychosis appears when

government persists in repeating this self-defeating play. Maybe twenty-first-century people will come to cherish their absurdities. (Wildavsky 1979: 307–8)

We urgently need to find a way of moving the discourse onto a different plane in respect of putting health *before* health care. As the Wildavsky quote makes clear, making that leap still defies us, whether we are politicians, professionals, managers, academics or members of the public. But make it we must for the sake of our health.

Index

Barnes, R., and Rathwell, T. 1993: *Study to Assess Progress in the Adoption and Implementation of Health Goals and Targets at the Regional and Local Levels.* Leeds: Nuffield Institute for Health, University of Leeds.

Barrett, S., and Fudge, C. 1981: *Policy and Action.* London: Methuen.

Beaglehole, R., and Bonita, R. 1997: *Public Health at the Crossroads.* Cambridge: Cambridge University Press.

Beck, U. 1992: *Risk Society.* Cambridge: Polity.

Belcher, P. J. 1999: *The Role of the European Union in Healthcare: Overview.* Zoetermeer: Council for Health and Social Service.

Berridge, V. 1999: *Health and Society in Britain since 1939.* Cambridge: Cambridge University Press.

Black, N. 2001: Evidence based policy: proceed with care. *British Medical Journal*, 323, 275–9.

Blackstone, T., and Plowden, W. 1988: *Inside the Think Tank: Advising the Cabinet 1971–1983.* London: Heinemann.

Blears, H. 2002: *The Challenges Facing Public Health.* Speech by Hazel Blears, MP, Minister for Public Health. Annual Scientific Conference of Faculty of Public Health Medicine, 27 June. London: Department of Health.

Bunker, J. P. 2001: The role of medical care in contributing to health improvements within societies. *International Journal of Epidemiology*, 30 (6), 1260–3.

Busse, R., Wismar, M., and Berman, P. (eds) 2002: *The European Union and Health Services: The Impact of the Single European Market on Member States.* Amsterdam: IOS Press.

Cabinet Office 1999: *Professional Policy Making for the Twenty First Century: Report by Strategic Policy Making Team.* London: Cabinet Office.

Cabinet Office 2000: *Reaching Out: The Role of Central Government at Regional and Local Level.* London: Performance and Innovation Unit.

Cabinet Office 2001a: *Better Policy Delivery and Design: A Discussion Paper.* London: Performance and Innovation Unit.

Cabinet Office 2001b: *Strengthening Leadership in the Public Sector: A Research Study by the PIU.* London: Performance and Innovation Unit.

Calman, K., Hunter, D. J., and May, A. 2002: *Make or Break Time? A Commentary on Labour's Health Policy Two Years into the NHS Plan.* Durham: University of Durham.

Calman, K. C. 1998: *The Potential for Health: How to Improve the Nation's Health.* Oxford: Oxford University Press.

Caulkin, S. 2002: Good money thrown at the bad. *The Observer*, Business Section, 21 July, 8.

Challis, L., Fuller, S., Henwood, M., Klein, R., Plowden, W., Webb, A., Whittingham, P., and Wistow, G. 1988: *Joint Approaches to Social Policy: Rationality and Practice.* Cambridge: Cambridge University Press.

Chapman, J. 2002: *System Failure: Why Governments Must Learn to Think Differently.* London: Demos.

Checkland, P. 1995: Systems theory and management thinking. In: M. Blunden, and M. Dando (eds) *Rethinking Public Policymaking: Questioning Assumptions, Challenging Beliefs*. London: Sage.

Clarke, M., Hunter, D. J., and Wistow, G. 1997: For debate: local government and the NHS: the new agenda. *Journal of Public Health Medicine*, 19 (1), 3–5.

Collins, D. 2000: *Management Fads and Buzzwords: Critical-Practical Perspectives*. London: Routledge.

Comack, M., Brady, J., and Porter-O'Grady, T. 1997: Professional practice: a framework for transition to a new culture. *Journal of Nursing Administration*, 27 (12), 32–41.

Commission of the European Communities 2000: *A Proposal for a Decision of the European Parliament and of the Council Adopting a Programme of Community Action in the Field of Public Health (2001–2006)*. COM(2000) 285 final. Brussels: Commission of the European Communities.

Commission of the European Communities 2001: *Amended Proposal for a Decision of the European Parliament and of the Council Adopting a Programme of Community Action in the Field of Public Health (2001–2006)*. COM(2001) 302 final. Brussels: Commission of the European Communities.

Coote, A., and Hunter, D. J. 1996: *New Agenda for Health*. London: Institute for Public Policy.

Cornford, J. P. 1974: The illusion of decision. *British Journal of Political Science*, 4, 238–9 [review article].

Cummins, S., and Macintyre, S. 2002: 'Food deserts' – evidence and assumption in health policy making. *British Medical Journal*, 325, 436–8.

Dahlgren, G. 1995: *European Health Policy Conference: Opportunities for the Future*, Volume II: *Intersectoral Action for Health*. Copenhagen: WHO Regional Office for Europe.

Dahlgren, G., and Whitehead, M. 1992: *Policies and Strategies to Promote Equity in Health*. Copenhagen: World Health Organization.

Davis, P., and Howden-Chapman, P. 1996: Translating research findings into health policy. *Social Science and Medicine*, 43, 865–72.

Degeling, P., Kennedy, J., and Hill, M. 1998: Do professional subcultures set the limits of hospital reform? *Clinician in Management*, 7, 89–98.

Degeling, P., Hunter, D. J., and Dowdeswell, B. 2001: Changing health systems. *Journal of Integrated Care Pathways*, 5, 64–9.

Degeling, P., Maxwell, S., Kennedy, J., and Coyle, B. 2003: Medicine, management, and modernization: a 'danse macabre'? *British Medical Journal*, 326, 649–52.

Department of Environment, Transport and the Regions 2000: *Local Strategic Partnerships: Consultation Document*. London: DETR.

Department of Health 1997: *The New NHS: Modern, Dependable*. Cm 3807. London: HMSO.

Department of Health 1998a: *The Health of the Nation – A Policy Assessed*. London: HMSO.

Department of Health 1998b: *Chief Medical Officer's Project to Strengthen the Public Health Function in England: A Report of Emerging Findings.* London: Department of Health.

Department of Health 2000: *The NHS Plan: A Plan for Investment, a Plan for Reform.* Cmd 4818. London: HMSO.

Department of Health 2001a: *Shifting the Balance of Power: Securing Delivery.* London: Department of Health.

Department of Health 2001b: *Tackling Health Inequalities. Consultation on a Plan for Delivery.* London: Department of Health.

Department of Health 2001c: *Vision to Reality.* London: Department of Health.

Department of Health 2001d: *The Report of the Chief Medical Officer's Project to Strengthen the Public Health Function.* London: Department of Health.

Department of Health 2001e: *Government Response to the House of Commons Select Committee on Health's Second Report on Public Health.* London: Department of Health.

Department of Health 2002a: *Shifting the Balance of Power: The Next Steps.* London: Department of Health.

Department of Health 2002b: *Tackling Health Inequalities: The Results of the Consultation Exercise.* London: Department of Health.

Department of Health 2002c: *Improvement, Expansion and Reform: The Next 3 Years Priorities and Planning Framework 2003–2006.* London: Department of Health.

Department of Health 2002d: *Managing for Excellence.* London: Department of Health.

Department of Health 2002e: *Code of Conduct for NHS Managers.* London: Department of Health.

Department of Health and Social Security 1976: *Prevention and Health: Everybody's Business: A Reassessment of Public and Personal Health. A Consultative Document prepared jointly by the Health Departments of Great Britain and Northern Ireland.* London: HMSO.

Dimmock, S., and Barnard, K. 1977: Relationships and communications. In: E. Raybould (ed.) *A Guide for Nurse Managers.* Oxford: Blackwell, 81–103.

Donaldson, L. J. 2002: Health services and the public health. *Journal of Epidemiology and Community Health,* 56, 835–40.

Donkin, A., Goldblatt, P., and Lynch, K. 2002: Inequalities in life expectancy by social class 1972–1999. *Health Statistics Quarterly,* 15, 5–15.

Drucker, P. 1955: *The Practice of Management.* London: Pan Books.

Drucker, P. 1990: *The New Realities.* London: Mandarin.

Duggan, M. 2001: *Healthy Living: The Role of Modern Local Authorities in Creating Healthy Communities.* Birmingham: Society of Local Authority Chief Executives (SOLACE).

Duncan, B. 2002: Health policy in the European Union: how it's made and how to influence it. *British Medical Journal,* 324, 1027–30.

Dunsire, A. 1978: *Implementation in a Bureaucracy.* Oxford: Martin Robertson.

Edmonstone, J., and Havergal, M. 1998: The third way: a new approach to management education in health care. *Health Manpower Management*, 24 (1), 33–7.

European Commission 2001: *The Internal Market and Health Services: Report of the High Level Committee on Health.* Health & Consumer Protection Directorate-General, Directorate G – Public Health. Brussels: European Commission.

European Health Management Association 2000: *The Impact of Market Forces on Health Systems: A Review of the Evidence in the 15 European Union Member States.* Dublin: EHMA.

European Health Management Association 2002: *EU Shortcuts.* No. 25. Brussels: EHMA.

Evans, R. G. 1995: Healthy populations or healthy institutions: the dilemma of health care management. *Journal of Health Administration Education*, 13 (3), 453–72.

Evans, R. G., and Stoddart, G. L. 1990: Producing health, consuming health care. *Social Science and Medicine*, 31 (12), 1347–63.

Exworthy, M., and Halford, S. (eds) 1999: *Professionals and the New Managerialism in the Public Sector.* Buckingham: Open University Press.

Exworthy, M., Berney, L., and Powell, M. 2002: 'How great expectations in Westminster may be dashed locally': the local implementation of national policy on health inequalities. *Policy & Politics*, 30 (1), 79–96.

Ferlie, E., and Fitzgerald, L. 2002: The sustainability of the new public management in the UK. In: K. McLaughlin, S. P. Osborne and E. Ferlie (eds) *New Public Management: Current Trends and Future Prospects.* London: Routledge, 341–53.

Fox, A. 1974: *Man Mismanagement.* London: Hutchinson.

Frenk, J. 1992: The new public health. In: Pan American Health Organization, *The Crisis of Public Health: Reflections for Debate.* Washington: PAHO, WHO, 68–85.

Friend, J. K., Power, J. M., and Yewlett, C. J. L. 1974: *Public Planning: The Inter-Corporate Dimension.* London: Tavistock.

Fulop, N., and Hunter, D. J. 1999: Editorial: saving lives or sustaining the public's health? *British Medical Journal*, 319, 139–40.

Fulop, N., Allen, P., Clarke, A., and Black, N. (eds) 2001: *Studying the Organisation and Delivery of Health Services: Research Methods.* London: Routledge.

Gillam, S., Abbott, S., and Banks-Smith, J. 2001: Can primary care groups and trusts improve the population's health? *British Medical Journal*, 323, 89–92.

Glouberman, S. 2000: *Towards a New Perspective on Health and Health Policy: A Synthesis Document of the Health Network.* Ottawa: Canadian Policy Research Networks.

Graham, H., Benzeval, M., and Whitehead, M. 1999: Social and economic policies in the UK with a potential impact on health inequalities. In:

J. P. Mackenbach and M. Droomers (eds) *Interventions and Policies to Reduce Socio-Economic Inequalities in Health*. Rotterdam: Department of Public Health, Erasmus University.

Greer, S. 2001: *Divergence and Devolution*. London: Nuffield Trust.

Greer, S., and Sandford, M. 2001: *Regional Government and Public Health*. London: Constitution Unit, University College London.

Gunn, L. A. 1978: Why is implementation so difficult? *Management Services in Government*, 33, 169–76.

Halpern, D., and Mikosz, D. (eds) 1998: *The Third Way: Summary of the NEXUS On-Line Discussion*. London: Nexus.

Hamer, L. 2000: *A National Review and Analysis of Health Improvement Programmes 1999–2000*. London: Health Development Agency.

Harding, A., and Preker, A. S. 2002: A conceptual framework for organizational reforms of hospitals. In: A. S. Preker and A. Harding (eds) *Innovations in Health Service Delivery, Volume 1: The Corporatization of Public Hospitals*. Washington: World Bank, 1–27.

Hardy, B., Hudson, B., and Waddington, E. 2000: *What Makes a Good Partnership? A Performance Assessment Tool*. Leeds: Nuffield Institute for Health.

Harrison, S. 1998: Implementing the results of research and development in clinical and managerial practice. In: M. Baker and S. Kirk (eds) *Research and Development for the NHS: Evidence, Evaluation and Effectiveness*. Oxford: Radcliffe Medical Press, 141–52.

Harrison, S. 1999: Clinical autonomy and health policy: past and futures. In: M. Exworthy and S. Halford (eds) *Professionals and the New Managerialism in the Public Sector*. Buckingham: Open University Press, 50–64.

Harrison, S., and Pollitt, C. 1994: *Controlling Health Professionals: The Future of Work and Organisation in the NHS*. Buckingham: Open University Press.

Harrison, S., Hunter, D. J., Johnston, I. H., Nicholson, N., Thunhurst, C., and Wistow, G. 1991: *Health Before Health Care*. Social Policy Paper No. 4. London: Institute for Public Policy Research.

Harrison, S., Hunter, D. J., Marnoch, G., and Pollitt, C. 1992: *Just Managing: Power and Culture in the National Health Service*. London: Macmillan.

Haynes, B., and Haines, A. 1998: Barriers and bridges to evidence based clinical practice. *British Medical Journal*, 317, 273–6.

Hazell, R., and Jervis, P. 1998: *Devolution and Health*. Nuffield Trust Series No. 3. London: Nuffield Trust.

Health Development Agency 2000: *Health Improvement Programmes (HImPs) 1999–2000. Conclusions and Recommendations of HDA's National Review*. London: Health Development Agency.

Health Development Agency 2001: *Health Improvement Programmes: Research into Practice*. London: Health Development Agency.

Health Service Journal 2002: Minister points Scotland to better health. *Health Service Journal*, 112, 14 November, 8–9.

Heclo, H. 1972: Policy analysis. *British Journal of Political Science*, 2, 83–108 [review article].

Heclo, H. 1975: Social politics and policy impacts. In: M. Holden Jr. and D. L. Dresang (eds), *What Government Does*. Beverly Hills, CA: Sage, 151–76.

HM Treasury 2002: *Opportunity and Security for All: Investing in an Enterprising, Fairer Britain: New Spending Plans 2003–6*. London: HM Treasury.

Higgins, J. 1978: *The Poverty Business: Britain and America*. Oxford and London: Blackwell and Robertson.

Hogwood, B. W., and Gunn, L. A. 1984: *Policy Analysis for the Real World*. Oxford: Oxford University Press.

Holland, W., Mossialos, E., and Permanand, G. 1999: Public health policies and priorities in Europe. In: W. Holland and E. Mossialos (eds) *Public Health Policies in the European Union*. Aldershot: Ashgate, 1–48.

Holland, W. W., and Stewart, S. 1998: *Public Health: The Vision and the Challenge*. London: Nuffield Trust [Rock Carling Fellowship 1997].

Hood, C. 1991: A public management for all seasons? *Public Administration*, 69 (1), 3–19.

House of Commons Health Committee 2001a: *Public Health. Second Report*. Volume I: *Report and Proceedings of the Committee. Session 2000–01*. HC30-I. London: HMSO.

House of Commons Health Committee 2001b: *Public Health. Second Report*. Volume II: *Minutes of Evidence and Appendices. Session 2000–01*. HC30-II. London: HMSO.

Hunter, D. J. 1980: *Coping with Uncertainty: Policy and Politics in the National Health Service*. Chichester: Wiley.

Hunter, D. J. 1982: Organising for health: the National Health Service in the United Kingdom. *Journal of Public Policy*, 2 (3), 263–300.

Hunter, D. J. 1983: Patterns of organisation for health: a systems overview of the National Health Service in the United Kingdom. In: A. Williamson and G. Room (eds) *Health and Welfare States of Britain: An Inter-Country Comparison*. London: Heinemann, 56–88.

Hunter, D. J. 1997: *Desperately Seeking Solutions: Rationing Health Care*. London: Longman.

Hunter, D. J. 1999: *Managing for Health: Implementing the New Health Agenda*. London: Institute for Public Policy Research.

Hunter, D. J. 2002a: England. In: M. Marinker (ed.) *Health Targets in Europe: Polity, Progress and Promise*. London: BMJ Books, 148–64.

Hunter D. J. 2002b: Wanless with a pinch of salt. *Health Service Journal*, 10 January.

Hunter, D. J. 2002c: A tale of two tribes: the tension between managerial and professional values. In: B. New and J. Neuberger (eds) *Hidden Assets: Values and Decision-Making in the NHS*. London: King's Fund, 61–78.

Hunter, D. J. 2002d: Management and public health. In: R. Detels, J. McEwen, R. Beaglehole and H. Tanaka (eds) *Oxford Textbook of Public Health*, Volume 2: *The Methods of Public Health*. 4th edn, Oxford: Oxford University Press, 921–36.

Hunter, D. J. 2003: *Public Health Management: Making it a World Concern. Report of WHO/University of Durham Meeting*. Geneva: WHO.

Hunter, D. J., and Berman, P. C. 1997: Public health management: time for a new start? *European Journal of Public Health*, 7 (3): 345–9.

Hunter, D., and Goodwin, N. 2001: How to get promoted. *Health Service Journal*, 19 July, 26–7.

Hunter, D. J., and Williamson, P. 1991: Comparisons and contrasts between Scotland and England. *Health Services Management*, 87 (4), 166–70.

Hunter, D. J., and Wistow, G. 1987a: *Community Care in Britain: Variations on a Theme*. London: King Edward's Hospital Fund for London.

Hunter, D. J. and Wistow, G. 1987b: The paradox of policy diversity in a unitary state: community care in Britain. *Public Administration*, 65 (1), 3–24.

Hunter, D. J., Fulop, N., and Warner, M. 2000: *From 'Health of the Nation' to 'Our Healthier Nation': A Case Study from England*. Policy Learning Curve Series No. 2. Brussels: European Centre for Health Policy, WHO.

Hunter, D., Marks, L., and Sykes, W. 2000: HImPs: learning from PCGs early experience. *British Journal of Healthcare Management*, 6 (4), 165–7.

Hunter, D. J., Shishkin, S., and Taroni, F. 2004: Steering the purchasers: the stewardship role of government. In: J. Figueras, E. Jakubowski and R. Robinson (eds) *Effective Purchasing for Health Gain*. Copenhagen: European Observatory on Health Care Systems.

Hunter, T. D. 1989: A service within a service: the National Health Service in Scotland. In: M. G. Field (ed.), *Success and Crisis in National Health Systems: a Comparative Approach*. New York: Routledge, 195–230.

Huxham, C. 1996: Advantage or inertia: making collaboration work. In: R. Paton, G. Clark, G. Jones, J. Lewis and P. Quintas (eds) *The New Management Reader*. London: Routledge, 238–54.

Independent Inquiry into Inequalities in Health 1998: Report of the Committee chaired by Sir Donald Acheson. London: HMSO.

Institute of Medicine 1988: *The Future of Public Health*. Washington: National Academy Press.

Institute of Medicine 2002: *The Future of the Public's Health in the 21st Century*. Washington: National Academy Press.

Jarrold, K. 1998: *Servants and Leaders: Leadership in the NHS*. Unpubd lecture.

Judge, K., and Mackenzie, M. 2002: Theory-based evaluation: new approaches to evaluating complex community-based initiatives. In: J. Mackenbach and M. Bakker (eds) *Reducing Inequalities in Health: A European Perspective*. London: Routledge, 300–12.

Judge, K., Barnes, M., Bauld, L., Benzeval, M., Killoran, A., and Robinson, R. et al. 1999: *Health Action Zones: Learning to Make a Difference*. PSSRU Discussion Paper 1546. Canterbury: University of Kent.

Kaufman, G. 1997: *How to be a Minister*. London: Faber & Faber.

Kelman, S. 1975: The social nature of the definition problem in health. *International Journal of Health Services*, 5, 609–38.

Kendall, L., and Harker, L. 2002: *From Welfare to Well-being: The Future of Social Care*. London: Institute for Public Policy Research.

Kernick, D. 2001: Evidence based policy: more fundamental concerns. *British Medical Journal*, 323, 275.

Kickbusch, I. 2002: Perspectives on health governance in the 21st century. In: M. Marinker (ed.) *Health Targets in Europe: Polity, Progress and Promise*. London: BMJ Books, 206–29.

Kickert, W., Klijn, E.-H., and Koppenjan, J. 1997: *Managing Complex Networks*. London: Sage.

Klein, R. 1989: *The Politics of the NHS*. 2nd edn, London: Longman.

Klein, R. 1996: The NHS and the new scientism: solution or delusion? *Quarterly Journal of Medicine*, 89, 85–7.

Lalonde, M. 1974: *A New Perspective on the Health of Canadians*. Ottawa: Minister of Supply and Services.

Law, C. 2001: Book review. *British Medical Journal*, 322, 560.

Legowski, B., and McKay, L. 2000: *Health Beyond Health Care: Twenty-Five Years of Federal Health Policy Development*. CPRN Discussion Paper No. H/04. Ottawa: Canadian Policy Research Networks.

Lewis, J. 1986: *What Price Community Medicine? The Philosophy, Practice and Politics of Public Health Since 1919*. Brighton: Wheatsheaf.

Lewis, S., Saulnier, M., and Renaud, M. 2000: Reconfiguring health policy: simple truths, complex solutions. In: G. L. Albrecht, R. Fitzpatrick and S. C. Scrimshaw (eds) *The Handbook of Social Studies in Health and Medicine*. London: Sage, 509–23.

Light, D. W. 1993: Conclusion: lessons from managed competition in Britain. In: D. Light and A. May (eds) *Britain's Health System: From Welfare State to Managed Markets*. New York: Faulkner & Gray, 161–72.

Light, D. 2000: The sociological character of health-care markets. In: G. L. Albrecht, R. Fitzpatrick and S. C. Scrimshaw (eds) *The Handbook of Social Studies in Health and Medicine*. London: Sage, 394–408.

Lipsky, M. 1980: *Street Level Bureaucracy*. New York: Sage Foundation.

Local Government Association and UK Public Health Association 2000: *Joint Response to the Public Health White Paper, 'Saving Lives: Our Healthier Nation'*. London: LGA.

Long, A. F. 1998: Health services research – a radical approach to cross the research and development divide. In: M. Baker and S. Kirk (eds) *Research and Development for the NHS: Evidence, Evaluation and Effectiveness*. Oxford; Radcliffe Medical Press, 87–99.

Loughlin, M. 2002: *Ethics, Management and Mythology: Rational Decision Making for Health Service Professionals.* Oxford: Radcliffe Medical Press.

Lukes, S. 1974: *Power.* London: Macmillan.

Macintyre, S. 2000: Modernising the NHS: prevention and the reduction of health inequalities. *British Medical Journal,* 320: 1399–400.

Macintyre, S., and Petticrew, M. 2000: Good intentions and received wisdom are not enough. *Journal of Epidemiology and Community Health,* 54 (11): 802–3.

Macintyre, S., Chalmers, I., Horton, R., and Smith, R. 2001: Using evidence to inform health policy: case study. *British Medical Journal,* 322, 222–5.

Mackenbach, J. P. 1995: Tackling inequalities in health. *British Medical Journal,* 310, 1152–3.

Mackenbach, J. P. 2002: Socio-economic inequalities in health in developed countries: the facts and the options. In: R. Detels, J. McEwan, R. Beaglehole and H. Tanaka (eds) *Oxford Textbook of Public Health,* Volume 3: *The Practice of Public Health.* Oxford: Oxford University Press, 1773–90.

Mackenbach, J., and Bakker, M. (eds) 2002: *Reducing Inequalities in Health: A European Perspective.* London: Routledge.

Mackenbach, J. P., and Stronks, K. 2002: A strategy for tackling health inequalities in the Netherlands. *British Medical Journal,* 325, 1029–32.

McCallum, A. 1997: Public health, health promotion and broader health strategy. In: S. Iliffe and J. Munro (eds) *Healthy Choices: Future Options for the NHS.* London: Lawrence & Wishart, 94–119.

McInnes, D., and Barnes, R. 2000: England: a healthier nation. In: A. Ritsatakis, R. Barnes, E. Dekker, P. Harrington, S. Kokko and P. Makara (eds) *Exploring Health Policy Development in Europe.* WHO Regional Publications, European Series, No. 86. Copenhagen: World Health Organization, 209–35.

McKeown, T. 1979: *The Role of Medicine: Dream, Mirage or Nemesis.* 2nd edn, Oxford: Blackwell.

McLachlan, G. 1987: A 'complaint of the common weill of Scotland'? In: G. McLachlan (ed.) *Improving the Common Weal: Aspects of the Scottish Health Service 1900–1984.* Edinburgh: Edinburgh University Press for Nuffield Provincial Hospitals Trust.

McNulty, T., and Ferlie, E. 2002: *Process Transformation? A Case of Reengineering in Health Care.* Oxford: Oxford University Press.

McPherson, K. 2001: Are disease prevention initiatives working? *The Lancet,* 357, 1790–92.

Marks, L. 2001: *Health Improvement Programmes and Tackling Inequalities in Northern and Yorkshire Region.* Durham and London: University of Durham and the Health Development Agency.

Marks, L. 2002: *Evidence-Based Practice in Tackling Inequalities in Health: Report of a R&D Project.* Durham: University of Durham.

Marks, L., and Hunter, D. J. 1999: *Health Improvement Programmes: A Review of Research: A Report commissioned by the Department of Health R&D Division*. Leeds: Nuffield Institute for Health, University of Leeds.

Marks, L., and Hunter, D. J. 2001: *From PCGs to PCTs: Work in Progress*. Bath: NHS Alliance.

Marmor, T. 2001: *Fads in Medical Care Policy and Politics: The Rhetoric and Reality of Managerialism*. London: Nuffield Trust [Rock Carling Fellowship 2001].

Mawhinney, B., and Nichol, D. 1993: *Purchasing for Health: A Framework for Action*. London: NHS Management Executive.

Mechanic, D. 1991: Sources of countervailing power in medicine. *Journal of Health Politics, Policy and Law*, 16 (3), 485–98.

Merkel, B., and Hubel, M. 1999: Public health policy in the European Community. In: W. Holland and E. Mossialos (eds) *Public Health Policies in the European Union*. Aldershot: Ashgate, 49–67.

Milburn, A. 2000: *A Healthier Nation and a Healthier Economy: The Contribution of a Modern NHS*. LSE Health Annual Lecture, 8 March. London: London School of Economics.

Milburn, A. 2002: *Tackling Health Inequalities, Improving Public Health*. Speech to the Faculty of Public Health Medicine. London: Department of Health.

Milburn, A. 2003: *Localism: from Rhetoric to Reality*. Speech to the New Health Network and the New Local Government Network. London: Department of Health.

Mintzberg, H. 1996: Managing government, governing management. *Harvard Business Review*, May–June, 75–83.

Mooney, G., and Loft, A. 1989: Clinical decision making and health care policy: what is the link? *Health Policy*, 11, 19–25.

Moore, M. 1996: *Public Sector Reform: Downsizing, Restructuring, Improving Performance*. Discussion Paper No. 7. Geneva: World Health Organization.

Moran, G. 1996: *Promoting Health and Local Government: A Report prepared for the Health Education Authority and the Local Government Management Board*. London: Health Education Authority.

Mossialos, E., and McKee, M. 2002: Editorial: health care and the European Union. *British Medical Journal*, 324, 991–2.

National Assembly for Wales 2001: *Improving Health in Wales: A Plan for the NHS with its Partners*. Cardiff: National Assembly for Wales.

National Audit Office 1996: *Health of the Nation: A Progress Report*. HC 656, Session 1995–96. London: HMSO.

Neighbourhood Renewal Unit and Regional Co-ordination Unit 2002: *Collaboration and Co-ordination in Area-Based Initiatives*. Research Summary No. 1. London: Neighbourhood Renewal Unit.

Nutbeam, D., and Wise, M. 2002: Structures and strategies for public health intervention. In: R. Detels, J. McEwen, R. Beaglehole and

H. Tanaka (eds) *Oxford Textbook of Public Health,* Volume 3: *The Practice of Public Health.* 4th edn, Oxford: Oxford University Press, 1873–88.

O'Neill, O. 2002: *A Question of Trust.* London: BBC [Reith lectures].

Osborne, D., and Gaebler, T. 1993: *Reinventing Government: How the Entrepreneurial Spirit is Transforming the Public Sector.* New York: Plume.

Parston, G., and Timmins, N. 1998: *Joined-Up Management.* London: Public Management Foundation.

Perkins, E. R., Simnett, I., and Wright, L. (eds) 1999: *Evidence-Based Health Promotion.* Chichester: Wiley & Sons.

Pettigrew, A., and Whipp, R. 1991: *Managing Change for Competitive Success.* Oxford: Blackwell.

Pettigrew, A., Ferlie, E., and McKee, I. 1992: *Shaping Strategic Change: Making Change in Large Organizations.* London: Sage.

Pfeffer, J. 1992: *Managing with Power: Politics and Influence in Organizations.* Boston: Harvard Business School Press.

Plsek, P. E., and Greenhalgh, T. 2001: The challenge of complexity in health care. *British Medical Journal,* 323, 625–8.

Plsek, P. E., and Wilson, T. 2001: Complexity, leadership, and management in healthcare organisations. *British Medical Journal,* 323, 746–9.

Pollitt, C. 1990: *Managerialism and the Public Services: The Anglo-American Experience.* Oxford: Blackwell.

Pollock, A. 1999: Devolution and health: challenges for Scotland and Wales. *British Medical Journal,* 313, 195–8.

Potter, I. 1998: *In the Name of Health – Shifting Paradigms, Shifting Perspectives: Canada's Experience in Adopting and Implementing a Population Health Perspective: An Overview and Update.* A background paper at the Cambridge International Health Leadership Program, Judge Institute of Management Studies, University of Cambridge, 15–22 April.

Preker, A. S., and Harding, A. (eds) 2002: *Innovations in Health Service Delivery,* Volume I: *The Corporatization of Public Hospitals.* Washington: World Bank.

Pressman, J. I., and Wildavsky, A. 1979: *Implementation.* Berkeley: University of California Press.

Research Unit in Health and Behavioural Change 1989: *Changing the Public Health.* Chichester: Wiley & Sons.

Rhodes, R. A. W. 1995: Foreword: governance in the hollow state: In: M. Blunden and M. Dando (eds) *Rethinking Public Policy-Making.* London: Sage, 1–6.

Richardson, A., Duggan, M., and Hunter, D. J. 1994: *Adapting to New Tasks: The Role of Public Health Physicians in Purchasing Health Care.* Leeds: Nuffield Institute for Health.

Ritsatakis, A. 2000: Learning from the past, looking to the future. In: A. Ritsatakis, R. Barnes, E. Dekker, P. Harrington, S. Kokko, and P. Makara (eds) *Exploring Health Policy Development in Europe.* WHO Regional Publications, European Series, Bo. 86. Copenhagen: WHO Regional Office for Europe, 347–87.

Ritsatakis, A., Barnes, R., Dekker, E., Harrington, P., Kokko, S., and Makara, P. (eds) 2000: *Exploring Health Policy Development in Europe*. WHO Regional Publications, European Series, Bo. 86. Copenhagen: WHO Regional Office for Europe.

Rittel, H., and Webber, M. 1973: Dilemmas in a general theory of planning. *Policy Science*, 4.

Rivlin, A. 1971: Obstacles to social progress: why can't we get things done. *Washington Post*, 22 July.

Robinson, M., McKee, M., and Coyle, E. 1996: *Health – Every Government Department's Business?* London: Royal Society of Medicine Press.

Sallis, J. F., and McKenzie, T. L. 1991: Physical education's role in public health. *Research Quarterly for Exercise and Sport*, 62 (2), 124–37.

Sandford, M. 2002: *A Commentary on the Regional Government White Paper, 'Your Region, Your Choice: Revitalising the English Regions'*. London: Constitution Unit, University College London.

Schon, D. 1973: *Beyond the Stable State*. Harmondsworth: Penguin.

Schon, D. A. 1991: *The Reflective Practitioner: How Professionals Think in Action*. Aldershot: Avebury.

Scottish Executive 2000: *Review of the Public Health Function in Scotland*. Edinburgh: Scottish Executive.

Scottish Executive 2001: *Our National Health: A Plan for Action, a Plan for Change*. Edinburgh: Scottish Executive.

Secretary of State for Health 1992: *The Health of the Nation: A Strategy for Health in England*. Cm 1986. London: HMSO.

Secretary of State for Health 1999: *Saving Lives: Our Healthier Nation*. Cm 4386. London: HMSO.

Smith, J., Walshe, K., and Hunter, D. J. 2001: Editorial: the 're-disorganisation' of the NHS. *British Medical Journal*, 323, 1262–3.

Society of Local Authority Chief Executives (SOLACE) 1995: *Lighthouses not Spotlights*. Birmingham: SOLACE.

Stewart, J. 1998: Advance or retreat: from the traditions of public administration to the new public management and beyond. *Public Policy and Administration*, 13 (4), 12–27.

Stiglitz, J. 2002: *Globalization and its Discontents*. London: Allen Lane.

Thompson, F. J. 1981: *Health and Policy and the Bureaucracy: Politics and Implementation*. Cambridge, MA: MIT Press.

Twaddle, A. C. 2002: Health care reform and global hegemony. In: A. C. Twaddle (ed.) *Health Care Reform Around the World*. Westport, CT: Auburn House, 341–91.

UNICEF 2000: *Child Poverty in Rich Nations*. Innocenti Report Card No. 1. Florence: UNICEF.

Walker, D. 2002: Labour's public service test: can they deliver on childcare? *The Guardian*, 27 August, 10.

Wanless, D. 2001: *Securing our Future Health: Taking a Long-Term View: Interim Report*. London: HM Treasury.

Wanless, D. 2002: *Securing our Future Health: Taking a Long-Term View: Final Report*. London: HM Treasury.

Webster, C. 1996: *The Health Services Since the War*, Volume II. London: HMSO.

Webster, C. 2002: *The National Health Service: A Political History*. New edn, Oxford: Oxford University Press.

Welsh Health Planning Forum 1989a: *Strategic Intent and Direction for the NHS in Wales*. Cardiff: Welsh Office.

Welsh Health Planning Forum 1989b: *Local Strategies for Health: A New Approach to Strategic Planning*. Cardiff: Welsh Office.

Whitley, R. 1988: The management sciences and managerial skills. *Organization Studies*, 9 (1), 47–68.

Wildavsky, A. 1979: *The Art and Craft of Policy Analysis*. London: Macmillan.

Wilkinson, D., and Applebee, E. 1999: *Implementing Holistic Government: Action on the Ground*. Bristol: Policy Press.

Wismar, M., Busse, R., and Berman, P. 2002: The European Union and health services – the context. In: R. Busse, M. Wismar and P. Berman (eds) *The European Union and Health Services: The Impact of the Single European Market on Member States*. Amsterdam: IOS Press, 17–29.

World Bank 1993: *World Development Report 1993: Investing in Health*. Oxford: Oxford University Press.

World Bank 1996: *World Development Report 1996: From Plan to Market*. Oxford: Oxford University Press.

World Health Organization 1985: *Targets for Health for All*. Geneva: WHO.

World Health Organization 1998: *Strengthening Public Health*. Copenhagen: WHO.

World Health Organization 2000: *The World Health Report 2000 – Health Systems: Improving Performance*. Geneva: WHO.

World Health Organization 2002: *The World Health Report 2002: Reducing Risks, Promoting Healthy Life*. Geneva: WHO.

References

Acheson, D. 1988: *Public Health in England.* Cmnd 289. London: HMSO [Acheson report].

Ackoff, R. 1979: The future of operational research is past. *Journal of the Operational Research Society,* 30 (2), 90–100.

Alderslade, R., and Hunter, D. J. 1994: Commissioning and public health. *Journal of Management and Medicine,* 8 (6), 20–31.

Allen, I. 1997: *Committed but Critical: An Examination of Young Doctors' Views of their Core Values.* London: British Medical Association.

Allison, G. T. 1971: *Essence of Decision.* Boston: Little, Brown.

Appleby, J. 1997: Feelgood factors. *Health Service Journal,* 107, 24–7.

Appleby, J., and Coote, A. (eds) 2002: *Five-Year Health Check: A Review of Government Health Policy 1997–2002.* London: King's Fund.

Audit Commission 2002: *Neighbourhood Renewal.* London: Audit Commission.

Bachrach, P., and Baratz, M. S. 1962: The two faces of power. *American Political Science Review,* 56, 947–52.

Bachrach, P., and Baratz, M. S. 1970: *Power and Poverty.* New York: Oxford University Press.

Baggott, R. 2000: *Public Health: Policy and Politics.* London: Macmillan.

Bakker, M., and Mackenbach, J. (eds) 2002: By way of conclusion: key messages for policy-makers. In: J. Mackenbach and M. Bakker (eds) *Reducing Inequalities in Health: A European Perspective.* London: Routledge, 337–42.

Barnard, K. 1998: *On Preparing the Future Servant Manager of Health* (unpubd paper).

Barnard, K. 2000: *Developing Policies and Building Partnerships for Health.* Paper presented at the European Public Health Congress, Istanbul, October.